D0991100

Julio Medem

Manchester University Press

Spanish and Latin American Filmmakers

Series editors:
Núria Triana Toribio, University of Manchester
Andy Willis, University of Salford

Spanish and Latin American Filmmakers offers a focus on new filmmakers; reclaims previously neglected filmmakers; and considers established figures from new and different perspectives. Each volume places its subject in a variety of critical and production contexts.

The series sees filmmakers as more than just auteurs, thus offering an insight into the work and contexts of producers, writers, actors, production companies and studios. The studies in this series take into account the recent changes in Spanish and Latin American film studies, such as the new emphasis on popular cinema, and the influence of cultural studies in the analysis of films and of the film cultures produced within the Spanish-speaking industries.

Already published

The cinema of Álex de la Iglesia   Peter Buse, Núria Triana Toribio
and Andy Willis
Emilio Fernández: pictures in the margins   Dolores Tierney

Julio Medem

Rob Stone

Manchester University Press
Manchester and New York
distributed exclusively in the USA by Palgrave

PN
1998.3
.M399
S78
2007

Copyright © Rob Stone 2007

The right of Rob Stone to be identified as the author of this work has been asserted by him in accordance with the Copyright, Designs and Patents Act 1988.

Published by Manchester University Press
Oxford Road, Manchester M13 9NR, UK
and Room 400, 175 Fifth Avenue, New York, NY 10010, USA
www.manchesteruniversitypress.co.uk

Distributed exclusively in the USA by
Palgrave, 175 Fifth Avenue, New York,
NY 10010, USA

Distributed exclusively in Canada by
UBC Press, University of British Columbia, 2029 West Mall,
Vancouver, BC, Canada V6T 1Z2

British Library Cataloguing-in-Publication Data
A catalogue record for this book is available from the British Library

Library of Congress Cataloging-in-Publication Data applied for

ISBN 978 0 7190 7200 0 *hardback*

First published 2007

16 15 14 13 12 11 10 09 08 07   10 9 8 7 6 5 4 3 2 1

**Arts & Humanities
Research Council**

Typeset
by Florence Production Ltd, Stoodleigh, Devon
Printed in Great Britain
by Bell & Bain Ltd, Glasgow

Para Esther

versity
Pittsburgh, PA 15213-3890

Contents

List of figures

Acknowledgements

This book was made possible by the collaboration of a great many people. Above all, *un fuerte abrazo a* Julio Medem for his time, candour and generosity. Special thanks are also due to Jesús Robles and Maria Silveyro of Ocho y Medio, Madrid, for their kindness, support and collaboration. Thanks also to Silvia Cotino Estornell and the marketing department of Sogecine-Sogepaq. All of the interviewees in this book gave generously of their time and hospitality and afforded me great honour. *Saludos de nuevo a* Javier Aguirresarobe, Iván Aledo, Teresa Asisi, Fernando Bovaira, Fernando de Garcillán, Kiko de la Rica, Carmelo Gómez, Silvia Gómez, Ione Hernández, Alberto Iglesias, Nancho Novo, Emma Suárez and Koldo Zuazua. Many thanks are also due to my student and teacher Helen Jones, who helped to shape the manuscript in a great many ways, to Isabel Santaolalla whose insightful writing and thoughts on Medem were a major influence on this book, and to Owen Evans, who not only carried out invaluable research on my behalf but was always good for coffee and advice. Thanks also to Silvia Gómez for welcoming me into Alicia Produce and our mutual friend Celia Valenciano for her gracious and valued collaboration. *Gracias también a* Caridad Iglesias Arroyo and to Fernando Carricajo Garrido for making Madrid my second home; Matthew Frost and Jonathan Bevan of Manchester University Press; series editors Nuria Triana Toribio and Andy Willis; Paul Smith of Metro-Tartan for inviting me to provide notes and commentary on the DVDs of Medem's films and Louise Anderson and Geoff Andrew for their invitation to curate a season of Basque cinema for the National Film Theatre in 2004. I would also like to thank the following colleagues and friends who supported me with their interest and collaboration: Elaine Canning, Tom Charity, Paul Cooke, María Delgado, Peter William Evans, Jennifer Green, Graeme Harper, Mostyn Jones, Raquel Linares, Alan O'Leary, Victoria Pastor, Alfredo Santamaría, John Sundholm, Eric Thau, Kevin Williams, Rhys Williams and Paddy Woodworth. Many people assisted me in the research of this book with contacts and information, including María José Ferrer, Elvira Herreira, Sonia Lozano and Verónica Roldán Bistagne.

Thanks also to the British Academy for their invaluable research grant, the University of Wales at Swansea for the sabbatical and to the Arts and Humanities Research Council for their granting of research leave during 2004. This book would not have been possible without their support.

And finally, *mil gracias a* Esther Santamaría Iglesias, who put up with it all, who transcribed endless hours of interviews and stood my research absences as stoically as she weathered my writing of the book, who listened and prompted, argued and inspired, all tirelessly and good-humouredly.

Rob Stone

Note on interviews

All translations are the author's own and all quotes are, unless otherwise stated, from the following interviews.

Julio Medem

[1] 30.1.02, Museo Chicote, Madrid.

[2] 10.1.03, Bar in Madrid.

[3] 14.7.03, Café del Oriente and Medem's editing studio in his flat in Madrid.

[4] 27.11.03, London Film Festival, day of screening of *La pelota vasca*.

[5] 23.4.04, Alicia Produce (Medem's production company) Madrid.

Nancho Novo [6] 13.2.04, Novo's home, Madrid.

Silvia Gómez [7] 13.2.04, Alicia Produce, Madrid.

Javier Aguirresarobe [8] 14.2.04, Aguirresarobe's apartment, Madrid.

Fernando de Garcillán [9] 16.2.04, Bailando Con La Luna, Madrid.

Kiko de la Rica [10] 16.2.04, Café Oriental, Madrid.

Ione Hernández [11] 18.2.04, Alicia Produce, Madrid.

Iván Aledo [12] 17.4.04, editing suite, Madrid.

Koldo Zuazua [13] 19.4.04 Alicia Produce, Madrid.

Emma Suárez [14] 20.4.04, Plaza Dos de Mayo, Madrid.

Carmelo Gómez [15] 20.4.04, Gómez's chalet, Madrid.

Alberto Iglesias [16] 21.4.04, Iglesias's chalet, Torrelodones.

Fernando Bovaira [17] 21.4.04, Sogecine, Madrid.

Teresa Asisi [18] 22.4.04, Los Mesones, Madrid.

1

Author, auteur, Aitor

Author

'I think my best work is still to come. Truly', says Julio Medem in what is an open-ended conclusion to his last interview for a book about him [5]. Nevertheless, he already enjoys a reputation in Basque, Spanish, European and even World cinema for the colourful eroticism, subjective camerawork, elaborate plotting, structural equations, straight-faced absurdity and obsessions with symmetry, duality and chance that characterise the films he has written and directed. *Vacas* (1992), *La ardilla roja* (*Red Squirrel*, 1993), *Tierra* (1996), *Los amantes del Círculo Polar* (*Lovers of the Arctic Circle*, 1998), *Lucía y el sexo* (*Sex and Lucía*, 2001) and the documentary *La pelota vasca: la piel contra la piedra* (*Basque Ball: The Skin against the Stone*, 2003) have gained him festival prizes, complex distribution strategies, quality DVD editions of his films, the backing of Spain's media giant Sogecine, a belated and problematic reputation as a political filmmaker and an increasing degree of autonomy that comes from co-financing his own features and making use of new technologies such as high definition digital video that he edits on his home computer. He also warrants this book, whose author has taken advantage of his being alive, busy and approachable to base it on a series of interviews and observational encounters that occurred throughout the making of *La pelota vasca*.

Justification for a book on Medem is complicated by the fact that any writing on a film director must position itself in relation to the debate over auteurism, 'a belief in the primary creative importance of the director in filmmaking, often combined with a critical advocacy of the works of certain strong, distinctive directors' (AHDEL 2000). Staunch auteurists favour the emancipation of the artist-director from structures that may be politically imposed, traditionally maintained or commercially tried and tested, and, moreover, hold that this is essential to the recognition of film as an art form. However, as film has become an increasingly complex subject for analysis, incorporating industry and audience studies, film theory, history and contextual analyses, so the study of a film director must engage with all these areas instead of an exclusive relationship with auteurism, the composition and performance of which maintains that a filmmaker's personal experiences act as catalysts for their representation on film and that a perception of the career of a director 'implies an operation of decipherment' (Wollen 1992: 590) of the semantic dimension of the work. Although this too is true with Medem, and it is to this end that the book is partly based upon the notion that interviews with him and with many of his collaborators would provide a stimulating polyphony in the manner of Medem's parallel work on *La pelota vasca* and thereby provide an introduction and accompaniment to the films which bear his name as writer and director.

Nevertheless, this strategy obliges the writer and reader to negotiate a path between the traps that, firstly, the many excerpts from those interviews should ever be treated as the last word on any of the subjects under discussion, and, secondly, that academic or critical interpretation should ever supplant the declarations of the speaker. There exists, after all, the problem of interpretation that is relevant to the task of accessing the subject of this book. Most interviewers are beholden to their interviewees for their time and willingness to be interviewed. In the case of infrequently observing and interviewing Medem over three years, the question of such access was paramount. This book was originally going to feature observation and interviewing of Medem while he made *Aitor: la piel contra la piedra* (*Aitor: The Skin against the Stone*), a coruscating, magical realist 'opera of the Basque conflict' [1]. Instead, Medem first set about *La pelota vasca* as a preparatory project for *Aitor* and as the documentary grew to envelop him so too did the controversy it engendered. In effect, observation and interviewing became unavoidably skewed to the subject and meaning of *La pelota vasca* and Medem's consequent experience of being at the centre of popular, political and media debate in Spain. Accordingly, this book became not only the study of a writer-director at work but an attempt to understand the character and context of a person who during this time was denounced by Spain's government, disowned by London's Spanish Embassy and vilified by public demonstrations outside the 2004 Spanish Film Academy Awards that threatened him with a banner stating *Contra el pelota vasco: la bala contra la nuca* (Against the Basque creep: the bullet against the nape). And during all this time Medem, like most of his collaborators, remained a generous, welcoming and forthright interviewee. To some extent, therefore, the kind of privileged access gained for this book invalidated immediate comeback, attack and contradiction, especially when the subject was at pains to defend himself elsewhere. Debate with Medem was often spontaneous, but our interviews were also not immune from his delivery of practised anecdotes and soundbites that have appeared in several media and attest to both his performance of auteurism and a fair shielding of his privacy.

All the interviews in this book were conducted in Spanish, which allowed for informality, wide-ranging discussion and a freedom of expression that also has much to do with Medem being both affable and intense. Any query about his films prompted him to reveal the intimate resonance of their content, but for a filmmaker whose work is so determinedly personal there must also be an allowance that such statements, some of which on *La pelota vasca* edge him close to a kind of martyrdom, are all part of the process of the creation of an auteurist persona that includes the films themselves and is integral to their reception. To the extent that Medem is largely the author of his own auteurism, the danger exists that interviewees' comments are used as mere illustration of an unchallenged status quo instead of as tools in an academic argument. Nevertheless, challenges to interviewees' contradictions, provocations and easy get-outs at the writing stage are arguably unfair. It is for this reason that each of the chapters on Medem's films are largely divided into a polyphonic account of the production history of each film in which interviewees are liberally referenced and juxtaposed with the declarations of others in the service of clarity and debate and, following this, a critical analysis of each film in which the interviews play no part, for any questioning of the role of the academic or critic is answered here at the point of the text, i.e. by exclusive concentration on the film. The divisions are not strict, however, because there can be no clinical separation of the films from their writer-director, nor of the writer-director from his social, political, industrial and creative context and collaborators.

Just as Medem's many collaborators engaged with their memories of working with him, so they propounded observations and theories about their relationships with each other and with Medem that were rarely separate from the praxis of performance. For reasons that had much to do with their own status, all of the interviewees were participants in the investment, construction and corroboration of Medem's auteurist trajectory. Actors often stressed how they had based their characters on Medem himself or on members of his family in full knowledge that they had enabled their writer-director to revisit and rework his childhood, youth, divorce and infatuations as well as family histories and legends in films that Medem was subsequently keen to disentangle and psychoanalyse in interviews, pressbooks and prefaces to his published scripts. Just as 'the auteur is the structuring principle of enunciation' (Corrigan 1991: 102), so the characters that are written, played, filmed, edited and marketed by Medem and his cast, cinematographers, editors and producers reveal a combined effort to render, evoke or sell some semblance of Medem's persona. This collaborative cultivation, refinement and promotion of Medem's auteurism also prompts an enquiry into whether the auteur theory fits Medem or whether Medem fits the auteur theory.

Auteur

The concept of auteurism came from literary studies and gained ground with the French New Wave at a time when formalist approaches to film studies were concerned with the deployment of ideologies to explain film as a symbolic system that sustained social, psychic and political relations. Louis Althusser claimed that an ideology was not a point of view but a process of investment in ideas that was evolving and contradictory (Althusser 1984). In tune with Structuralism, semiotics and psychoanalysis, the auteur theory pushed film studies to maturity as a 'self-contained, disciplinary movement [that] redeemed cinema from the material and historical determinants of the marketplace' (Nichols 2000: 36) but ironically converted artistic merit into a commodity based on authority and style. In the 1970s, ideological film criticism that was politically motivated or oriented fuelled feminist approaches to film analysis, while the prevalent contemporary approach wields a politicised concern with perception and cognition and seeks to disable and dissect the commodity of auteurism, seeing cinema as 'a socially constructed category serving socially significant ends' (Nichols 2000: 37) from which the auteur is excluded in case artistry, emotional investment, aesthetic idiosyncrasies and oft-repeated obsessions should spoil the calculus.

What is most often deemed important in relation to the figure of the film director is 'how a filmmaker [. . .] intended a work to be categorized' (Corrigan 1991: 103) and this has much to do with the importance of cult viewing in relation to auteurism, where the auteur operates 'as a commercial strategy for organizing audience reception, as a critical concept bound to distribution and marketing aims that identify and address the potential cult status of an auteur' (Corrigan 1991: 103).

Medem has become increasingly autonomous by co-financing his films to the extent that his auteurism illustrates the notion of a 'commercial strategy for organising distribution and audience, constructed by and for commerce' (Corrigan 1991: 104) and might even be classified in terms of the 'commercial performance of the business of being an auteur' (Corrigan 1991: 104). Medem has also employed technologies that permit greater control of this 'business' such as the high definition digital video of *Lucía y el sexo* and the synergetic distribution of *La pelota vasca* as a commercial feature, a television series and a seven-hour version on the three-disc Spanish DVD with all its extras. All of this makes him an ideal case study for the prolongation of theories of auteurism into contemporary cinema in line with Corrigan's affirmation that they were originally 'tightly bound to changes in production and distribution strategies, such as the rise of an international art cinema and the introduction of an Arriflex camera, all of which encouraged reconceptualizing films as more personal and creative documents' (Corrigan 1991: 104).

However, it can seem as if the study of filmmaking has been replaced by the study of film-watching to the extent that voyeurism, once a cornerstone of Truffaut's testimonial to Hitchcock's auteurism, has become the prerogative of the audience. Since the 1970s the auteur theory has lost ground to what Andrew Sarris called 'the temptations of cynicism, common sense and facile culture-mongering' (1985: 536) that were led by the barrage of criticism from such as Pauline Kael (1985: 541–52), as well as a panoply of alternative critical approaches, many of which emanated from the cultural studies approach of university departments of modern languages where foreign films were largely the subject of contextual analyses. Under the sub-heading 'Authorship in European Cinema: The Canon and How to Challenge It' in her chapter in *The Oxford Guide to Film Studies*, Ginette Vincendeau attests that 'the rise of cultural studies produced a (critical) devaluation of art cinema and European auteurs, and arguably of

European cinema altogether', (1998: 445) but that recent years have seen a 'renaissance of film history' (1998: 445) that has allowed for a changing critical discourse in relation to auteurism. Vincendeau writes: 'If understood in an industrial, social and cultural context, as opposed to just as an expression of genius, [the concept of the auteur] can still illuminate areas of European film history that remain unknown' (1998: 445). Because this book takes that as given, so the interviewing and analysis of Medem and his collaborators makes its enquiry not just historical and contemporary, but also artistic and industrial, as well as international, European, Spanish and particularly Basque.

In relation to the international context, Nick James writes in *Sight and Sound* that 'the feature film, being a hybrid work created by a team of craftspeople rather than by a solo artist, is constantly vulnerable to the opinion that it's more a form of entertainment than of art. That view predominates in the US and UK media (even though everyone still pays lip service to the auteur)' (2005: 3). Festivals used to be about debate, now they are mostly about publicity, with the most photogenic or charismatic of directors (and Medem is both) almost as valuable as their stars in terms of gaining recognition and markets for a film. The cult of the auteurist persona is clearly essential to the funding, distribution and marketing strategies that thrive on the notion of the film director as auteur in apparent defiance of the view that a director is nothing more than the sum of his or her social interaction, cultural influences, commercial negotiations and self-fulfilling promotion: in sum, that the figure of the auteur is the selfish receptor of all the acclaim that would otherwise be shared out between the film's cast, writer, cinematographer, editor, producer and even its interpretative audience. Critics argue that the film director is similar to the conductor of an orchestra, the choreographer of a dance and the editor of a book not its writer, yet the celebration of the film director as auteur by audiences, critics, festivals, producers, marketing campaigns and the film director himself or herself, for all its pretension, assumption, snobbery and blinkered bloody-mindedness remains, for better or worse, integral to the recognition of film as a unique art. Correlatively, the extant notion of contemporary auteurism maintains the notion of the emancipation of the artist from the industry that encloses him or her by purveyance of personal obsessions, themes, experiences or aesthetics in a body of films or *oeuvre*. Although Geoffrey Nowell-Smith warns that 'the defining characteristics of an author's work are not necessarily those which are most readily apparent' (1968: 10), in

Medem's case the cyclical structures, subjective camerawork and sensual imagery do amount to 'a hard core of basic and often recondite motifs' (Nowell-Smith 1968: 10) that also testify to the obsessive repetition that often lies beneath the auteurist guise of reinvention.

It might be said that auteurism is recognised at the point where it is the film's director not its star, script or genre that attracts funding. Medem's engagement with the kind of literary and philosophical influences that underpin much 'high art' European cinema has resulted in the attractive and bankable style, tone and content (especially sexual) of his films on the international festival circuit and market that is also receptive to his use of new technologies such as digital video. Medem certainly functions as a self-conscious construct with auteurist ambitions that rhyme with funding, production, marketing and distribution strategies in Spain and elsewhere. He shares these commercial strategies as well as an urge to develop intriguing narrative, aesthetic and structural strategies with several of his contemporaries such as Wong Kar Wai, Pedro Almodóvar, Michael Haneke, Atom Egoyan, Lukas Moodysson, Michael Winterbottom, François Ozon and Tom Tykwer, all of whom share a vague new sense of modernism in which narrative codes are knowingly played, displayed and replayed. However, what has proven most crucial to critical appreciation and audience awareness of Medem's uniqueness is his thematic, structural and aesthetic way with juxtaposed subjectivities. Indeed, the link between subjectivity and Medem's auteurism is strengthened by his method of authoring scripts by successively assuming the first person perspective of his main protagonists and thereafter tying these separate versions into a whole that is subsequently disentangled by the filming and editing of juxtaposed subjectivities, a strategy identified by Paul Julian Smith, who dubbed him 'the cineaste of subjectivity' (2000: 146).

Claims on Medem's auteurism combine Smith's appreciation of his subjectivity with an indulgence of his solipsism and a justification of authorial punctuation in the service of emotion, reflection and melancholy, but often separate him from the traditions, legacy, clichés and contemporary context of Spanish and especially Basque cinema. Viewing his films, interviewing their writer-director and reading the other interviews he has given would have you believe that Medem is (to borrow Sarris's premise of the 'three concentric circles' of the auteur theory [1992: 597]), a craftsman with an original eye, a stylist with a sense of humour and an auteur with his heart on his sleeve; but whether a career built on centripetal introspection can survive the gradual centrifugal dispersion of any meaning other than the intensely personal in his films is an increasingly urgent question that only his next few films can answer. Unlike one of Medem's greatest avowed influences, the Russian filmmaker Andrei Tarkovsky, with whom his films share a somewhat comparable aesthetic, Medem's concerns are more personal than existential. In the extraordinarily resonant *Mirror* (1974), for example, Tarkovsky reflects on his childhood as symbolic of the destiny of the Russian people, but even when exploring the theme of human duality in *Tierra*, Medem's resolution is a comparatively non-resonant exorcism of his own marital problems. If Tarkovsky makes the personal political, Medem makes the personal even more personal.

Yet, look also to Alfred Hitchcock, Luis Buñuel, Yasujiro Ozu, Federico Fellini, Krzysztof Kieślowski, Víctor Erice and Wim Wenders for Medem's forebears in a diachronic genealogy of interpretative and emotional challenges that includes Hitchcock's subversion of heroic protagonism and fearful adoration of women, Buñuel's Surrealist provocations and deliberately unreliable narratives, Ozu's observance of human needs and failings, Fellini's sentimental absurdity, Tarkovsky's meditations on the mythic contextualisation of human endeavour, loss and longing, Kieślowski's games with fate and chance, Erice's struggle to reconcile human endurance with the poetry of the everyday, and Wenders forebearance with grief and passion, all of which are present in the films written and directed by Medem. However, Medem may also be categorised synchronically alongside contemporary filmmakers who are exploiting new production and distribution technologies and whose affined traits include the tension between minimalism and hyper-emotionalism in the films of Lars Von Trier, the emotional abandon and subsequent regret of characters in the luscious films of Wong Kar Wai, the civilised orgy of human connections that is filtered through film, art, opera and music in the work of Pedro Almodóvar, the arousal and confusion of passions in films directed by David Lynch, the weaving of humans into the landscape by means of choral voiceovers in the work of Terrence Malick, the transcendence of dislocated individuals in the films of Tom Tykwer, and the 'what if?' games with misfits played by Atom Egoyan. Like them, Medem demands an interdependent emotional and intellectual response, where to understand one has to be moved: 'When I present a film, I suggest people leave their minds open. Let the ideas be born of the emotional movement and not the other way round' (Stone 2001: 180).

These filmmakers of the new millenium are also engaged in the dynamic process of undoing the relationship of film to generic, political, social, industrial, commercial, artistic and technological traditions so that new relationships may be attempted. Rearrangements of film grammar, for example, encompass the subversion of narrative codes, genre conventions, the star system and audience expectations in the same way in which the Romantics once undid Classicism. Classical art presented order and inspired objectivity in an audience that had no option but to agree with the artist on a common meaning, whether it was the glory of some religious figure or the status of the subject of a commissioned portrait, but Romantic art invited the audience to contend with the ambiguities of the image and take part in the discovery of its meaning, which, like beauty, was often found in the eye of the beholder. Like the Romantic artists and poets, the aforementioned filmmakers do not provide meanings unless the audience is prepared to engage imaginatively and emotionally with their original characters, structural innovations and stylistic idiosyncrasies, which in turn are the factors that encourage claims of auteurism by critics, fans, producers, publicists and often the filmmakers themselves.

John Orr identifies the context and dominant theme of contemporary European cinema as a 'brittle world of disconnected beings adrift in a sea of transient encounters' (2004: 300). He suggests that these filmmakers, like their critical and public fan-base, see the world in a much more fractured manner than is commonly supposed by mainstream cinema and politics and he identifies 'a key metaphysic of immanence in the new [European] cinema' (2004: 315). Yet pantheism is not limited to Europe, for the moody musings of Medem are arguably more comparable to the films of China's Wong Kar Wai than to the austere, quarrelsome cinema of Haneke and Moodysson, while Medem's subjective camerawork is also a feature of films as varied and important as *Lola rennt* (*Run, Lola, Run*, 1998), *Fa yeung nin wa* (*In The Mood For Love*, 2000), *La Pianiste* (*The Piano Teacher*, 2001) and *Lilja 4-ever* (*Lilya 4-ever*, 2002) to name but a few. Although film authorship is commonly recognised by its uniqueness and contrariness (which is often identified in opposition to Hollywood), Medem is only one of many contemporary filmmakers who stake a claim on auteurism in their dealings with film traditions, industry and audiences. Other weapons fast becoming the clichés of contemporary arthouse cinema, which Vincendeau identifies as 'a useful polemical and marketing tool' that is nonetheless 'a largely aesthetic category', (1998: 441–2) include out-of-field techniques that counter obsessive framing, the subversion of artifice by a foregrounding of the filmmaking process and the dispassionate long-take travelling shots that present, perhaps, the greatest challenge to the neurotic, fast-cutting of Hollywood.

In addition to these concerns, Medem's films must be located within the problematic belief system that European films are commonly perceived as having a national identity that, from the Oscars to the university departments in which they are often studied, is largely determined by language. This makes the movement away from seeing the director as muse-driven artist towards a view of him or her as an intermediary between industry and audience all the more amenable to the critics and academics for whom European cinema is seen as enclosed within an institution and a category of aesthetics, sub-divided into languages and separated into categories of high and low art that shepherd their distribution, prefigure their reception and inspire academic territoriality. A brief survey of Medem's academic standing in the UK and the USA reveals that only *Vacas* has truly entered the canon of films as academic texts in departments of Hispanic studies and courses on Spanish cinema, and it duly warrants a chapter to itself (by Isabel Santaolalla) in *Spanish Cinema: The Auteurist Tradition* (1999) edited by Peter William Evans and a sub-chapter in Mark Allinson and Barry Jordan's *Spanish Cinema: A Student's Guide* (2005). By way of contrast, the academic study of *Los amantes del Círculo Polar* and *Lucía y el sexo* is more often within courses on European cinema, Postmodernism and other theories of the present and future condition of cinema and culture that can be opportunistically illustrated by recourse to their fragmented or fractal narratives.

What is problematic about this emancipation of filmmakers such as Medem and Almodóvar from studies of 'national' Spanish cinema and their situating in a wide-ranging discussion of European or World cinema is their estrangement from the culture, art, traditions, society, politics and history that has formed them and informed the films they have written and directed. The fact that Medem was born into Franco's dictatorship, spent his infancy in the 'traitorous province' of the Basque Country, his elitist education in Madrid and came of age in 1975, the year that the dictator died, certainly demands a contextualisation of his social, political and academic formation within a state defined by the Spanish brand of Catholic-backed Fascism, while the additional fact that his own declarations encourage this is only extraneous to independent academic enquiry. In comparison, critics, audiences and academics constantly search for autobiographical resonance in the films of Pedro Almodóvar, but for all the exuberance of earlier works such as *La ley del deseo* (*Law of Desire*, 1987) and the refined artistry of later films such as *La mala educación* (*Bad Education*, 2004), Almodóvar remains a far more reclusive personality in the films he writes and directs than Medem, who, in addition to working off personal experiences, casts actors who look like him and, indeed, deliberately impersonate him onscreen due to their conviction that characters such as J in *La ardilla roja*, Ángel in *Tierra* and Lorenzo in *Lucía y el sexo* are manifestly Medem. That Medem is so adept at spinning tales of his films' geneses, personal resonances and emotional repercussions in interviews is eagerly supported by a burgeoning cult around his auteurist persona and such comments as Carmelo Gómez's assertion that 'his films are him. They're his time, his rhythm, his way of looking. They're him!' [15]. What must be investigated is how this 'him' is as much a product of social, political and cultural events and circumstances in a specific Spanish and Basque context as it is of the personal experiences that he espouses.

Fans of Medem tend to empathise with his existentialism and appreciate the relative optimism of his films, which also distances him from the 'tendency towards realism' that Elizabeth Ezra identifies in contemporary European cinema (2004: 15). In contemporary Spanish cinema, where the social realism of Fernando León de Aranoa (*Los lunes al sol/Mondays in the Sun*, 2002) and Iciar Bollaín (*Te doy mis ojos/Take My Eyes*, 2003) seems to exist in opposition to the 'shameless and deliberate affront to the liberal middle-class sensibilities of democratic Europe' that Núria Triana Toribio identifies in the superficially crass and commercially triumphant *Torrente* films (2004: 149), Medem is both applauded and derided as an auteur. Triana Toribio also attests that 'Julio Medem's cinema can be understood as an instrument by which the discourse that locates the Spanishness of Spanish cinema in high art and the intellectual traditions of the country is maintained' (2003: 149), but just as Medem's Basqueness bests his Spanishness, so the traditions are not all intellectual. For example, although many argue that *Lucía y el sexo*, which consecrated Medem's status in Spain and elsewhere, including the USA, was a 'high art' hit because of its artful symbolism and intriguing structure, others put the blame on a frequently naked Paz Vega. Yet both views are correct as both connect with traditions in Spanish cinema.

The films written and directed by Medem cannot be generically pigeon-holed as can those by his Spanish peers Álex de la Iglesia (*Acción mutante/Mutant Action*, 1993; *El día de la bestia/The Day of the Beast*, 1995) and Alejandro Amenábar (*Tesis/Thesis*, 1996; *Los otros/The Others*, 2001). Nor can his stylisation, which seems opposite to the realism favoured by Bollaín and León de Aranoa, be grouped with the composite art of Almodóvar. His films do, however, hark back to the *cine metafórico* (metaphorical cinema) of the dictatorship (1939–1975) that was associated with dissident filmmakers such as Juan Antonio Bardem (*Calle mayor/Main Street*, 1956), Carlos Saura and the producer Elías Querejeta (*Ana y los lobos/Ana and the Wolves*, 1972) and owed a long-standing debt to the Surrealist films of Luis Buñuel, whose influence is foregrounded in a fairly explicit link across the decades between the sliced cow's eye in *Un chien andalou* (*An Andalusian Dog*, 1929) and the many bovine eyes of *Vacas*. For reasons that included a fear of censure and punishment, these filmmakers used allegory, metaphor and the common vehicle of a suffering female protagonist who bore the weight of their symbolism to subvert a tradition of religious education based on parables and thereby communicate an alternative view of Spain to the most astute of domestic audiences and the most sympathetic of foreign critics. Although popular Spanish cinema of the dictatorship contained its own idiosyncratic filmmakers and a range of subversive elements (see Triana Toribio 2002; Lázaro Reboll and Willis 2004), the influence of *cine metafórico* on Medem, particularly his belated though avowedly life-changing first viewing of *El espíritu de la colmena* (*The Spirit of the Beehive*, 1973, directed by Víctor Erice and produced by Querejeta) should not be undervalued; for, even if it is likely exaggerated, the fact that Medem should assert its truthfulness is evidence of his own ambitions.

Secondly, just as subtitled sex is a long-established attraction of the arthouse, so the liberalness that followed the repeal of censorship in Spain in 1979 was a key factor in the international success of Spanish films with sexual themes and explicit content such as *¡Átame!* (*Tie Me Up! Tie Me Down!*, 1990), *Amantes* (*Lovers*, 1991) and *Jamón, jamón* (1992) and remains a factor in the success of films written and directed by Medem. Moreover, while *Vacas*, *La ardilla roja*, *Tierra* and *Los amantes del Círculo Polar* include sexual content, the fact that *Lucía y el sexo* is Medem's most explicit and most profitable film to date is surely not coincidental. In it he typically overvalues sex in an adolescent manner, treating it as sacred while his use of it skirts the profane. Moreover, the observation that Medem's own endeavour is echoed by his apparent alter ego in the film, the writer Lorenzo (Tristán Ulloa), only adds to this film's interrogation of the requirements, responsibilities and indulgences of authorship. Thus, as an example of how Medem's films must be contextualised within Spanish cinema, the overwrought hallowing of sexual and suffering women in his fictions must be recognised as connecting with both the lineage of abused and saintly females in the *cine metafórico* and a tradition of sexual content in Spanish cinema of the democracy.

Aitor

Of all possible contexts, however, it is that of the Basque Country and Medem's Basqueness that is the most critically undervalued. Medem is German-Basque on his father's side and Spanish-French on his mother's, but it is the Basqueness of his birth that most indelibly marks his work. Medem's early critical writings in the Basque newspaper *La voz de Euskadi* (*The Voice of Euskadi*) attest to an envious affinity with the directors associated with the New German Cinema, which he addressed as a model for the incipient post-Franco Basque film industry. Yet, until *La pelota vasca* so thoroughly reversed the trend, dwindling references to Basqueness in Medem's fictions prompted many to lose sight of the most prevalent line of enquiry into his own authorial relationship to film. However, as Isabel Santaolalla has so insightfully argued of *Tierra*, Medem's 'process of separation and distancing from the [Basque] mother land is a necessary strategy geared towards self-examination and self-definition [as] only through a dynamics of differentiation can an individual acquire self-knowledge' (1998: 333). Indeed, analysis of the films that Medem has written and directed reveals that before the ambition of the overtly political *La pelota vasca* and the as yet unfilmed *Aitor* he had already explored his fractious bloodline in five fictions, but without attaining peace of mind: a troubled immersion in paternal Basqueness that prompts a final but doomed recourse to a maternal France at the end of *Vacas*, a practical yet fantastical split from vengeful Spanishness with *La ardilla roja*,

a final flight from commitment to the land to flirtation with the sea in
Tierra, and a doomed attempt at reconciliation with his German
ancestry in *Los amantes del Círculo Polar*. Was it any wonder that the
protagonists of *Lucía y el sexo* had all sought refuge on a floating desert
island?

The conflict within a divided self, the duality that it engenders and
its correlative symmetry, is an earnestly personal predicament for
Medem, who in the midst of the furore over *La pelota vasca* that formed
the background to our interviews was always keen to stress this aspect
of his persona:

> I think there has always been something inside me that I needed to
> express since I was a boy. Because I was living between Madrid and the
> Basque Country I was very aware of how the Basque Country was seen
> from Madrid and of how Madrid was seen from the Basque Country. I felt
> a foreigner in both places. What I saw was that there was no wish
> to comprehend the divide. There are certain sentiments that come
> with feeling you belong to a place, to a collective, to a place that is
> misunderstood, and in my case that was doubled. [4]

It therefore seems that, by default as it were, it was Medem's wish to
comprehend the divide that in our first meeting and interview in
January 2002 [1] prompted him to assert the imminent production of
his ambitious *Aitor* and simultaneously accede to the proposal for this
book at a time when he was giddy from the scuffle for distribution
rights to *Lucía y el sexo* at the 2002 Sundance Film Festival and
cautiously optimistic of that same film's chances at the impending
Spanish Film Academy Awards. It was then that Medem performed
this pitch for his long-gestating project *Aitor*:

> Imagine that all the souls of the people that have died in the past, present
> and future because of the Basque conflict fall from the trees, and as they
> fall they sing. It will have this great choral effect. It's going to be so
> powerful. [1]

He described the eponymous Aitor as an impassioned soul whose
experiences of the Basque Country's purgatory between the past and
the present required more research if the film was to function as he
intended. Thus, he explained, he was duly working on a preparatory
documentary project called *La pelota vasca* based on his interviews with
a wide range of politicians, academics and activists about the history,
cultural identity and politics of the Basque Country.

Over two years later in our last interview in April 2004 [5] Medem proffered the second draft of the script for *Aitor* that he had finished just two days previously: a tale in two parts that is unified by the complex characterisation of Aitor, a filmmaker whose efforts at uniting the living lead him to reconciliation with the dead. The first part moves from the summer of 1976 to that of 1978, while the second takes place between the beginning of 2003 and that of 2004. *Aitor* takes the Basque conflict head-on before swerving onto a metaphysical plane mixing film, fact and fiction, torture and terrorism, spirits and singing souls, guilt, romance and redemption of a kind. Characters exist in halls of mirrors, seeing themselves multiplied in their younger selves, in their parents and in their representation by actors in a film-within-the-film. At one point, the spirits confront Aitor with the convoluted abstraction of his film-within-the-film and he admits, 'Mis metáforas se pegan unas contra otras' (Medem 2004: 61) (my metaphors are fighting each other). This revelatory exchange was also Medem's diagnosis of the problems still remaining with the project. Whereas in our first interview he had aimed for optimism, hope and humour, the experience of making, releasing and defending *La pelota vasca* had turned *Aitor* into a story of ageing, regret and frustration. It had become an examination of authorship and the problematic representation of political realities and violence through symbolism, analogy and metaphor. Like all of Julio Medem's films, therefore, *Aitor* is largely about Julio Medem. It reflects his experience of making *La pelota vasca* and his temporary reversal of the 'process of separation and distancing' (Santaolalla 1998: 333) that occurred during the writing of this book.

But with *Aitor* shelved – '*Aitor* demands distance from *La pelota vasca* and all that surrounded it' [4] – Medem subsequently returned to this process of separation and distancing with *Caótica Ana* (*Chaotic Ana*, 2007), 'a kind of farce' [4] about a young painter and believer in reincarnation, who pursues her vocation in Ibiza before returning to Madrid under the patronage of a millionaire much taken with her art, where she meets and falls in love with a young Morroccan. It may be that *La pelota vasca* exorcised the concerns that were crucial to Medem's formation and creativity but were nonetheless inhibiting of the more frivolous, sensual and commercial aspect of his fictions. Or it may be that *Caótica Ana* will act as counterweight to the complex seriousness of *La pelota vasca*, thereby allowing Medem to regain his balance and honour his increasingly vague commitment to make *Aitor*. For the moment, regrettably, it means that this book has no chapter on

Aitor. Instead, it begins with a biographical account and details of his academic and professional formation that include excerpts from his aforementioned critical writings. It also includes analyses of Medem's short films and the narrative strategies, character quirks and themes that would become particular and recurring in his work. It examines the five fiction films he has so far written and directed for their increasingly insular focus on relationships subject to chance, symmetry and reincarnation and it tracks political resonances that lead into his only documentary to date. Yet the absolute key to these films by Julio Medem is always resolutely Julio Medem.

In the entirety of Medem's *oeuvre* there is nothing that so explicitly defines his cinema as a moment in *Clecla* (2001), his three and a half minute contribution to the annual online No-Todo Film Festival, in which he asks his daughter Alicia how she knows her imaginary friend Clecla is there. 'Because she loves me', replies Alicia of a relationship made real by the emotion invested in it. And if Alicia is the link between Clecla and Julio Medem, then Alicia's way of seeing the world is also crucial to her father's relationship with film. For imaginary friends made real by the emotion invested in them abound in his worlds too, including the nationalist myth of the Basque Country in *Vacas*, J's creation of the perfect girlfriend from the emotional and physical wreckage of Sofía in *La ardilla roja*, Ángel's angel in *Tierra*, Otto's Ana and Ana's Otto in *Los amantes del Círculo Polar*, Lorenzo's Elena, Elena's Lorenzo and, most optimistically of all, Lucía's Lucía in *Lucía y el sexo*. The ruse also involves all those in *La pelota vasca*, 'the most controversial thing to hit Spanish cinema for years' (Tremlett 2003: 16), who thanks to Medem appear to be having an orderly discussion about the Basque conflict, which makes it the most fantastic gathering of all. Medem commonly interprets coincidence and fate as malleable in the face of emotion and empowers his characters to seek out their own happy endings, while, for audiences who likewise seek joyful resolutions, Cristina, Sofía, Ángel, Ana and Lucía all find their soul mates at the end of Medem's films: Peru, J, Mari, Otto and Lorenzo, respectively. It is only Otto in his half of *Los amantes del Círculo Polar* who stubbornly refuses to invest emotionally in his relationship with Ana and therefore suffers her tragic death in his version of events. Correlatively, there is a risk that Medem may exhaust or reduce his emotional commitment to the films he makes and thereby staunch his creativity.

There is also concern that Medem is presently a director with an authorial identity that is international, national (Spanish) and regional (Basque) and indeed continually in flux between them all, because 'today's auteurs are agents who, whether they wish it or not, are always on the verge of being consumed by their status as stars' (Corrigan 1991: 106). For example, Medem found it impossible to resist the invitation to contribute a five-minute film to the nineteen others in the portmanteau *Paris, je t'aime* (2007) for the thrill of finding himself in the company of Tom Tykwer, the Coen brothers, Alexander Payne, Isabel Coixet, Gus Van Sant, Alfonso Cuarón, Walter Salles and Olivier Assayas amongst others; but then he struggled to fit the tiny project into his pre-production schedule for *Caótica Ana* and bowed out late in 2005 to be replaced by Christopher Doyle. The gap between ability and ambition widens beneath the tightrope that contemporary filmmakers are required to traverse. But, such disappointments apart, this book attests that it is in the career-long formation of his self as subject that Julio Medem, the auteur, is a fantasy made real by the emotion he has invested in its making.

2

A sense of nobility: the making of Medem

For one whose films are so preoccupied with fabulism in national and personal histories, Medem is academically precise about his own lineage:

> The name Medem is German, although its origin is Scottish. It becomes German in the eighteenth century, Prussian to be exact. In my family there has always been a sense of belonging to nobility. [5]

Medem's German grandfather was a giant of 1.96 metres who died in Berlin of renal failure just before the Spanish Civil War but is remembered as Aki, the uphill skier, in *Los amantes del Círculo Polar*. He was survived by Medem's Valencian grandmother, who is recalled as Elena the Valencian cook in *Lucía y el sexo*, who took her son, Julio Medem San Juan, out of a German boarding school and the Hitler Youth to bring her children back to Spain and the Nationalist zone of Madrid at a time when the country and its cities were fragmenting into Republican and Nationalist territories. By 28 March 1939, when Francoist forces marched into Madrid, the Civil War was over and the city was in ruins.

Meanwhile, Medem's mother, Margarita Lafont Mendizábal grew up in the Basque resort of San Sebastian with her French father and Basque mother. Her post-war courtship and marriage to Julio Medem San Juan occurred in a Spain that was ignored by foreign powers and isolated from foreign influences by the Francoist regime. The Allies saw Spain as a remnant of the Fascism it had just eradicated in Europe and it was not until 1953, when Franco's febrile anti-communism was adjudged compatible with American foreign policy, that a treaty with the USA allowed for the establishment of American military bases near Madrid and Cadiz in return for foreign investment in Spanish goods, raw materials, industries and services. Thereafter, internal reforms by technocrats heralded a softening of the more hardline aspects of Francoism and led to the Stabilization Plan of 1959, which centred on plans for the liberalisation of the economy as demand for labour in new industries and services in the growing cities grew to the extent that agriculture now took up only 40% of the workforce. The Catholic Church still controlled education, oversaw social practices and kept the family unit sacrosanct and symbolic of its intensely patriarchal hierarchy, but fresh optimism twenty years on from the Civil War meant that 1958 still holds the record for the highest ever birth rate in Spain. Julio Medem Lafont San Juan Mendizábal, the eldest of five children for the Medems, was born in the Basque coastal town of San Sebastian on 21 October in the baby boom year that pushed Spain's population above 30 million.

Medem was joined by a brother Alberto in 1960 and his sister Ana in 1962, by which time the family had moved to Madrid, 'so I have hardly any memories of San Sebastian' [5]. Later came Sofía, who would be wardrobe assistant on *Lucía y el sexo*, and brother Álvaro, ten years Julio's junior. The city that took them in was sprawling onto the surrounding plains and tagging outlying villages with its public transport system. The unchecked growth wreaked havoc with town-planning and migrant settlements turned the city's outskirts into slums, but the centre of Madrid was vibrant. Medem's father was a draughtsman who worked in the studio above the family home, while his mother was a clothes designer whose shop Chavales (Kids) provided an exclusive outlet for her designer label Lafont, which was worn by the newest generation of Spain's aristocracy and the gaining middle classes.

Although Spain was yet to shrug off the rural poverty that had been exacerbated by the Civil War, the urban lower classes accepted a patient truce with the more repressive aspects of the dictatorship as social improvements and trickle-down wealth improved life in the city. The harshest policies of Francoism were directed at the provinces of Galicia, Catalonia and the Basque Country, where languages other than Spanish were outlawed, universities were closed or reduced to teaching sciences and local government was stripped back to administrative bodies that took their orders from Madrid. The adolescent Julio Medem lived these divisions in his own family:

> My father had two cousins with hunting reserves in Ciudad Real and Andalusia. These are very right-wing people; very good people that I love very much. With them I learnt what it was to live comfortably in the

Francoist regime. But I also learnt what it was to be Basque because I'd spend each summer in San Sebastian with my uncle and grandfather [on my mother's side]. My grandfather had lost his brother in the trenches during the First World War. He loved my father very much, but he was against the Nazis and against Franco, so I also experienced anti-Franco sentiment and the clandestine dissidence of some of my relatives. [5]

The knowledge of this extant conflict and duality was crucial to the developing political awareness of Medem, even as he typically experienced it at a sulkenly personal level:

I didn't have an infancy that I liked very much. I suffered a lot from feeling misunderstood. Nobody at home knew what I was like. I had a brother who was very extrovert and funny, while I was introverted, strange and fragile. At the time it was just too difficult for me to explain myself at home. I got embarrassed and used to think that they would never understand what I was about. My father never understood me and that was a hard thing to take. [5]

An introverted childhood is a common sympton of many filmmakers for whom refuge in the cinema leads to ambitions to express oneself on film. In Medem's case, this ambition was hastened by his father's own interest in recording his hunting exploits on Super-8. Says Medem:

He'd turn his films about hunting into little fictions and all of us in the family were his actors. And, because I liked the camera so much, when I was fourteen he showed me how to frame correctly, something that he did perfectly. That's how I discovered I could be a filmmaker, because of working with Super-8. I felt confident with the camera. [5]

This opportunity for bonding apart, however, Medem argued constantly with his father, who he describes as 'a man without a clear ideology' [5], and it is remarkable how fractious fathers complicate the plots of *Vacas*, *La ardilla roja*, *Tierra* and *Los amantes del Círculo Polar*.

An increasingly introverted Medem also discovered a talent for running when, at the age of ten, he found himself well out in front of forty other children in a school race and, as he asserts, 'by the time I was fourteen they were calling me SuperMedem' [5]. He also discovered a talent for the high jump, the long jump, the pole vault, the 1000 metres and broke the Spanish hurdling record, which made him a candidate for the Olympic Games until he diverted all his energy into writing:

I began to write because I fell in love with my neighbour. I was getting good grades and running well and doing it all for her. I put her on this special balcony in my subconscious from where I imagined her watching me. But she rejected me and I lived my infatuation in private. We saw each other every weekend and I loved her secretly, suffering all the time. Besides poems, I wrote the story of my life and called it *Mi primer día* (My First Day). It was my whole life in just one day. I was in love and this story was of how I dreamed things might be. I wrote and rewrote this story for a very long time. Nobody has ever read it. [5]

There is clearly a dark side to this formative obsession with engineering a fearful, masochistic mythology about a female that is resurrected in *La ardilla roja* and *Lucía y el sexo*, but Medem is more concerned with the convolution of his sculpted tale, which he tells because its postscript corroborates his notion of a life that, as Ana says in *Los amantes del Círculo Polar*, can be told by linking up coincidences: 'Many years later I discovered that the grandmother of this girl I'd been so in love with had been the lover of my grandfather in Zaragoza. So we were family, blood relatives' [5].

At fourteen Medem went to Madrid's exclusive El Pilar Secondary School to be taught by Marianist monks, who he claims 'made us feel we were the leaders of a Spain that had to be a certain way and no other, and the rest of the population was scum' [5]. One of his classmates was the dictator General Franco's grandson, J. Cristóbal Martínez Bordiú, while pupils at this elite school included José María Aznar (President of Spain 1996–2004) and many of the key financial and political figures of his administration. However, Medem asserts that his schooling had the opposite effect to that desired by increasing his contrary awareness of the social and political divisions and developments in Spain and so isolating him from his classmates: 'During the last three years of the dictatorship I was known as "the Basque" at my school' [5]. By 1970 the EEC had signed a preferential trade agreement with General Franco that exploited the tourist boom and ignored political oppression in order to attract foreign investors and on 8 June 1973 the hardline Admiral Carrero Blanco became president of the Council of Ministers, effectively assuming the Presidency of Spain as substitute dictator for a rapidly ailing Franco. However, on 20 December 1973 Carrero Blanco was assassinated by ETA when his chauffeur-driven Dodge Dart was blown over rooftops by a bomb containing 100 kilos of explosive. This killing removed the most serious obstacle to reform and allowed for Spain's relatively peaceful

and administrative transition to democracy following the death of
Franco on 20 November 1975. Says Medem: 'When Carrero Blanco
was killed, I said it was a good thing. Then when Franco died everyone
was distraught except for a Basque friend and I. We celebrated his death
with champagne in the schoolyard' [5].

Spain changed so quickly then that Medem, like many of those who
came of age at such a momentous time, was disoriented by the choices
thrown up by political, social and moral flux. His infatuation with his
neighbour, his running and obsessive rewriting of *Mi primer día* all
fizzled, but his enthusiasm for film endured. His father may have
taught him how to film and edit but he also kept his equipment under
lock and key. Only when he bought a new camera did he sell his old one
on to his eldest son, who had to save up his pocket money to buy it.
Thus equipped, the seventeen year old Medem set to the nocturnal
creation of fictions by rousing his sister Ana to film in secret around
their home, an experience that is echoed in the relationship of Otto
and his stepsister Ana in *Los amantes del Círculo Polar*. By setting up
his camera in various places and editing the shots together, Medem
began to understand that film could be, as he says, 'a portal into a
space and a time that was open to infinite, manipulative possibilities'
[5]. This imagined world made real on film was an arena for tangible
representations of his subconscious and a medium for the realisation
of illusionary places, times, atmospheres and relationships between
objects and people. The moviola was like one of the mechanisms in his
films identified by Peter William Evans that induce 'awareness of
parallel real and imagined worlds' (2004: 262). In it he discovered a
place where his filmed self looked back and conversed with his
watching self. Filmmaking turned an incomplete reality into a fictional
whole, where, for example, thanks to skilful editing Medem might be
with the girl that he had so often written about in *Mi primer día*. It was
also at this time that Medem encountered the psychotherapeutical
teachings of Sigmund Freud:

> Freud's book *The Interpretation of Dreams* fell into my hands. I was
> fascinated and read it all, read everything I could about the subconscious
> and psychoanalysis. And when I used to make my Super-8 films I'd
> always say that one day I'd manage to capture on film a piece of time and
> space from my subconscious. I always thought that some day I could
> unload my subconscious onto film without being aware of it, without
> even thinking rationally about it. [5]

The coincidence of Freud and film in late adolescence had a determinant effect on Medem, but any greater ambitions for film-making were postponed while he set to the more practical career of medicine. In 1976 Madrid had two state universities that took students from catchment areas that bore suspicious correspondence with the upper and lower class areas of the city. Because of his elitist schooling, Medem should have gone to the Autonomous University, but because there were so many applicants (a consequence of the record birth rate of 1958) places were limited to those with a final school grade of 7.4 or above and Medem had only 6.9. He spent a year sitting in on classes at the more proletariat Complutense University, where he met his first wife, Lola Barrera, and one year later went to Soria to begin his studies before moving to San Sebastian, his birthplace, where his university place was assured. Because there were few students on his course, Medem enjoyed a literally hands-on education in anatomy:

> The whole year we had this body without a head. It was a vagrant who had died from the cold. We kept him in formaldahyde at weekends. He was like a dried ham. It gave us the chance to study anatomy in great depth. [5]

Perhaps, after so much tortuous, adolescent introspection, Medem's delightful experience of dissection should not be undervalued for it carries a personal echo of the development of the sciences in the eighteenth century and the consequent denigration of spirituality in favour of a new focus on the body as the source of life's ills and fortunes. Thanks to medical research, which explored and charted the skeletal and muscular basis of human expression, the body became responsive and objectified and the concept of identity was transferred from a consideration of one's spiritual health to a notion of individuality that was contained and supported by the physical body. This new process of self-determination obviated the need for religious, royal or paternal approval for one's actions and provided the foundation for a revolutionary concept of citizenship that would hasten the French Revolution. It also forced a reconsideration of the distinctions in masculine and feminine behaviour and posited a revision of traditional gender roles. Similarly, Medem's lessons in anatomy briefly lessened his obsessions with abstract imaginings and tortuous psychology. After defining himself by his psychological frustrations for so long, he became aware that character and selfhood were also physical qualities and it is therefore perhaps a consequence rather than a coincidence (though Medem typically delights in claiming as one) that he met his wife Lola while a student of general surgery.

Lola Barrera is from Madrid and her parents are from the Canary Islands so the only way that she could complete her studies in San Sebastian alongside Medem was if they were to marry. 'We, who were adamant we were never going to be wed, suddenly found ourselves obliged to get married' recalls Medem [5]. But following five centuries of staunch Catholicism in Spain there was no real alternative to a church ceremony for atheists who had only recently been empowered to declare themselves as such. Moreover, civil weddings required months of paperwork in pursuit of a certificate that would be held in social disregard, whereas the Church could arrange a marriage in fifteen days.

> We told a priest in Madrid that we weren't believers or practising church-goers, but could he please do us this favour of marrying us. And he did. During the ceremony he asked all present to pray for us so that we'd get our faith back. Everyone laughed and my faith never returned. I don't think they prayed hard enough. [5]

Newlywed, Medem left for San Sebastian by way of Navarre and the Valley of Baztán (where *Vacas* would be filmed) and arrived just in time for his exams.

Medem graduated from the University of the Basque Country in 1985 with a degree in medicine and general surgery, but unlike Lola he would never practise medicine, being too distracted by film. His work on Super-8 began with the short films *El ciego* (*The Blind Man*, 1974), *Los jueves pasados* (*Thursdays Past*, 1977) and *Fideos* (*Noodles*, 1979), which begins in an abstract manner before revealing itself to be a plate of noodles being consumed as they are filmed from beneath a transparent plate. He had continued making films throughout his studies, *Si yo fuera un poeta (Antonio Machado)* (*If I were A Poet [Antonio Machado]*, 1981) and *Teatro en Soria* (*Theatre in Soria*, 1982), which was his last film on Super-8 and in which appears the cowardly male who ventures beyond his imagination and is transformed against his will by contact with reality – a prototype for the Medem archetype as represented by Manuel Irigibel in *Vacas*, J in *La ardilla roja*, Ángel in *Tierra*, Otto in *Los amantes del Círculo Polar* and Lorenzo in *Lucía y el sexo*. *Teatro en Soria* is a portrait of a young man in his flat in Soria who never leaves home, just spends all his time in this enormous glass balcony. When at last he goes out, he feels he is being observed from his own balcony and, says Medem, 'he misses himself because he's no longer there' [5].

1983 to 1985 are what Medem calls his 'film buff years, when I really found out which filmmakers I liked and I really liked auteurist cinema: Bergman, Tarkovsky, the French New Wave, Fellini, Buñuel. Antonioni, Pasolini and Visconti's first films – just stunning!' [5]. He was greatly impressed by his belated first viewing of *El espíritu de la colmena* (1973) and other key Spanish films of the transition, including *Arrebato* (1979) and the first works of Pedro Almodóvar. During this time he learned enough to demand greater aesthetic and narrative ambition from the films he watched and began writing film reviews for the specialist magazines *Casablanca* and *Cinema 2002* and the Basque newspaper *La voz de Euskadi* (*The Voice of Euskadi*), which has a mix of articles in Spanish and the Basque language of Euskera and was obsessed with the rocker Frank Zappa. Medem's enthralment to German cinema is a constant in his film reviews and features. His account of film noir (1983b: 35) honours the psychological effect of Expressionist lighting, while the complementary treatise on Fritz Lang includes the observation that 'sus películas reflejaban una forma de angustia paranóica, la del hombre acosado' (1983c: 26) (his films reflected a form of anguished paranoia, that of the hounded man), which is a trait of Medem's own films. Special editions of *La voz de Euskadi* dedicated to the annual San Sebastian Film Festival are heartily biased towards Basque filmmakers, though Medem is an exacting critic with passionate ideas about auteurist filmmaking that encompass the artistry of any number of a director's collaborators.

> The spectacle of talent is what I like. I also want to feel myself seduced by the artists behind the film. There is one artist who is the auteur and there are all the other artists, like the composer of the music. [5]

In a revealing review of Volker Schlondorff's *Un amour de Swann* (*Swann in Love*, 1983), Medem posits a celebration of New German Cinema as an auteurist model for an emerging Basque cinema and claims that Wim Wenders, Werner Herzog and Rainer Werner Fassbinder came from 'una concepción crítica que ya les venía perfectamente planteada, por lo que les fue sencillo independizarse para crear un fructífero cine de autor' (1984a: 21) (a critical concept that was already perfectly grounded, which is why it was easy for them to become independent in order to create a fruitful auteurist cinema). For Medem, auteurist filmmakers, who can be composers, editors, cinematographers and any actors of note, are go-betweens in the relationship between the artistic, social and political commitments of a national cinema. However, it is the emancipation of the director from the social and political context of his or her formation that intrigues him the most. Eulogies to Wim Wenders abound, most particularly in reference to the German director's America-set *Paris, Texas* (1984), which Medem describes as 'esperando con educada obediencia a que la razón le dé pista libre en los momentos claves' (1984a: 21) (waiting with polite obedience for reason to show the way at crucial moments). Even if, as he diagnoses of Mansur Madavi's *Dicht hinter der tur* (1984), the director's quirks 'parecen caprichos privados a los que nadie tiene derecho a acceder' (1984b: 35) (seem like private fancies to which nobody has right of access), Medem's critical writings maintain his conviction that symbolic and emotional resonance should be the aim of any director.

Medem's most revealing critical writing is in the service of combative articles on Basque cinema. In a piece entitled 'La creatividad en desuso' (1984c: 44) (Creativity in Disuse) he admits that Basque cinema may not yet exist, but in attempting to qualify and clarify its nature he analyses *La conquista de Albania* (1983), *La muerte de Mikel* (1983) and *Akelarre* (1983) and concludes that 'son vascas porque sus directores, sus temas y su financiación es vasca' (1984c: 44) (they are Basque because their directors, themes and financing are all Basque). In *Cinema 2001*, Medem delivers an epic essay entitled 'Cine vasco: una historia interrumpida' (Basque Cinema: An Interrupted History) in which he claims that 1983 'es el año de la esperada revolución cinematográfica vasca, que goza, por lo demás, de claras posibilidades de continuidad' (1983a: 21) (is the year of the long-awaited revolution of Basque cinema, which also possesses clear possibilities of continuity). For Medem, a unique Basque cinema may be distinguished by 'un cierto espíritu del País Vasco, una estética genuina y distinta [y] un peculiar sentido narrativo' (1983a: 25) (a particular spirit of the Basque Country, an authentic and distinct aesthetic [and] a particular understanding of narrative). He praises the directors Antxon Eceiza, Iñaki Núñez and Imanol Uribe and effects an accumulative celebration of left-wing, avant-garde Basque filmmakers that is tempered by warnings about the need to protect and serve 'el sentido de manifestación cultural con posibilidades de continuidad' (1983a: 28) (the sense of cultural representation and the possibilities of continuity). He approaches arguments surrounding the validity of a Basque-language cinema but is diverted by questions of funding before concluding that 'ya por el proceso de identificación nacional, ya como instrumento para exportar nuestra cultura, el cine vasco necesita urgentemente descubrirse, llegar a su mayoría de edad' (1983a: 29) (Basque cinema urgently needs to define itself, to come of age for the sake of national identity and the exportation of our culture). Above all else, this article is indicative of Medem's Romantic commitment to his Basqueness, which was commonly considered latent until *La pelota vasca*, when his opponents signalled his diluted bloodline, ignorance of Euskera and residency in Madrid as evidence of his opportunism. Yet the reacquaintance with his birthplace that resulted from the expediency of his studying at the University of the Basque Country and his resultant defence of 'nuestra cultura' (our culture) is vital to an understanding of his career.

In addition, it was also at this time that Medem began reading Latin American literature and was fascinated by magical realism: 'Once I started *Cien años de soledad* [*One Hundred Years of Solitude* by Gabriel García Márquez] I couldn't put it down. I dreamed about it. It influenced me immensely' [5]. In discussion, Medem does not distinguish between the magical realism of Garcia Márquez, which is concerned with the fabricated and literally fantastic such as ghosts, and the truly fantastic or 'marvellous real' of writers such as Alejo Carpentier, which deals with what is unfamiliar or 'an unexpected alteration of reality' (Carpentier 1995a: 86) from a European perspective but very real in Latin America, such as a cloud of butterflies obscuring the sun. These distinctions, which are blurred in *Vacas*, were also largely ignored by the Basque authors, musicians and filmmakers of the 1970s and 1980s, whose enthusiasm for Latin American literature was based on their recognition of a kindred spirit of vindicatory creativity borne of a post-colonial sensibility that reflected an affined desire to break away from imperial Spain and create an identity midway between long-held traditions and a progressive relationship with its past and present oppressors (Spain and the United States). Although the consideration of the Basque Country in terms of post-colonialism is massively problematic, the exemplary projection of an idealised homeland in Latin American literature did inspire many, including the Basque author Bernardo Atxaga, who reimagined the maligned Basque Country of the dictatorship in his epic, multi-strand narrative novel *Obabakoak* (1988). *Obabakoak* would exert a powerful influence on Medem when he wrote *Vacas* and, in return, Atxaga has the privilege of providing the introduction and conclusion to *La pelota vasca*. Moreover, Medem's response to the 2005 film *Obaba* (2005) directed by Montxo Armendáriz was one of disappointment at not having directed the film of the only book he had ever wanted to adapt for the screen.

The result of these self-professed 'film buff years' of 1983–85 was that Medem was estranged from his university studies in medicine and a routine and respected middle class career path by a confluence of Freud, Latin American literature, a belated viewing of *The Spirit of the Beehive*, the hobby of Super-8, a critical immersion in cinema and, most decisively, the exhilarating possibility of belonging to a Basque film movement that might have something of the auteurist character of New German Cinema about it. With great seriousness he dedicated himself to the writing of scripts in which he reworked Basque themes and symbols from myth and literature, developing obsessions that would result in *Vacas*, percolate through *La ardilla roja*, *Tierra*, *Los amantes del Círculo Polar* and *Lucía y el sexo* and eventually boil over into *La pelota vasca* and the writing of *Aitor*. Although all of Medem's fictions prior to *La pelota vasca* share a journey motif that takes his characters far from the Basque Country, this is not evidence of his estrangement from it but of his search for a vantage point from where to look back on the entire history and expanse of his birthplace. This only seeming separation from the Basque Country has been expertly identified by Isabel Santaolalla, who diagnoses his 'emotional and creative liberation from the nationalistic demands of Basqueness', but concludes that, 'a safe distance from the object of desire is necessary in order to prevent excessive identification with the object of the look' (1998: 334). For Santaolalla, Medem's 'distancing from his native landscapes is to be seen as a necessary step towards the exploration of his innermost personal or communal fears and/or desires' (1998: 334). Indeed, the deliberate, studious and experimental trajectory that Medem pursues between 1983 and the release of *Vacas* in 1992 is so determinedly adherent to his own published writings on Basque cinema that Medem appears to have met the challenge he set others.

His three unfilmed scripts from this period are the medium-length *La leche Basterretxe* (1984) that he defines as 'a Surrealist film about Basque cinema' [5], the full-length *Entre dos mares* (1986) and *Mari en la tierra* (1987). In *La leche Basterretxe*, a man enters his home and on the second floor finds a group of film fans watching the silent Basque melodrama *El mayorazgo de Basterretxe* (1927). He looks out the window and feels as if he were walking through a landscape of moving green mountains, where he comes across an *aizkolari* (Basque woodsman) chopping logs. Driven by hate, the *aizkolari* hurls his axe into a nearby forest, where he believes his enemy is hiding (Heredero 1997: 569). This image would be subsequently relocated at the centre of *Vacas* (and re-inserted at the centre of *La pelota vasca* too) because the axe (with a snake coiled around it) is the symbol of the Basque terrorist group ETA and therefore a potent indication of Medem's enduring commitment to the political history of the Basque Country. As Medem recounts, his script for *Entre dos mares* also attests to a development of archetypical themes.

> It's about someone who leaves the sea after twenty years away and returns to his village. His father has died leaving him a small house and a car. When he takes the car and tries to leave, a cow on its way to the slaughterhouse blocks his way. He hits it, the cow dies, and he falls into a state of shock and has to stay in the tavern until his car is fixed, where he meets people who come from the rural world but always breakfast early and then go to the slaughterhouse. Because he's been away twenty years he feels as if he's between two seas. [5]

Here is a prototypical construction by Medem: the psychological trauma of a character estranged from the time and space of his normal habitat, a journey prompted by fate and thwarted by chance, an animal catalyst (probably the same cow that blocks the road in *Vacas*), and a human protagonist who misses out on reconciliation with the patriarch but recognises the possibility of a metaphysical deliverance that he is too weakened by incertitude to pursue.

Recycling is even more evident with *Mari en la tierra*, for Medem drew on this script based on the legend of a Basque witch in order to guide the actress Silke in her characterisation of Mari in *Tierra*. During that film's shoot he even proposed the filming of *Mari en la tierra* by a crew of ten on 16mm in black and white as an appendix to the main feature, but his producers baulked at the expense. Instead, he reworked the script into a diary for Mari that was published with the script for *Tierra* by Planeta (Medem 1997). Bearing in mind Medem's technique of writing scripts by assuming the first-person subjectivity of his characters, the preface to Mari's diary is revealing of his mindset at the time:

> Quiero convertirme en una escritora de éxito, pero no sé escribir. [. . .] Sólo necesito ser sincera, es decir, poner cualquier cosa. Eso incluye

mentir. [. . .] Y como tampoco sé muy bien a qué debo tener respeto, pues
. . . ¿por qué tenerlo? Así que soy libre. [. . .] Pretendo no mirar hacia
delante, no saber hacia dónde voy, sólo sorprenderme viajando por
lugares en los que no he estado nunca. [. . .] Sólo espero pacientemente
a llegar, dentro de diez años [. . .] a convertirme verdaderamente en una
escritora leída por millones de personas. (Medem 1997: 17–18)
   (I want to become a successful writer, but I don't know how to write.
[. . .] I only need to be sincere, that's to say, to write whatever comes to
mind. And that includes lying. [. . .] And as I also don't know who or what
I should be respectful of . . . well, why be respectful? So I'm going to be
free. [. . .] I'm going to try not to look ahead, to not know where I'm going,
just surprise myself by travelling through places I've never been before.
[. . .] I only patiently hope to manage, within ten years, to become a real
writer who is read by millions of people.)

To further this ambition, Medem enrolled on a course in
professional video in 1984 that was sponsored by the local council of
Guipuzcoa and by 1986 he was working on such disparate projects as
a pilot programme of an aerobics class for Spanish television and a
promotional documentary about tourism entitled *San Sebastián:
dentro del mar*. He graduated to 35mm when he began working with
a group of filmmakers benefitting from subsidies awarded by the
autonomous Basque government, which had dedicated 5% of its entire
budget to the revitalisation of Basque cinema, and in 1986 he created
Grupo Delfilm with Luis Campoy and wrote, produced, edited and
directed *Patas en la cabeza*. *Patas en la cabeza* illustrates what Medem
describes as 'the impulse of a character to communicate, to talk and to
begin a relationship with someone, with a girl that he hardly knows'
[5]. It begins with a seagull in flight and cuts to a travelling shot of a
young couple striding determinedly along a suburban street, the young
man speaking archly of fate: 'Sometimes chance or destiny can be
organised and, on occasion, manipulated. These can be opportunities!'.
The man (played by Joaquín Navascués, who Medem had admired in
Arrebato) implores his companion to arrange a meeting with a friend
of hers, with whom he is eagerly obsessed: 'I was able to imagine her
perfectly. In my bed. I spent the whole night watching her.' This echo
of Medem's infatuation with his neighbour is easily spotted, but
Medem is also critical of his alter ego, allowing the woman to describe
him as 'infantile, insecure, immature, obsessive . . . '. Gradually, the
successive backwards-forwards travelling shots amount to a symmetry
that clarifies how the friends are actually engaged in the invention of

this other woman because their shared illusion of her is a way for both these timid romantics to be together. *Patas en la cabeza* contains several of Medem's aesthetic and thematic characteristics such as the display of juxtaposed subjectivities and the invention of fantasy lovers. It also includes a shot of the man leaning on the railings above the crashing waves on San Sebastian beach like J in *La ardilla roja* and bemoaning his ineffectual romantic and suicidal impulses – 'Who knows, I might even kill myself!' – as well as a foretaste of the geometric puzzle of *Los amantes del Círculo Polar* and a precursor of the writer Lorenzo's escape hole at the centre of *Lucía y el sexo*: 'By the way', says the young man, 'I'm going to write a novel. I'm going to write it backwards from the end to arrive at the superficial, the beginning of the work. What is most clear to me, most precisely, is that that in the middle there's a comma, just like that, to relax.' *Patas en la cabeza* was selected for the San Sebastian Film Festival and won the main prize in the Basque Film Festival in Bilbao.

The following year Medem collaborated on the script, direction and editing of José María Tuduri's *Crónica de la segunda guerra carlista* (*Chronicle of the Second Carlist War*, 1987), which prepared him for *Vacas* by immersing him in the history of the Basque Country and Carlism, the nineteenth-century protest movement in rural Catholic Spain. He also scripted, directed and edited *Las seis en punta* (*Six O'Clock Sharp*, 1987). The most explicitly Surrealist of his films, *Las seis en punta* tells of a pre-pubescent boy who brings his dream of an older female guardian-friend to life but is unable to control the nightmare that becomes of it. Medem claims the idea came to him suddenly at night, but that 'it was a great effort to transcribe it afterwards because I could so easily have fallen into the trap of imposing an order and a narrative sense that just wasn't needed' [5]. Medem received funding from the Basque Government on this film and began his long-term collaboration with the composer Alberto Iglesias, who had scored many recent Basque films. 'It was a kind of free university amongst friends', says Iglesias of the time. 'We made short films very quickly and without much money; maybe that's why my score is so minimalist. I bought a Chicco baby-rattle, which is one of the most amazing instruments I've ever known. It's the Stradivarius of baby-rattles' [16].

Las seis en punta is distinguished by agile camerawork, minimalist mise en scène, the bleached colours and the menacing atmosphere conjured by the score. The boy returns home from school to be greeted by a young woman who waits on him with a birthday cake for someone about to turn thirty. He sneezes but fails to dim the birthday candles and blows open all the doors in the apartment instead. He slides a present across the table to the woman and she unwraps a watch showing six o'clock sharp. Having misplaced his spectacles, Ignacio pinches the glass cover from the Dalíesque watch and uses it as a monocle, causing the woman to lose the minute hand, which sticks in her forearm like a needle and causes her to deflate (clock hands are needles – *agujas* – in Spanish, hence the titular wordplay). Medem claims *Las seis en punta* is Surrealist because 'the elements appear in relation to what comes immediately afterwards' [5]; but more than this objective rationalisation of the events onscreen, the film reveals a sinister undercurrent to the imaginings of a lonely, frustrated child. Medem agrees:

> My films always have a lot to do with my childhood. I've been very immature and I still am. I had a very long adolescence. There's a part of me, my inner child, that's useful for inventing characters. [5]

Las seis en punta was screened during the San Sebastian Film Festival and won the Telenorte prize for best Spanish short film in the Bilbao International Film Festival. This success prompted Medem to approach the Basque producer Elías Querejeta, a key figure of the dissident cinema under Franco, in the hope of securing financing for *Entre dos mares*. Querejeta declined, but at the time he was keen to nurture new filmmakers who might provide fresh perspectives on the evolution of democratic Spain and after a viewing of *Las seis en punta* he invited Medem to submit a proposal for a Spanish National Television (TVE) project entitled *Siete huellas* (*Seven Imprints*, 1988) to be made up of seven half-hour films on 35mm by debutante writer-directors. Medem's *Martín* was episode six, co-written with Juan Manuel Chumilla and made with a semi-professional crew that included Alberto Iglesias and cinematographer Gonzalo Fernández Berridi, who had shot *Patas en la cabeza* and would film *La ardilla roja* and *Los amantes del Círculo Polar*. With the full weight of Querejeta's production company behind him, however, Medem was forced to compromise his auteurist ambitions and entered into a conflictive working relationship that resulted in a satisfactory but unremarkable feature.

Martín begins with images of hunters that recall, deliberately it would seem, key films with a hunting theme produced by Querejeta such as *La caza* (*The Hunt*, 1965), *Pascual Duarte* (1975) and *Furtivos* (1975), which symbolically and metaphorically exploited the passion for hunting of the dictator. In *Martín*, two huntsmen toting shotguns approach a hut from which emanates a banshee-like wail, but this is revealed to be a film on television watched by Martín (played by Miguel Ángel García, the teenage Peru in *Vacas*), his deaf and dumb father and his stern and frumpy mother, who is the housekeeper of a block of flats in whose basement they reside. By juxtaposition Medem builds the tension between the televised film and the reaction of the family as the hunters burst into the hut with shotguns blasting to disempower the spell of the wailing that comes from their target: a frantic blonde. But the denouement is pre-empted by Martín's mother's superior agility with the remote control. Martín, with his imagination about what happens next on overdrive, is sent off to bed. Still troubled, he spends the next morning sitting on the kerb outside the apartment block in a deserted midsummer Madrid. He is another in a long line of children in Spanish cinema struggling to make sense of a world ruled by adults who understand things even less, such as Ana (Ana Torrent) in *El espíritu de la colmena* and *Cría cuervos* (*Raise Ravens*, 1975), both produced by Querejeta. Martín's friends are all at the beach and television news items on frolicking holidaymakers intensify his isolation. When a mysterious young woman (Laura Bayonas) comes to stay in the penthouse apartment, Martín, whose regular chores include watering the plants of absent tenants, is relieved of the task. Concerned about one dying ficus, he exhorts her to care for it but is dismayed by discovery of its empty pot and shredded branches in her rubbish. However, upon stealing onto her balcony, he discovers she has pruned and replanted it. He also discovers her portfolio of stills from films in which she has appeared, including one of her bewigged, blonde and playing dead as the wailing woman of the previous evening's film. Unable to make sense of the coincidence, he spends a night in terror that is exacerbated by a thunderstorm and various horror movie clichés, but the next morning the woman leaves in a taxi, pausing only to explain her profession of actress to Martín, whose final enlightenment about the reality of this fantasy woman allows for her farewell smile to be subjectively freeze-framed in his memory and behind the closing credits.

The experimentation and originality of *Las seis en punta* and *Patas en la cabeza* is absent from *Martín*, which instead exploits the kind of generic horror clichés that Medem would thankfully not return to until the overwrought scene of the dog attack in *Lucía y el sexo* in 2001. Unlike his peers Alejandro Amenábar (*Tesis*, 1996) and Álex de la Iglesia (*El día de la bestia*, 1995), both of whom have spun horror film conventions into self-reflexive essays on genre dynamics, Medem treats genre conventions derisively as a last resort for the sensationalist plot machinations of *Martín* and *Lucía y el sexo*, but without the wit nor irony of his aforementioned peers. It seems unlikely that Medem would have maintained a distinguished career in film had he directed the generic scripts of others, for his skill and artistry stems from enthusiasm for projects that are based upon his exploration of themes with personal resonances. It was therefore extremely fortuitous, though Medem would no doubt call it coincidental, that the 1980s were a time of experimentation and self-discovery for those who the historian John Hooper calls *The New Spaniards* (1995), when political, sexual and creative autonomy was its own retort to the censorship of the past. The repeal of censorship in 1979 prompted the Spanish public's brief fling with pornography and a more elitist but no less passionate reacquaintance with a backlog of unseen arthouse cinema before settling down to the more conventional pleasures of uncut Hollywood product. At the same time, the phenomenon of Madrid's *movida*, during which the marginal characters, sexualities and lifestyles of the capital's nightlife were relocated at the centre of contemporary Spanish culture, showed that anarchy was within reach of even the most staid and stagnant of arts. Music went glam, art went pop and drugs went well with everything. However, Medem was not a part of this. Instead, at the time he was unemployed, living in the Basque mountains on the single wage of his doctor wife and caring for their infant son Peru. In recalling this time, he describes a struggle against depression, insomnia and boredom that was alleviated by writing the script of *Vacas* and a series of short stories that each turned on the notion of a lie, one of which would become *La ardilla roja*. He also latched on to the cultural revolution that was taking place in the Basque Country and connected with artists, writers, musicians and filmmakers who had a common desire to promote the revitalisation of Basque culture and identity. Unlike Madrid's *movida*, however, which recklessly, frivolously and dogmatically ignored the consequences of its excess and extravagance, this Basque cultural movement was conscious of its social, political, linguistic and artistic responsibilities.

In 1989 Medem won a commission to write, direct and edit a short feature called *El diario vasco* that was to educate schoolchildren about the workings of a newspaper and in 1990 he was selected by the European production company Romana San Paolo Audivisi to represent Spain in an international project called *100 Minutes of Young European Cinema* for which ten directors had been chosen (two from each co-producing country: France, Italy, Germany, Great Britain and Spain) to make a short film for a television project with the umbrella title of *El lenguage de los sentimientos* (*The Language of Feelings*). Medem also edited Germán Beltrán's short film *La espalda del cielo* (1988) and Koldo Eizaguirre's *El puente* (1990), while writing and reworking scripts that included the medium-length *Peru, el hogar del arquitecto* (*Peru, The Home of the Architect*, 1988) and the full-length *Vacas*, for which he received a development award of 1,500,000 pesetas from the ICAA (Instituto de la Cinematografía y de las Artes Audiovisuales).

Meanwhile, Felipe González's Spanish government weathered corruption scandals that prompted public disillusionment (*desencanto*) with a democracy that was barely a decade old. Many of the financial architects of Spain's fast-track capitalism in the eighties such as Mario Conde and the head of the national bank, Mariano Rubio, were indicted to testify before enquiries into insider trading and were shortly thereafter imprisoned. In the Basque Country, the 1988 Ajurea Anea Pact against violence and towards the reincorporation into civil life of reformed and pacifist ETA activists had been sidelined by terrorist attacks, the dissention of Herri Batasuna (the political party associated with ETA) and González's government's adoption of the very tactics of indiscriminate terror that had characterised both the Franco regime and ETA's own strategy (see Woodworth 2001). The beginning of the 1990s also brought a reduction in the Basque government's investment in Basque cinema and an awareness that the lack of a cultural productive tradition meant that the strategy intended to create trade and a cultural identity through the professionalisation of filmmaking personnel largely backfired, when most left the Basque Country to seek work in Madrid, including Medem, whose attempts at securing funding in Madrid at a time of such political turmoil, particularly for a script like *Vacas*, must be seen as symptomatic of the changes in Basque film culture, as well as timely, bold and naive. If, as suggested, Medem had indeed set the bar high for a 'New Basque Cinema' and taken a decade-long run up to *Vacas*, he could not have landed in Spanish cinema at a more fractious or propitious time.

3

The other side of the hole: *Vacas* (1992)

The state monopoly of television in Spain ended in 1989 when Spanish Canal Plus was formed to win one of three independent television franchises. The others went to Antena 3 (part-owned by ABC) and Tele 5 (part-owned by the Italian mogul and politician Silvio Berlusconi). This Spanish wing of Canal Plus, the multinational European satellite subscription television company, was part-owned by Prisa and French Canal Plus. As the channel took off, it changed the viewing habits of 'a nation of TV addicts, [for] the Socialists' decision to allow competition on television is likely to be seen with hindsight as one of their most valuable contributions to the consolidation of democracy, comparable with their taming of the army' (Hooper 1995: 306). Its programming also created new sources of financing for Spanish filmmakers that revolutionised the way that films were produced, marketed and distributed. Prior to the 1990s, explains the producer Fernando de Garcillán, 'Spanish cinema had an antiquated structure that was weak and obsolete with terrible production criteria, very little development money and very poor post-production facilities' [9].

Successive government policies have since pushed the Spanish film industry towards the kind of independence that carries with it a boom or bust mentality, but back in 1991 the establishment of Sogetel, the film production wing of the Sogecable group, provided impetus for the revitalisation of Spanish cinema, for Sogecable's links with Prisa prompted their participation in the long-term plan to channel domestic product into the programming of Canal Plus. To win one of the independent television franchises, Prisa had agreed to reserve 25% of its screenings for Spanish films, before realising that the present output of the film industry barely measured up to their generosity. Nevertheless, with an obligation to the government and a correspondent self-serving interest in supporting Spanish cinema, Sogetel (renamed Sogecine in 1997) sought out independent companies such as Bailando con la Luna (Dancing with the Moon, a line from *A Midsummer Night's Dream*), whose managing director, Fernando de Garcillán, had moved into film production after assisting his brother in that role on Pedro Almodóvar's *Laberinto de pasiones* (*Labyrinth of Passions*, 1982). Says Garcillán:

> What happened next was that loads of scripts started arriving, especially when people knew there was a big production company with lots of resources backing us. And one day, amongst the mountains of scripts that I had, there was one with a curious cover, a collage of photographs, called *Vacas*. I picked it up and read it and it was marvellous. I'm talking about the original script, because the one filmed was much shorter. The original was just beautiful, a museum piece. I read it and called Julio. [9]

With Sogetel behind Bailando con la luna, *Vacas* would mark a new way of filmmaking in Spain that was based upon independent financing, pre-sold distribution rights to the new private television channels, American-style publicity, innovative strategies for attaining foreign sales and a fresh emphasis on the notion of the filmmaker as auteur that made him or her the figurehead of a film's commercial campaign, one that exploited popular and critical support for the autonomy of the creative individual as emblem of a nation's progressive sense of identity. Previously, producers had all baulked at the weirdness of the script that Medem had proffered on his search for financing in Madrid and suggested that he at least change the title. Medem had returned to the Basque Country and written a supposedly more commercial script called *La ardilla roja*, only to receive the call from Fernando de Garcillán ten days later. 'He told me that he wanted some pretty cows for the coming year, for the Berlin Film Festival. It was a dream come true', says Medem [5]. Contracts were signed in March 1991 and filming began in July. *Vacas* was one of only 52 feature-length films made in Spain in 1992, compared to 137 in 2002 (ICAA 2003). Sogetel assigned a budget of just 165,000,000 pesetas and fitted this peculiar project, its debut director, cast of relative unknowns and risky subject matter amidst a roster of expensive star vehicles such as *Una mujer bajo la lluvia* (*A Woman in the Rain*) with Ángela Molina and Antonio Banderas, *Demasiado corazón* (*Too Much Heart*) with Victoria Abril and *Yo me bajo en la próxima, ¿y usted?* with Concha Velasco and José Sacristan, none of which are remembered with much affection, if at all.

The shooting script of *Vacas* is credited to Michel Gaztambide Muñoz and Julio Medem Lafont and is dated 29 July 1991 in Medem's hometown of Amasa in the Basque province of Guipuzcoa. *Vacas* tells of a feud that rages between three generations of two rival Basque families, the Irigibels and the Mendiluzes, beginning with the second Carlist War of the nineteenth century, in which the Basque defence of the *Fueros* (laws based on a privilege of autonomy that had protected the Basque Country from absolutism) was allied to Catholic, conservative Carlists fighting for the establishment of a separate line of the Bourbon family on the Spanish throne. Instead of jingoism, however, *Vacas* illustrates the jealousy, incest and ancient, inbred conflicts that hindered the Basque Country's progress into the twentieth century. Indeed, the film ends just as the Spanish Civil War is beginning in 1936. For the script of a debutant director, *Vacas* certainly presents the kind of cavalier attitude to formal narrative conventions and aids to audience comprehension that would cause most producers to pass even if it were not also told from the viewpoint of cows. Far from chaotic, however, the shooting script is precisely divided, sequential and structured. The inside cover of the copy held in the offices of Medem's production company Alicia Produce (Medem and Gaztambide 1991) reveals a folded map of the villages where it was filmed, Arrondo and Bearzun. Exclamation marks cover every page like splattered flies, while copious notes on costumes, house plans and camera placements fill the margins. The first page presents a listing of the four chapters that is numbered, chronological and timed.

I.	El aizkolari cobarde	(1875)	10 min.		
II.	Las hachas	(1905)	20 min.		
III.	El agujero encendido	(1915)	30 min.		
IV.	Guerra en el bosque	(1936)	35 min.	(Medem and Gaztambide 1991: 1)

However, this simple index suggests nothing of the conundrums of time and space within, nor the actors in multiple roles. To aid comprehension, the second page offers this crib:

	1875	1905	1915	1936
Carmelo	30†			
Juan	Born	30	40	61
Catalina	Born	30	40	America
Paulina		55–60	†	
Peru		Born	10	31

Manuel	30	60	70	†	
Ignacio		30	40	America	
Madalen		30	40	61	
Cristina		6	16	37	
Middle sister		8	18	–	
Older sister		10	20		
Ilegorri	10	40	50	71†	
Lucas		10	20	41†	(Medem and
					Gaztambide 1991: 2)

Thereafter the script offers a balanced, finely crafted framework for evocative imagery that is plagued by terrible doodles. Surprisingly for a filmmaker with such a pronounced visual sense, disproportionate stick-men and malformed animals prove that Medem cannot draw, though the misshapen menagerie does attest to his frustrating struggle to match imagery to the words on his page. He describes the initial script as 'skeletal' [5] and confirms that the idea for *Vacas* came from his observation of rural Basque customs while tending his son Peru and the script that he had written in 1984 called *La leche Basterretxe*, which included the image of an *aizkolari* hurling his axe at an unseen enemy:

> One morning, he's in front of his house and training, when he hears his rival training in the forest. He can't bear the rhythm of their axes. That was it: this idea of rivalry. I always say the main problem in the Basque Country is between the Basques themselves. The axe is the symbol of ETA, that was very clear to me. The only thing the *aizkolari* can do is hurl his axe against the forest. [5]

This shot, which appears at the centre of *Vacas*, reappears at the centre of *La pelota vasca*, where it punctuates demands for ETA to leave the Basque people in peace and serves as a reminder of the cyclical nature of both the Basque conflict and the films of Medem. 'I re-use that shot because that's how my films began. It's what I've always wanted to express', he explains [5]. In *Vacas*, the impact of the axe sends out concentric shockwaves that resonate at the beginning and end of the film, travelling a spiral route through cyclical narratives that spin above each other and create the central void of *Vacas*, the hole in the wizened tree.

'What's on the other side of the hole?' As the aged Manuel Irigibel (Txema Blasco) answers the child Peru: 'The same as here or similar. You are on the other side.' The cyclical narrative of *Vacas* spins around this hole like a broken record, revealing how the successive generations are destined to repeat the mistakes of the past. Moreover, a retrospective analysis of Medem's fictions demands an Alice-like journey down this hole to pass through *La ardilla roja*, *Tierra* and *Los amantes del Círculo Polar* in order to emerge into sunlight through the hole that exists at the centre of *Lucía y el sexo*; for this is the loop that has allowed Medem to endlessly rework his symbols and protagonists in the hope that unsatisfactory realities can be rectified in a fantasy world. Nevertheless, although schematic symbolism and geometric structures are common tropes in films written and directed by Medem, he denies any cold-bloodedness in his calculations of symmetry and cyclical narratives and claims that the emotional effect of the images is his true objective. He reasons that the four chapter headings in *Vacas* are props for an emotional synthesis of imagery that is conditioned by applied meaning rather than its function within the syntax of a conventional narrative. In other words, as Medem declares:

> *Vacas* is a Surrealist film because of how things happen. Nothing happens for a reason or a pre-established narrative. There's no prior debate, nor any dominant logic. Things happen according to the most insane pleasure emanating from a place that is so near to what is dreamed. [5]

Declaring a film to be Surrealist suggests that its meaning is only found in the subconscious of its audience; however, the Surrealism that Medem claims for *Vacas* is only part of a medley of associated elements that includes magical realism, the 'marvellous real' and the fanaticism of extremist Basque nationalism. Played straight, *Vacas* would be like Pietro Mascagni's *Cavalleria Rusticana*, 'a myth that was something akin to the official ideology of the Sicilian Mafia for nearly a century and a half' (Dickie 2004: xiv), but thankfully it is also magical realist, fantastic, parodic, postmodern, ironic and Surrealist. The virtue of this mix is that *Vacas* consequently illustrates the close, overlapping relationship of these elements in order to reveal the irony that illusions of the Basque Country as a progressive, independent nation are based on allusions to a mythic race, nation and masculinity that have fuelled the delusions of nationalist fervour that inhibit the nation's progress in the real world.

Magical realism is present in the paradox of the union of opposites like life and death in the portal of the hole in the tree as well as in the tensions that exist between the feudal, rural past of the Basque Country in the nineteenth century and its uneasy progress towards industrialisation in the twentieth century. Most emphatically, because

magical realism brokers no conflict between a rational view of reality
and a deadpan acceptance of the supernatural, the film punctuates the
historical reality of successive civil wars with images of such supernatural portent as the scything scarecrow, the tree hollow, the watchful
cows and the reincarnation of its single protagonist played by Carmelo
Gómez as Manuel, Ignacio and Peru Irigibel, whose lives illustrate the
moral and physical deterioration of the Basque Country by typifying
magical realism's concept of time as 'exist[ing] in a kind of timeless
fluidity' (Flores 1995: 115). As in Latin American literature, where the
deadpan juxtaposition of real and ordinary events and unreal, fantastic,
dreamlike elements expresses a contrast between European rationality
and a primeval understanding of the world through the irrational
elements of indigenous faiths and superstitions, so *Vacas* juxtaposes
this evolving character played by Gómez, who begins by escaping
the Carlist War and ends by escaping the Spanish Civil War, with the
stagnating myths of his homeland. Manuel (when played by Gómez,
not Txema Blasco as an aged man, whereupon he becomes a separate
character), Ignacio and Peru Irigibel combine to make a single pilgrim
who, like the audience, must distinguish between what is traditionally
understood as the literal fantastic of magical realism (such as the spirits
of the woods, the cows and the tree hollow) and that which only seems
fantastic because of the way it is represented by extremist Basque
nationalism, such as ancient racial purity, virtuous superiority and
the righteousness of fighting for this cause in repetitive civil wars. The
distinction is frustrated, however, because Medem combines the fabricated magic of the myths of Basque superiority (which stem from the
often histrionically racist writings of the father of Basque nationalism
Sabino Arana (1865–1903) and his idea of the Basques as a special race
with a land of their own) with his own no less artificial conjuring of
magical and supernatural elements from the Basque landscape. That
is to say, unable to separate his pantheistic reverence for the land, its
flora and fauna from the nationalist hagiography of its people, Medem
may sometimes seem as guilty as Arana of romanticising Basqueness.

On the other hand, the 'marvellous real' (Carpentier 1995a: 75–88),
which only seems fantastic because it is strange to foreign observers
but is found, as Alejo Carpentier said of Latin America, 'en vuelta de
cada esquina, en el desorden, en lo pintoresco de nuestras ciudades, en
los rótulos callejeros o en nuestra vegetación o en nuestra naturaleza
y, por decirlo todo, también en nuestra historia' (Anon 2004) (around
every corner, in disorder, in our picturesque cities, in street signs or in

our vegetation or in our nature and, to cap it all, in our history), is largely suffocated and driven out by the twin deceivers of bizarre camera angles and political agitprop. What is missing from *Vacas* is any corrective sense of ordinariness, which would be an impossibly dull conclusion for Medem, who can't resist the temptation to err towards mythopoeia. There is nothing mundane or routine about this representation of rural life, as there is in reality and in realist films such as *Tasio* (1984, produced by Querejeta and directed by Montxo Armendáriz), for example. Representations of the rural Basque Country thus fall prey to that which Alejo Carpentier describes as 'an amplification of the scale and categories of reality perceived with particular intensity by virtue of an exaltation of the spirit that leads it to a kind of extreme state' (Carpentier 1995a: 86) because the exaltation of the spirit is the product of either nationalist rhetoric or cinematic artistry, which, from the time of the Nazi propaganda film *Triumph of the Will* (1935) have been infamously conjoined on film.

Like Manuel feigning death to escape the trenches, Ignacio escaping to America and Peru escaping to France, however, Medem escapes the trap of matching the fabricated Basqueness of Arana with the no less fabricated Basqueness of his own film by recourse to Surrealism because, although the representation of the Basque Country as object of desire is fabricated by mise en scène and montage, the effect of the artifice is incalculable and the subconscious tremors it provokes are disturbing. Whereas 'magic realism, unlike the [. . .] surreal, presumes that the individual requires a bond with the traditions and the faith of community, that s/he is historically constructed and connected' (Foreman 1995: 286), Medem's Surrealism is designed to subvert the discourse of fabricated Basqueness by provoking subconscious misgivings that suggest how the difference between the Basque utopia and the Basque dystopia is subjective, being based upon an emotional response that arises from a subconscious reaction that may be prey to exploitation by such forces as radical nationalism but is still potentially unique and subversive. Says Medem: 'Surrealism interests me because one sees an image without explanation, but as soon as one starts to analyse it, it acquires one' [5]. In *Vacas* situations accumulate that have more to do with tone and atmosphere but they acquire meaning by imposition, and vice versa, for Medem also deconstructs myths of Basqueness in order to reveal the political spin that went into their making. In sum, Medem clearly has his cake and eats it with *Vacas* as regards its Romantic and magical realist construction of myths of

Basqueness, and its Surrealist and ironic deconstruction of them. More specifically, Medem looks back to Romanticism in his recreation of the film's bellical and pastoral settings so beloved of radical Basque nationalists, but uses Surrealism (which André Breton considered the heir to Romanticism) to subvert this contact with the mythic past. Whereas a traditional, Homeric narrator was an objective, unimpeachable guide, a Romantic narrator played games with facts, offering biased, unreliable exposition. However, a subsequent literary surge in experimentation involving multiple narrators or views from the same narrator at different times and a shuffled deck of flashbacks and flash-forwards offering hindsight and premonition as a way of questioning the veracity of events and their telling meant that a reader not only had to evaluate the facts but also the way they were presented. The result was that no single, reliable, definitive narrative perspective was discernible and the break-up of the narrative was correlative with a lack of any adequate explanation for unfolding events that often folded back in on themselves in a Surrealist manner. In his second manifesto, Breton admitted that 'we [the Surrealists] are quite willing, historically, to be considered today as the tail, but then such a prehensile tail' of Romanticism (1962: 184). This admission was pragmatic, even opportunistic, for Surrealists look backwards for selfish reasons, hoping to justify their questions by finding universal, cyclical incidents of their asking just as Medem similarly aspires to a shift from the concrete reality of historical events to the suggested intangibility of a world beyond human conflict and reason, where liberation is realised in the infinite, and therefore often ends up going round in circles, trapped in a cyclical patterning that is crucial to his films. Indeed, it is even possible to trace Medem's progress through Surrealism's three phases of evolution, the Freudian, the metaphysical and the Marxist, whereby his films can be seen to demonstrate the evolution of incidental dream imagery (*Vacas, La ardilla roja, Tierra*) through structural metaphors (*Los amantes del Círculo Polar, Lucía y el sexo*) towards a cumulative politicisation (*La pelota vasca* and *Aitor*).

Surrealism makes interpretation a challenge because it upsets traditional notions of structure and style and demands of the audience a more active participation in a process of decipherment that is simultaneously sabotaged by the writer-director's positioning as unreliable narrator, all of which is also indicative of the movement from Classicism to Romanticism to Surrealism that in *Vacas* is represented respectively in terms of the relationship between the objective historical truth of events such as civil wars, the nationalist conversion of those events into myth and the filmmaker's subversion of their details. *Vacas* may tell of three generations from two rival Basque families during the traumatic evolution of the modern Basque Country from the Second Carlist War of 1875 to the start of the Spanish Civil War in 1936, but it maintains that history is not reality but a subjective interpretation of it, one that suits the beholder and may be opportunistically imposed upon others. Indeed, so subjective may be the propagandist interpretation of reality by a strand of Basque nationalism that it conjures up the landscape of myth. In *Vacas* there is history: a chronological and captioned delineation of the passing decades that are pegged to successive civil wars. There is myth: the legends that form four chapter headings as if the film were comprised of separate fables about the archetypical character played by Gómez, a pilgrim to the progress of the Basque Country, who is reincarnated three times as a victim of its revolving stagnation. And floundering somewhere in the middle there is a lost reality lived by characters moving between these dual narratives. However, there is also an emerging intra-history (a subjective, emotional experience of truth) in the evolving artistic sensibilities of painting (Manuel), photography (Peru) and film (Julio Medem), while, as Joseba Gabilondo has recognised, 'the suturing element that makes allegory filmically possible in *Vacas* is the camerawork, which constructs a point of view that cannot properly be called mythical or historical' (2002: 269).

David Lean's *Lawrence of Arabia* (1962), Stanley Kubrick's *Barry Lyndon* (1975), Terrence Malick's *Badlands* (1974) and *Vacas* all have protagonists that are caught between their enslavement to the myth that they aspire to embody (uniter of the Arabs, roguish noble, James Dean, *aizkolari*) and their awareness of the flaws in their own hagiography (sadism, passivity, vaingloriousness, cowardice). These characters are all bullied by expectations of masculinity as they respond to unstable myths of nationhood in relation to natural and temporal frontiers. There, respectively, the butting together of Occidental and Oriental territories during the First World War, the tension between static social strata and shifting national boundaries in eighteenth-century Europe, and the wilderness of Dakota in an America turning in on itself during the isolationist 1950s: here, the violent, troubled emergence of the modern Basque Country. Medem's characters typically embody a duality that is, characteristically for his films, exacerbated by their operating in both fantastic and real worlds. Similarly postmodern approaches to the role of the individual in the construction of a myth of nationhood such as Jacques Audiard's *Un héros très discret* (*A Self-Made Hero*, 1995), Michael Verhoeven's *Das schreckliche mädchen* (*The Nasty Girl*, 1989) and Robert Zemeckis's *Forrest Gump* (1994) have all focussed on the forging of a modern national identity during warfare (World War Two for France and Germany, Vietnam for the USA). *Vacas* involves a similar juxtaposition of both hagiographic and deconstructivist means of representing nationhood on top of which Medem employs a subversive, Postmodern sensibility in his parodic recycling of the conventions of the literary and cinematic Basque pastoral and bellical saga.

What emerges as the key question here is the subjectivity of the writer-director, especially one who is making his directorial debut. In order to balance the realist and Surrealist elements, Medem should maintain an ironic distance from the more bizarre imagery so that the realism is not compromised, while simultaneously respecting the historical veracity of events so that the reality of the nationalism that he aims to deconstruct does not disintegrate into fantasy. Like mixing too many colours, however, *Vacas* ends up a bit of a sludge. The emotionally, ideologically and physically exiled character(s) played by Gómez should provide the distance that Medem proves unable to maintain with his camera, for he is too enamoured of the imagery of landscapes, *aizkolariak* and Emma Suárez, but this three-in-one character is a too-malleable cypher who appears and reappears at the centre of the film's four chapters in order to represent little more than a cyclical understanding of time and Medem's correlative rejection of narrative linearity, one that nevertheless leads to an emotive conclusion that it is only irony and paradox that remain constant in the recurring social and political aspirations of the Basque Country.

It is usually the case that natural and supernatural cycles culminate in life-affirming optimism that, in turn, inspires the struggle to realise a political ideal through revolution, but *Vacas* is not life-affirming. On the contrary, it is a film about stagnancy, decay and death. However, the original script had ended with a fifth chapter, but, as Fernando de Garcillán recalls, '*Vacas* was a difficult production because resources and time were tight. As soon as we started working we knew it was impossible and that we had to cut the script. Cutting the last chapter was Julio's choice' [9]. Medem, however, remembers things differently: 'After saying it would be made, they told me to cut 20% of the script or it wouldn't be. It was horrible' [5]. The jettisoned final chapter begins where the finished film ends, with the sound of flies emanating from the tree as Cristina and Peru ride away from the Basque Country to France. The buzzing accompanies the camera as it glides through foliage and falls into a space that is wet and deep in which the buzzing is replaced by the murmur of voices. A point of light gets bigger until we find ourselves in an art gallery that is empty of people but adorned with large black and white photographs of cows. A poster announces the exhibition is called VACAS and a superimposed title states 'Brasilia 1990'. Applause is heard. People begin to fill the gallery. Some stop and look directly at the camera, thereby suggesting that the subjective viewpoint is that of a cow in one of the photographs. The eighty-five-year-old Peru appears and people congratulate him. He too looks at the camera and Medem cuts to his point of view. The final reverse shot is of an enormous photograph of the head of a black and white cow and an eye that stares at us, covered in flies. As a final chapter, this sequence would at least add optimism that relates to the creativity of the exile and its transformation into what Edward Said described as 'a potent, even enriching, motif of modern culture' (2002: 173). Yet Medem's cutting of this sequence is testimony to the pressures under which he was working, not the least of which was the need to conform to the practicalities of a budget. In fact, after the film was finished, he cut another twenty minutes from the film because it was decided it was too long, though Fernando de Garcillán states, 'we discussed it and decided what to cut. Julio was very smart and *Vacas* is as good as it is precisely because of what he cut out' [9].

On its preview of films in production in 1991, the Spanish film magazine *Fotogramas* struggled to find something encouraging to say about this peculiar Basque period film with the strange name and Surrealist ambitions and opined that from the evidence of its few publicity stills *Vacas* would at least offer an opportunity to see the actress Emma Suárez in pigtails. Medem guffaws at this reminder but Suárez (Madrid, 1964) was indeed the only known member of the film's cast and crew, having begun her acting career at fifteen. Suárez is sharp, funny, flirtatious, impassioned and spontaneous. Her description of her character Sofía in *La ardilla roja* will run to a dozen adjectives before she admits that she has moved on to describing herself. She claims 'making *Vacas* was like living a fairy-tale' [14] and professes no fashionable preference for the theatre, naming Gena Rowlands and Jeanne Moreau as her idols. She was acting in the short film made by José Luis Acosta for Querejeta's *Siete huellas* series when she met Medem, who she describes as:

> Someone with a great deal of talent and a profound sensitivity, something special to say and a unique way of expressing it. He communicated all the purity, strength and passion of someone who is just beginning and needs to express himself. There was a special bond between us. When he gave me the script for *Vacas* and the part of Cristina, he rescued me from a senseless type of cinema. The part was unique. It was all Julio's work. It was his world. [14]

This world was more difficult to enter for Carmelo Gómez (León, 1962) who had studied acting before playing minor roles in *El viaje a ninguna parte* (1986) and *Bajarse al moro* (1988). Medem had seen him in a television series and thought he was a non-actor cast for his physical suitability. Gómez was actually performing nightly in the theatre and doing the daily round of auditions. His audition for *Vacas* was a direct address to camera, but, as he would with Nancho Novo, Tristán Ulloa and, arguably, Paz Vega, Medem found something of his reflection in the actor's onscreen close-up. Indeed, as shall be seen in analysis of the films he has written and directed, Medem's transposition of personal experiences and family myths and histories into the imaginary Others of his scripts and films has made him an increasingly ripe subject for Lacanian analysis and the relational strand in psychoanalysis that emphasises recognising the multiple self in attachments to others. Jacques Lacan wrote of the unconscious as a social being and spoke of a child's passage through a mirror stage, in which it had to learn to envisage itself from outside before it could attain an internal identity (see Lacan 1991; Fink 1999). Yet Medem, like many Surrealists and psychologists, has always refused to dismiss the reality of an unconscious mind, believing it to be real and precise. The repeated casting of Gómez and Novo, both of whom resemble Medem and chose to purposefully imitate him in their portrayals, has created a constant notion of the alter ego in his films that corresponds to the 'prolonged stage of adolescent romanticism' that Thomas Schatz sees in auteurism (1992: 655). In other words, Medem is still the baby in the mirror, who, believing himself in control of the imagery in a film that was a reflection of his own concerns and obsessions, succumbed to the narcissism of seeing his internal identity represented by an actor with the charisma and virility of Gómez.

Even so, Medem's working methods were at odds with Gómez's classical training from the School of Dramatic Arts, which left him, as

Gómez recalls, with 'Stanislavsky on the brain and on my shoulders, thinking there's a method above all else and that the actor and his character are the most important thing' [15]. Hitchcock famously referred to his actors as cattle, but Medem turned that metaphor into reality, subordinating his cast to equal status in his composition as the cows. The difficulties encountered by Gómez were compounded by his need to differentiate between characters at different ages, though the range of the saga was also challenging for Suárez, who played Cristina from sixteen to thirty-seven. Nevertheless, matching Gómez to Suárez is one of Medem's greatest achievements, for through *Vacas*, *La ardilla roja*, *Tierra*, early plans for *Lucía y el sexo* and the films of Pilar Miró (*El perro del hortelano* [1996] and *Tu nombre envenena mis sueños* [1996]) they have sparred and sparked like protagonists in their own life-long film noir. Says Gómez:

> The best thing that's ever happened to Emma and I is that we've never gotten involved. All the desire you see between us onscreen is real. There's a tremendous sexual tension between us and the great thing is we've kept it going, Emma for her reasons and me for mine. We have a deep understanding. It's something that we keep topped up with potential. She'll call me and say, 'Shall we meet for lunch . . . together?'. It doesn't matter if we meet or not, the potential is always there. [15]

To prove it, he interrupts the interview to phone her on his mobile, checks which anecdotes about Medem she has already revealed and engages in a rally of teasing catch-ups before concluding with a teasing farewell. 'You see? Pure sex!' he grins, packing the phone away like a handgun [15].

They rehearsed together in Madrid's Retiro Park as Medem filled out his cast with actors who would become regular faces in his films: Txema Blasco, Karra Elejalde and, as the young Cristina, Ane Sánchez, who Medem discovered by visiting schools to audition girls who looked like Suárez. As Catalina Mendiluze, Medem managed the coup of Ana Torrent, who had played the infant Ana in *El espíritu de la colmena* and therefore symbolised an ambitious intertextuality. As the five-week shoot drew near, however, Medem succumbed to panic. The only way to get another week without upping the budget was to film without direct sound, which would entail the long but comparatively cheap process of dubbing. To compensate for shooting a silent film, Medem sent his sound technician into the woods to record authentic sounds of chopping wood and nature, such as the buzzing of flies in a tree, which would be added in post-production. *Vacas* was mostly filmed chronologically, but budget restrictions again meant the initial and most expensive scenes of the Second Carlist War were especially rushed. Medem: 'We shot the first chapter in just two and a half days. That's fourteen minutes of the whole film! Incredible! I've never known stress like it!' [5].

The young crew were talented but relations between Medem and cinematographer Carles Gusi were tested by Medem's constant need to check through the viewfinder and not mended until Medem asked him to collaborate with Javier Aguirresarobe on *Tierra*. Medem recalls:

> I'd come from making short films, from a very visual and atmospheric arena in which I felt very secure and comfortable. I had no experience of a big crew or of actors. When we started filming, I picked up the camera and Gusi thought I was possessive and didn't trust him. I admit I wanted the images to have the life that I'd dreamt they would have, of Basqueness, of the language, of gestures, of looks, of silence. I suppose I treated the actors that way too. [5]

But he grew increasingly despondent at the rushes and passed an unsatisfactory rought cut to Alberto Iglesias (San Sebastian, 1955), who received the edited film in its silent form, free of all dialogue and sound effects.

Although Iglesias and Medem share a birthplace and neither speak Euskera, Iglesias expresses nothing of the fractured identity that so defines Medem. Iglesias claims not to think of himself as Basque, preferring instead 'the sensibility of the exile' that allows him to 'have lots of roots in many different places because of the people you know. The education of a musician resides in learning that music is a universal language' [16]. Iglesias studied composition under Francisco Escudero (1913–2002), who had written the first opera in Euskera and was dedicated to the construction of a canon of Basque music (see Vallejo Ugarte 2002), but Iglesias had no interest in the project and studied in Paris, Milan and Barcelona before moving to Madrid in 1982. Thus he had initially been only a peripheral member of the group of new Basque filmmakers of the late 1970s and it was his brother José Luis, a filmmaker who died in 1988, who put him in touch with them. Iglesias scored *La conquista de Albania* (1983), *Fuego eterno* (1984) and *La muerte de Mikel* (1983) before collaborating on *Las seis en punta* with Medem, for whom, 'Alberto's music is a marvel. If my films move people, it's largely thanks to him' [5]. In his return to the Basque traditions that inform the music for *Vacas*, Iglesias knowingly risked invoking the national music of the Basque Country that he had abandoned:

> We live surrounded by this problem in the Basque Country: To what extent should we put national or territorial identity above all else? I leave it behind. For the score of *Vacas*, I did no research at all. Instead of playing a *txistu* (Basque flute), I played two metal flutes and it sounded just the same. What I meant to show is that, fortunately, traditions resemble each other. [16]

In this respect, Iglesias's score for *Vacas* can be understood to resonate with an irony that is appropriate to the film as a whole. Where a supposedly traditional Basque musical heritage is being imitated and duplicated by Iglesias, so too are myths of Basque origins, masculinity and racial purity being mimicked by Medem. Iglesias read the script to gain an idea of the spirit of the film, but then allowed the silent images to lead him on emotionally: 'With Julio, I allow myself to be provoked by his films, especially at the beginning. It's as if I were returning emotions, as if I were the audience's subconscious. The music had to say everything in a film without words. But then isn't that the dream of every musician?' [16].

Once the score was fixed and the dubbing was performed, a final trim left Fernando de Garcillán with the onerous task of marketing *Vacas* by way of what he terms 'American-style marketing [that] was quite innovative for that time, quite advanced and very brave' [9]. He experimented with distribution strategies and publicity at a time of massive changes in the Spanish film industry that included the renovation and remodelling of venues into multiplexes, a consequent increase in the number of screens, the emergence of Sogetel and other independent companies, the privatisation of Spanish television, the cautious interest of domestic and foreign audiences and, most emphatically, the appearance of a wealthy youth audience in Spain with an educated taste for the bizarre, that was primed to welcome such a film.

The Spanish poster provided a line drawing of a cow on a white background and, lying in the grass at its feet, the severed hands from Picasso's painting *Guernica*, which commemorates the bombing of the Basque town by German planes during the Spanish Civil War. The allusion was extraneous, but the tensions it evoked were commanding and in Medem, who won the Spanish Film Academy Award for Best

Debut Director, there was another hoped-for auteur to place alongside Pedro Almodóvar, thereby perhaps fulfilling Carlos F. Heredero's prophesy that 'as long as the national cinema boasts at least one such auteur per generation, many dismeanours of the commercial sector of its industry can be forgiven' (Triana Toribio 2003: 149).

Vacas was released in Spain on 26 February 1992 and took the small but significant equivalent of €370,703 from 152,031 spectators (Sogecine 2004). It was sold to ancillary markets in twelve foreign territories including Germany, France and Sweden, where it performed particularly well. The Swedish and German posters played up the director's Prussian surname and the auteurist peculiarities were highlighted in posters of the cow's eye that, as with much of the European marketing, encouraged cine-literate critics to refer to Buñuel's *Un chien andalou* (1929), an earlier piece of Spanish Surrealism in which a cow's eye is substituted for that of a woman. *Vacas* received the Golden Grand Prize in the New Filmmakers section of the 1992 Tokyo International Festival and the 1993 Sutherland trophy for 'the most original and imaginative first film' from the British Film Institute. It has since become a key film on university courses on post-Franco Spanish cinema in the UK and has been programmed in retrospectives of contemporary Spanish cinema, Basque cinema and, of course, the films of Julio Medem at Manchester's Cornerhouse, Cardiff's Chapter Arts Centre and London's National Film Theatre.

The importance of *Vacas* to the study of Spanish cinema and, more specifically, Basque cinema is that it signifies neither a continuation nor a break from politically-charged cinematic traditions in Spain and the Basque Country, such as accounts of the Civil War and the rural sagas of early Basque cinema (e.g. *El mayorazgo de Basterretxe*, 1929) and Spanish cinema of the late dictatorship (e.g. *Furtivos/Poachers*, 1975; *Pascual Duarte*, 1975), but a refreshingly fearless approach to their legacy. Most definitely, *Vacas* is also a revisionist spin on the deferential sagas, both literary and cinematic, that accompanied the emergence of the autonomous Basque region in the early years of democracy, when the newly autonomous Basque government invested heavily in the cultural resurrection of the nation. However, as with Bernardo Atxaga's epic novel *Obabakoak*, *Vacas* demands that its audience reflect on the ironies of recycling generic and narrative conventions while exhibiting a begrudging, frustrated and insistent respect for the suffering humanity within. In the first tale of *Obababoak*, Atxaga's adolescent protagonist is transformed by a view of his Basque village that corresponds to an indoctrinated nationalist ideal, 'verde, ondulado, salpicado de casas blancas; la clase de paisaje que todo adolescente intenta describir en sus primeros poemas [. . .] Comenzaba a sentirme eufórico' (Atxaga 1998: 57) (green, rolling hills, spattered with white houses; the type of landscape that every adolescent tries to describe in his first poems [. . .] I began to feel euphoric). The opening sequence of *Vacas* effects a similar representation of mythic Basqueness in its representation of an associated masculinity in the figure of the *aizkolari*, but deconstructs it by mise en scène and montage that renders this Basque woodsman a near abstract symbol of male aggression against the pure, sacred, feminine ideal of the landscape that is central to Basque mythology. The film's red credits blink upon the screen as Medem imitates the montage of the *pelotari* (*pelota vasca* players) in Néstor Basterretxea and Fernando Larruquert's *Pelotari* (1964) by constructing a mythopoeic notion of time and space about the figure of the aizkolari by juxtaposing shots from a multitude of angles, in which the phallic axe is presented as a symbol of masculinity that is associated with hate, being part of the symbol of the Basque terrorist group ETA, while, by opposition, the close-up shots of the hacked log are rendered explicitly vaginal. Correlatively, the *aizkolari*'s splitting of the log suggests the violence against the uterus and its bearer that will be echoed throughout the film. In this *aizkolari* battling to destroy the female beneath his feet, there is a symbolism that unites the abuse of women with the rape of the land and is later linked to the affinity that exists between females and cows, which like all animals may symbolise a Jungian appreciation of the unconscious. Iglesias's score offers alternate beats on piano and strings that exaggerate an underlying conflict and this mythified image of masculinity is ultimately undermined by the first chapter heading, 'El aizkolari cobarde' (The Cowardly Aizkolari), because this oxymoron is clearly anathema to the mythic sense of masculinity that powers and props up nationalist beliefs. Instead of a paragon, Medem provides a paradox.

Gradually, the film reveals itself as a fearful, Freudian dream of the idealised femininity of the Basque Country and a Nietzschean nightmare of the fall of its neurotic, fractious males. Perhaps most explicitly, the tree hollow with the burning hole that gives its name to the film's third chapter has an opening that 'clearly represents the female sexual organ, that inscrutable threshold to the depths of life [and] clearly takes on a further political dimension, evoking the idea of the Basque Country – the *motherland* – as insatiable devourer of its offspring.' (Santaolalla 1999: 319). The conflicts between masculine and feminine traits, subjectivities, motifs and characters is an enduring theme in the films written and directed by Medem, but *Vacas* is unique to date in that the conflict is also historical. The events that Medem pegs to successive civil wars reveal how the male's aggressive reaction to anxiety over trying and failing to live up to a mythic masculinity was appropriated and redirected towards military campaigns and how one ironic consequence of this channelling of male anxiety and aggression into sanctioned violence was the formulation of undeserving heroes. In contrast to notions of genetic purity and mythic masculinity, however, the swaggering disguise that results from all this male bravura, braggadocio and hatred is revealed as the main inhibitor of progress, one that is echoed in the many contemporary civil wars in Africa, for example, in which machine-gun-toting males, who commonly utilise rape as a military strategy, rip apart nations that are barely held together by females who typically take on the burdens of sustenance and shelter. In ancient times, maternal figureheads in such societies as the Basque and African were promoted into sacred figures of fecundity and oneness with the earth, but the irony of civil warfare is that it destroys the very country that is being fought for. The male in *Vacas* 'shapes the earth' (Perriam 2003: 72), but this is more the product of destruction than design.

The consequences of this violence are illustrated in the film's post-credit sequence on the front line trenches in Vizcaya during the second Carlist War, where Carmelo Mendiluze's virility and valour is shored up before a battle by news of his new-born son, while that of Manuel Irigibel (Carmelo Gómez) is already shown to be falling behind the legend of great *aizkolari* that precedes him. Carmelo is hit in the neck and Manuel fakes a wound, daubing his face with the blood that gushes from Carmelo's jugular; but the fountain of blood that causes Carmelo's death also gives life to Manuel. Carmelo's last words – 'I'm not dead' – are prophetic in the sense that he lives on in Manuel, if only as a malignant growth on his conscience that many years later the aged Manuel will attempt to exorcise in a painting of two cows lying in that very same trench, one spouting blood from its neck.

Manuel fakes death and is loaded onto a cart piled high with corpses. As the cart trundles through a forest, his naked, bloodied body emerges from between male legs, thereby offering a horrific parody of birth, while the male cadavers that birth him provide a nightmarish satire of

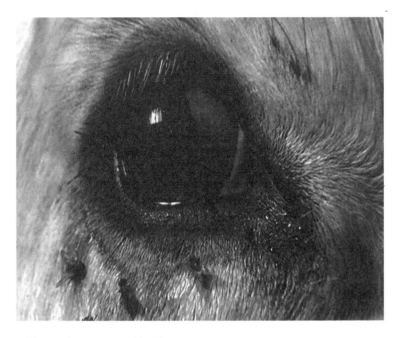

1 The cow's eye as portal in *Vacas*

stagnancy. Manuel drops to the ground like a helpless infant, keeping aloft his bloodied, broken leg like a severed umbilical cord, and this travesty of childbirth is juxtaposed with the film's primary symbol of motherhood, the benign, maternal gaze of a cow. Manuel stares fearfully at the animal and sees the reflected abyss of his crime of cowardice behind the flies that swarm around her eyes. Apart from its allusion to the close-up of the cow's eye in *Un chien andalou*, the shot allows for the juxtaposition of the subjectivities of Manuel and the cow that expresses both transcendence and metamorphosis and enables the audience to assume ownership of this reciprocal gaze. As in the script's discarded final chapter, the device of juxtaposing reciprocal subjectivities allows the audience to assume one and then the other, thereby moving through time and space as the journey to the film's second chapter begins through the iris of the cow. This journey thirty years into Manuel's future to find his aged, crippled self (Txema Blasco) painting a cow that is held by his three granddaughters is accompanied by the sound of buzzing flies that is suggestive of the infection that

Manuel carries with him and that nature and its female representatives appear to suffer by contagion with the male.

The child Cristina believes she is posing for her portrait but, although Manuel assures her this is true, his painting is only of the cow. Notions of sacred symbols that correspond to Basque myths of motherhood and its relationship to the earth resonate queasily in such imagery and dialogue. *Vacas* illustrates Freud's assertion that a fear of the female gives rise to her fetishisation by ill-functioning males, whose placing of real females on pedestals entails the imposition of fictions that ironically oppress the subjects they are intended to flatter. Such actions correspond to the Catholic cult of the Virgin, of course, and an essential part of Sabino Arana's ideology of ideal Basqueness was devout Catholicism, which he considered to be an essential part of the Basque identity. However, this is an early example of imbalance in the film that is caused by Medem failing to maintain an ironic distance from the more bizarre imagery and it comes from his typical indulgence towards the cowardly male protagonists of his fictions. *Vacas* is about three generations of snivelling Irigibels, J in *La ardilla roja* can't even pluck up the courage to kill himself and Ángel in *Tierra* lives in fear of responsibility. In *Los amantes del Círculo Polar* Otto lets his fear distance him from Ana, while Lorenzo, the worst of all, runs away from a dog's savaging of his child in *Lucía y el sexo*. But, despite their cowardice, Manuel, Ignacio and Peru Irigibel, J, Ángel, Otto (at least in one ending) and Lorenzo all end up with gorgeous and adoring young women. Equidistance can therefore be read as condoning the actions of these men, which supports Paul Julian Smith's argument that *La pelota vasca* offers an apology for terrorist violence (2004: 45). In *Vacas* the cow that observes Manuel in the earlier scene exudes a censorious godliness that is overridden by its maternal indulgence of this suffering infant, which is also a characteristic female response to the child-man protagonists of the films written and directed by Medem. Here, the regenerative powers of the womb are invoked like a spell that allows Manuel to journey through the eye of the cow and return to the transformative space of the uterus, an ability that is referenced later when the aged Manuel looks through the eye of a cow to determine her pregnancy in a shot that was realised by simply zooming away from Txema Blasco peering through a hole in a black sheet, thereby rendering in magical realist terms something which might otherwise have represented the 'marvellous real' in which 'the strange is commonplace and always was commonplace' (Carpentier 1995b: 104), because some Basque and, indeed, Welsh farmers do maintain that a cow's pregnancy can be detected in her eyes.

Manuel is thus 're-born' thirty years later in the second chapter 'Las hachas' (The Axes), a title that insists the conflict is far from over, but not as his aged self, now played by Txema Blasco, whose fractured psyche is symbolised by the splint around his leg, but as his son Ignacio, who is played by Carmelo Gómez. Ignacio's daughter Cristina (Ane Sánchez, who will be replaced as an adult by Suárez) tires of posing and runs after the cow but enters a dense forest that submerges her in the landscape of fairy-tale in which she is filmed from a furtive distance as if the subjectivity belonged to the wolf and she were Little Red Riding Hood. Cristina thus resembles the eternal female in a primordial forest, where the sexual potency of the wolf, vampire or snake is often symbolic of the savage and corrupted side of masculinity. Indeed, it is portentous that she should soon come across her father while he is chopping 'vaginal' logs just before he is distracted by movement amongst the ferns and chases a shadow through the undergrowth until he catches Catalina Mendiluze (Ana Torrent), the sister of his arch-rival Juan Mendiluze, who is thereafter targeted as the object of his desire.

Chris Perriam observes of Gómez that 'the reappearance in the narrative of his same strong facial features allows a masculine line of continuity to compete with the feminine' (2003: 72). This continuity is highlighted in the duel of *aizkolariak* (plural of *aizkolari*) that is arranged by Ilegorri (Karra Elejalde) between Ignacio and Juan, the sons of the fathers who met in the trenches in the film's first chapter. The repetition of that conflict is also underlined by Lucas, son of Ilegorri (and played by the same boy who played Ilegorri as a child) running along the brow of the hill as did his father, when a boy, above the trenches. A wager of 700 *reales* is placed with the cow as collateral and Manuel paints the number on her portrait as if she were branded with that sum, but the duel between the adulterous Ignacio and the incestuous Juan is really a contest for Catalina, thereby suggesting, again, how a woman is equal to a cow. As the duel begins, the montage of the opening credits is repeated with the juxtaposition of a myriad different angles of aizkolari chopping wood; only this time there are two men, whose resultant fragmentation prohibits any identification of individuality and instead produces an evocation of a conflictive duality that is also that of the Basque Country. The duality of Ignacio and Juan, like that of their fathers before them, can only be resolved in the third generation of Irigibels and Mendiluces with the character of Peru, whose physical union of the bloodlines (for he is the son of Ignacio Irigibel and Catalina Mendiluze) is allied to a healing of the fractured male psyche in its estrangement from the Basque Country. This duality of two generations and its resolution in a third over four chapters combines a structural equation with a Postmodernist questioning of identity achieved by the effect of the film's formal structures on the film's theme. Just as the structure questions the nature of history and identity, so too do Manuel and the film's audience, which allows the film's subversion of a chronological history and the principles of its enunciation in nationalist dogma to prompt a questioning of those same elements in reality. For now, however, the cycle of destruction against the land that is perpetrated by the competition between Ignacio and Juan receives due comment in the shot of a cow dropping a pat as the buzzing of flies restates the depth of infection caused by such violence.

In a vain attempt at exorcism, Manuel Irigibel creates the tokenistic figure of the skeletal, scything *segalari* (scarecrow) that he fits with his red Carlist beret and which was designed by the Basque artist Vicente Ameztoy (San Sebastian, 1946). In common with many Basque artists and sculptors, Ameztoy is concerned with representations of space and the elements that have forged the Basque landscape that, in turn, has defined the Basque people. Ameztoy: 'La gente y el paisaje son mis principales fuentes de inspiración. El paisaje de Euskadi es el que más he trabajado [. . .] . Son las personas en relación con este paisaje lo que con mayor frecuencia se puede observar en mis cuadros' (Sala 2001) (The people and the landscape are my main sources of inspiration. The landscape of Euskadi is what I've worked on the most [. . .] . The relation of the people to this landscape is what is mostly seen in my paintings). Ameztoy and Medem, like the Basque sculptors Jorge Oteiza (1908–2003) and Eduardo Chillida (1924–2002), are obsessed with physical space as the absence of something that is yearned for, such as an identity. The void that Medem sees in the mist-shrouded valley, in the traditional but derelict farmhouses or *baserri*, in chopped logs, in the eyes of cows and in the tree hollow is similar to the hollowed-out vacuums created by Oteiza and Chillida, who both made sculptures to frame empty spaces, such as Chillida's *El peine de los vientos* (*Wind Comb*, 1973), a modern iron sculpture embedded in the rocks at the water's edge in San Sebastian that funnels the wind through its twisted structure to provide a metallic ululation, and

Oteiza's *Construcción vacía* (*Empty Construction*, 1957) which treats iron like a card that has been cut into to create a jagged maze and then pulled apart, and was erected alongside it in 2002.

Iron and stone against the wind and the sea are characteristic elements of the Basque Country that have been trained but never tamed in its cultural expression. Just as Basque artists and sculptors decided that the shape of their work was not as important as the spaces within and around them, so Basque filmmakers have commonly positioned their protagonists in relation to the landscape that is emphatically also both around and within them. Basque documentaries such as *Ama lur* (1968) offered tapestries of rural Basqueness that interwove human and natural elements, cycles and histories, while the fictional *Tasio* 'stresses the centrality of the rural environment to [the] sense of identity' (Jordan and Morgan-Tamosunas 1998: 48) of the eponymous charcoal-burner in Navarre and *El espíritu de la colmena* also renders its isolated humans in reductionist scale to their environment. The making of *Vacas* coincides with the beginnings of the move from modernism to postmodernism in contemporary Basque culture that was capped by the opening of the Guggenheim Museum Bilbao in 1997 and, as Joseba Zulaika argues, the installation of Jeff Koon's *Puppy* (1992) on the pavement outside. *Puppy* is a monstrous floral sculpture of a West Highland terrier that constitutes a break from the modernist aesthetics of artists such as Oteiza and Chillida and is best understood from an ironic perspective that illustrates the subversive potential of irony in Basque culture (Zulaika 2004). Furthermore, Koon's non-Basqueness perhaps reflects the postmodernist emphasis on collage that chimes with a new sense of post-industrial Basqueness, one that accepts and even celebrates a collage of identities, nationalities and languages, at least in its cities, that might be thought all-encompassing were it not for the controversy over the genealogical collage of the blood-line of the non-Euskera-speaking Basque-French-Spanish-German Medem that provoked such debate at the time of *La pelota vasca*.

Rather similar to the 43-feet tall *Puppy* made of 70, 000 fresh flowers over a stainless steel armature holding over 25 tons of soil is Ameztoy's *segalari*, with its skeletal frame and leprous skin of moss. Even so, it is more of a soldier than Manuel ever was and its resemblance to the scything Tarot figure of Death is a bitter illustration of his own death in life. Manuel's most succesful creation of an effigy is, however, his son Ignacio, who is identical in appearance to Manuel when younger (being played by Gómez) but apparently much less of a coward. Ignacio is possibly an improved version of his father: a superior re-telling of the myth, who returns to the homestead with a horse and cow bought with his prize money from the regional competition of *aizkolariak*. His mythic Basque masculinity is best embodied by Gómez as Ignacio when the strapping actor is onscreen beside the frail Txema Blasco as his father, but the actor's masculine beauty undermines the film's critique of its meaning, much like Gómez's charismatic portrayal of an ETA terrorist in *Días contados* (1995) severely problematises that film's representation of his crimes. As Perriam states, 'Gómez is associated with, enriches, and embeds stock images of masculinity in spite of the film's strong flight away from the sociological into the anthropological and mystical, and in spite of its urge to be ambiguous' (2003: 72). Gómez truly grounds *Vacas*; but he also represents the metaphysical triumph of his father, whose transcendence of a miserable mortality circumscribed by his act of cowardice is made possible in this stereotypically more heroic new version of himself. The irony of Ignacio's incarnation of a Basque myth of superior masculinity that rules the land with its hateful axe is that, instead of positioning him as evidence of the Basque myths and propaganda that perpetrated the purity of the race and its landscape, Medem presents him as charismatic idol of a people who, through rivalry, incest and warfare, destroy themselves and the landscape that generates them like a cancer devouring skin.

Typically of Medem, this landscape is as psychological as it is physical, and as Juan and Ignacio both train with their axes, the interweaving of Basque history and myth seems to separate like a clefting of the mind. The year is 1905 and while Ignacio strides into the new century a real champion whose progressive modernity is illustrated by his successive returns from prize-winning contests with a cow, then a horse, then a car, Juan is forever tied by his grudge to a period marked by the Carlist Wars of the nineteenth century, one that would be transformed by the nationalist movement of the twentieth century into a mythic and nostalgic Basque past. Juan howls in frustration and hurls his axe into the forest at a rival he can no longer see, but whose incessant, rhythmic axe-blows insist upon the passage of unremitting real time in contrast to the stalled mythic time in which he remains. History and myth are split by the impact of the axe in the forest, leaving Juan in a world of heartfelt extremism where notions of masculinity, honour and nationhood support his beliefs in his own violent actions and where the reasons for his hatred, including the death of his father, are always recent and pertinent to his cause.

The victorious Ignacio claims Juan's sister Catalina as his prize and their copulation in the forest is rendered with a tracking shot that passes beside them and comes to rest on the tree hollow, the vaginal qualities of which are enflamed and duly give rise to the title of the third chapter: 'El agujero encendido' (The Burning Hole). The hollow is lit by the sacrifice of a female mammal, including a mouse, a pregnant boar in the memory of Manuel, the moral ruin of Catalina's pregnancy and unmarried motherhood and the diseased cow. Here, the earth and the moon, fecundity, maternity, the womb and the motif of a transformative hole that echoes the eternal circle are conjoined in the universal myth of a cyclical, regenerative Mother Earth, but the male flipside of this Basque spiral is the equally cyclical resumption of civil wars and rivalries. The scene where a calf is pulled from its mother's womb by Ignacio is perhaps the film's single naturalistic moment in its documentary-like observation, but it is also, literally, a vicious tug-of-war between the pre-perceptual calm of the uterus and its place at the centre of panacean myths of universal femaleness and the violent, specifically Basque myths of nationhood that exist beyond it. Like Macduff this calf is untimely ripped from its mother's womb and, as the Civil War approaches, the forest closes in on the Irigibels and Mendiluces as it does for Macbeth.

Irony is also cyclical in *Vacas*, for although legends of heroic *aizkolariak* are undone by Manuel's cowardice, it should be noted that he provides faithfully for his family for more than thirty years. On the other hand, the legends are reinstated by his son, Ignacio, a great *aizkolari*, who abandons his wife and children. Ignacio's triumph appears total but is hollow in its celebration of myths of Basqueness and masculinity that disguise his own moral failings and rewrite the history of cowardice in his family for, in the wake of Ignacio's triumph, his crippled father is redeemed, transformed into what the unscrupulous Ilegorri calls 'a hero of the Carlist war.' It is very unlikely that Manuel ever told of his cowardly escape from the trenches, but it should be remembered that the only witness to his playing dead was Ilegorri as a child, who has grown up to become a profiteering Basque fabulist exploiting and inventing the myths that *Vacas* is all about. Although he is observed by his wife, when Ignacio returns from the contest he kisses another woman holding a baby who, it is implied, is another trophy won by the mythopoeia of his masculinity. The ironic juxtaposition of his physical prowess and moral collapse with the converse of his father is expressed in his declarations to the press: 'This is my father. He's

2 Manuel (Txema Blasco) fabricates an image of Basque nationhood in *Vacas*

never taught me anything, but he's my father'. Ilegorri may claim that, like hate, 'el hacha se lleva en la sangre' (the axe runs in the blood) but Manuel duly ignores the celebrations as he searches for the illegitimate Peru – 'Speaking of blood, where's my grandson?' – thereby challenging the mythopoeia by insisting upon Ignacio's failure to embody familial and paternal responsibilities.

Most pointedly, Manuel is intrigued by the function of the camera in this process of myth-making because it represents a means of transforming fantasy into a reality that is more definitive and enduring than his scarecrow and paintings. He sends Peru to steal the camera and subsequently poses his family and their possessions in a *tableaux vivant* of a Basque rural idyll that he constructs according to Basque dogma. Thus, he confirms the status of the female by ordering his daughter-in-law to go stand by the cow and, when satisfied, poses on a log in front of the simulacrum of immaculate Basqueness and allows the camera to commemorate his representation of a nationalist ideal. Except, as one of his granddaughters enquires: 'Who takes the picture?'

With no film in the camera and nobody under its cape, the camera simply stands on its tripod in an empty field. The sequence thereby questions the nature of authorship in the production of history, myth and reality, drily and erroneously concluding (as does Cristina) that, 'the camera takes the picture itself, isn't that right, grandfather?' Manuel's pride in fabricating this illusion of wholesome Basqueness therefore stands as testament to the propaganda of racial purity, unbroken tradition and familial unity that was exhorted by Basque nationalists. Manuel the madman, it seems, has momentarily convinced himself of its reality by creating this mythic illusion out of a family that is falling apart. The contemplative framing of the Irigibel family facing the unmanned camera in *Vacas* actually indicates the stagnancy of the subject and impatience with the intransigence of Basque nationalism. Medem's take on this Basque meta-hierarchy is parodic, though he also reveals that any move away from such conventions demands a more dynamic approach to the art of representation, which is precisely what was advocated by Romanticism, which ignored established hierarchies, erased firm outlines and natural perspectives, broke with colour schemes and logic and ignited the imagination of the viewer, who became uncertain of whether he or she shared the perspective of the artist, thereby destabilising a sense of what the picture represented, especially when Romanticism gave rise to Surrealism.

Medem similarly constructs *Vacas* as a film in which Romantic and Surrealist ambitions coincide, in which he presents a Surrealist interpretation of a romantic object of desire: the Basque nationalist dream of a rural Basque utopia. As desire creates a Surrealist object, so did Basque nationalism turn the Romantic ideal of Basque nationhood into an expression of the oppressed, collective Basque subconscious, especially because the pleasure afforded by this view of a Basque utopia was heightened by its being forbidden under Francoism. This desire to render on film a fetishistic vision of a rural Basque utopia that is the objective of the aforementioned documentary *Ama lur* (1968), for example, (see Stone 2006) also reveals that the function of *Vacas* is 'to illustrate how [. . .] the expression of romantic literary attitudes lends itself to interpretation in the light of surrealist goals' (Matthews 1976: 15). Manuel's oneiric, panegyric idyll is therefore undone by the intrusion of Peru, his beloved but illegitimate grandson, whose pale youth belies his embodiment of the disruptive truths beneath the lies of this pretty picture. Peru dips under the cape and looks through the camera to see a father and a family that spurns him. His subjectivity is then appropriated by Medem, whose iris-out completes the picture by expressing the antique theatricality of a silent movie in its frozen fanfaronade of a magical realist fabrication of Basqueness, while the iris-in triggers a cut to the juxtaposed authenticity of natural imagery, with the close-ups of insects, lizards, beetles and fungi that suggest 'lo fantástico' as briefly as the birth of the calf indicated the barely appreciable counterpoint of naturalism.

The myths of Basqueness that resonate in the figure of the *aizkolari*, in nationalist rhetoric and in the pastoral and bellical films of the 1980s that were subsidised by the Basque government are all parodied in *Vacas*. The film culminates in an accumulation of transgressive acts and violent impulses directed towards females that accelerates the infection in the forest. Juan tries to rape his own sister, the cow falls sick and Cristina empties its infected milk beside the tree while Peru wears the camera on his head and focusses on Cristina's breasts, thereby equating once more the link between females bound to suffer. Manuel nears insanity as a consequence of his nationalistic fusion of history and myth, and of reality and fantasy, in his creation of the family portrait and tests the limits of his metaphysical powers by painting the sick cow with bloody stumps and then, because reality is the first victim of mythopoeia, chopping off its hooves to create the mitigating fantasy of his painting out of the painful reality of the animal. Peru is convinced that Juan has killed his mother and flees to the forest but is caught by Juan, who forces him into the hole in the tree whose vaginal aspect is enhanced by its being draped with the flesh and blood of the dead cow. Juan pushes Peru back into the womb because he clearly wishes this bastard son of Ignacio and his sister had never been born. Yet, the thresholds of birth and death are conjoined in the minds of humans, whose only possible frame of reference for what death might entail results from a subconscious memory of birth. The cycle of life and death is therefore associated with imagery of a uterine passage, while the belief that dying signifies transcendence to another world is also suggestive of a cyclical rebirth. Thus, Peru is not killed but returned to life by the sudden news from Ilegorri that his rightful parents are waiting to take him with them to America: the New World.

The fates of Manuel, Ignacio and Peru thus effect a complex illustration of the evolution of a troubled Basque masculinity in relation to national identity and historical events in which, as María Pilar

Rodríguez states, 'se combinan los exilios interiores y exteriores' (2002: 95) (interior and exterior exiles are combined). The psychological exile of Manuel and the physical exile of Ignacio renders them both victims of the nostalgia that is associated with nationalist myths of a strong and ancient Basque identity that was based upon displays of masculinity that Sabino Arana once contrasted mightily with the Spaniard's lack of same: 'El bizkaino es de andar apuesto y varonil; el español, o no sabe andar [. . .] o si es apuesto es tipo femenil' (1965: 627) (The Vizcayan walks confidently and in a manly fashion; the Spaniard does not know how to walk, or if he does, he is of feminine type).

The subsequent abandonment of Cristina and Manuel in the fairy-tale forest effects a timeless purgatory between this mythic Basque Country and its increasingly decrepit rural reality that involves the 'chilling of romantic style, which treats lovers and insects alike' (Auty 2004: 276) that characterises Terrence Malick's *Days of Heaven* (1978). Fragments of Peru's letters are answered by Cristina, who cannot write nor adequately reason: 'At last I saw a wild boar in the forest, but it didn't get caught in the trap. Of course, that would have been difficult because I saw it in a different forest.' As they wander, Cristina dictates her replies to an increasingly senile Manuel, who gradually fails to take note of her thoughts, while the stalking camera reveals her ageing into spinsterhood and the curtailing of her maternal potential. 'I want to leave', she says, but doesn't. And as the fourth chapter 'Guerra en el bosque' (War in the Forest) begins, Cristina's pigtails are beginning to look unseemingly girlish on a woman of thirty-seven. The banging shutters on the abandoned *baserri* of the Mendiluces sound like echoes of axe blows in an otherwise silent, abandoned valley, when the grown Peru (Gómez again) surprises Cristina by taking her photograph with a camera that recalls the one whose magical realist fabrication of a happy family was once achieved by Manuel. To emphasise this function of the camera Medem once again appropriates the subjectivity of the mechanism by juxtaposing uniquely cinematic representations of the couple's views of each other, cutting between reverse dolly shots in which the camera is pulled away from the subject as it simultaneously zooms in (a technique invented by second unit cameraman Irmin Roberts on *Vertigo* [1958]), thereby causing the forest to fall away as Cristina and Peru maintain the same stature. This technique effectively removes them from the forest in a moment of transcendence from the fiercely antagonistic nationalist clichés that are about to go to war around them. Just as their instincts simmer awkwardly and incestuously (for Ignacio is father to them both) beneath talk of Peru's American wife and daughter, so the eternal feud that defines their family history is absorbed into the Spanish Civil War. Still estranged from their surroundings by their feelings for each other, they assess the practical reality of their encounter by revising their place in the conjoined history and myth of their dead grandfather's paintings, each of which is revealed as an allegorical comment on the saga, including the aforementioned pictures of the two cows in the Carlist trench and the one of the cow with bloody stumps as well as a picture of Cristina and Peru sat back to back on a two-headed cow like a fairy-tale pushme-pullyou that shows how the long-standing conflict between their families has not resulted in their separation but in their interdependency. *Vacas* thus contends that the Basques are defined by the consequences of hatred, just as Basque nationalism was shaped by the hostile rhetoric of the writings of Sabino Arana and ideas of the modern Basque Country have been skewed by the terrorist activities of ETA. *Vacas* suggests that the Basques have to let go of the axe or at least bury the hatchet, but it offers no solution to these problems and even fails to convincingly unite its star-crossed proto-lovers, partly because Peru must remind Cristina of the father who abandoned her (for they are both played by Gómez), thereby adding symmetry, incest and cyclical happenings to a relationship overflowing with Medem's main obsessions.

Peru embodies the Nietzschean union of warring opposites in his mix of Irigibel and Mendiluze blood as well as a consequent potential for balancing the contrary traits of cowardice and bravery, progeny and childlessness, madness and sanity, fantasy and reality, and history and myth, for in sum he seems a sensitive, modern man, refined by his time in America and returned as a mere observer of the Basque Country and its conflict in his role as photographer. But for all the testosterone in *Vacas*, 'patriarchal power is circumscribed by and subsumed into a semi-mystical matriarchal structure' (Perriam 2003: 73). Indeed, in as much as Carmelo Gómez could ever be feminised, Peru is a more hesitant, delicate character with a slightly higher voice, especially when speaking (dubbed) English. As the war penetrates the forest, moreover, it is Madalen, Ignacio's abandoned wife, who takes charge, ordering women and children to the shelter of her house and the men into the woods to meet the opposing army, thereby illustrating how males in a matriarchal society are often burdened with embodying the ideal of *machismo*, never more so than by a vengeful Madalen who, one may surmise, believes that all *aizkolariak* deserve each other. Cristina also takes charge, leading Peru into the forest like his guide back into Basqueness while boys with pitchforks swarm around them and the Spanish Civil War routs myths of Basque superiority from the landscape, replacing them with the centralist, Francoist equivalent. Before they can escape, however, Cristina is traumatised by the killing of Ilegorri's son Lucas and falls into a semi-catatonic state caused by the infection of hatred and war that is symbolised by the buzzing of flies that emanates from within her. Peru surrenders himself to distract their pursuers and his stuttering protests of neutrality are met by jeers; yet, in this calculated gesture of cowardice, Peru is ironically rather brave. He assures Illegori that Lucas has escaped (a lie, perhaps a myth in the making) and accepts his fate in front of a firing squad until the aged Juan, whose madness has found its home in Francoism, rescues him by identifying his nephew as the grandson of two heroes who died together in the Carlist trenches. This reconciliation between the two families underlines the duality embodied by Peru, whose bloodline is equal parts Irigibel and Mendiluze, and calms the film's juxtapositioning of the Romantic dreams and Surrealist nightmares of Basqueness, prompting Cristina to wake serenely from her coma. 'I've seen grandfather', she says, referring to Manuel, and Peru, remembering Juan, concurs, though like Cristina he has come so close to death that he might also be referring to Manuel, the grandfather they share, who is on the other side of the hole. 'I'm going to dedicate my life to you', says Peru, whose deeds begin with a fairy-tale escape from the forest on horseback; but Cristina has no more patience for such fantasies of masculine prowess and expresses greater pleasure at the reality of food in the saddle-bags.

The ending is ambiguous: in leaving the Basque Country with Cristina, Peru repeats the moral transgression of their father Ignacio by doubtlessly abandoning his own American wife and children, but he also corrects Ignacio's dereliction of duty by rescuing Cristina from the Basque Country. In the final shot, the camera moves into the transformative dark of the tree hollow as the buzzing increases and Cristina's voiceover – 'we are arriving' – indicates there might be a better world on the other side of the hole. Indeed, if Medem does conjure optimism from this stalling of a film made from a curtailed script, it is because of his literally personal connection to the characters onscreen. For Peru is also the name of Medem's own son (who would play the infant Otto in *Los amantes del Círculo Polar*) and so his indulgence of this character suggests a parallel genealogy in Medem's own family history. If Peru Irigibel is Medem's son, this makes Medem into Ignacio and, consequently, Manuel Irigibel into Medem's own father, whose history begins not in the Carlist War but where *Vacas* ends, at the beginning of the Spanish Civil War. Thus, the cycle of events may be continued in Medem's own family because that same year Medem's grandmother brought his German-born father to live in the Basque Country, where Medem was subsequently born. At the moment Peru leaves, Medem's father arrives. But Medem, like Ignacio, later left the Basque Country and only returned there around the time of the birth of his own son Peru, who he was caring for while he wrote the script for *Vacas*. Peru, like his namesake, is clearly a symbol of cyclical reconciliation with the Basque Country in whom Medem no doubt hopes to see, as all fathers do, an improved version of himself. *Vacas* is not just Medem's artful positioning as a Basque filmmaker in relation to Basque nationalism and Basque cinema, it is also an ironic reflection on his feelings about Basqueness and the emotional investment in its meaning that he makes with this film and his own son.

4

Eyes that entangle:
La ardilla roja (1993)

Vacas may have made little money in Spain, but it was the international sales that convinced Sogetel of the profits to be gained by investing in Medem as auteur. The boom in private European television channels, satellite broadcasting, rental and sell-through video, the spread of consumer electronics through peripheral ancillary markets including Africa, Asia and the breakaway states from the Soviet Union made for a massive variety of market-places avid for commercial product. Thus, in addition to the lucrative Latin and South American markets, where Spanish films enjoyed easy distribution, Spanish cinema became a saleable commodity in an increasingly hectic worldwide trade in audio-visual product in which the brand names of Pedro Almodóvar and Antonio Banderas, for example, were heartily endorsed by international icons like Madonna, who had described Banderas as 'the sexiest man alive' in *In Bed With Madonna* (1991). In post-Gulf War America, new independent production and distribution companies led by Miramax were keen to acquire European arthouse films like *La Double vie de Véronique* (*The Double Life of Veronica*, 1991) and use canny marketing and Oscar campaigns to push them into multiplexes, where they turned a surprising profit.

In addition, while the route of independent filmmakers to arthouse audiences and the attendant cult of auteurism that was pioneered by the Sundance Film Festival worked for Steven Soderbergh and Quentin Tarantino, whose films expressed a keen awareness of European cinema and sensibility while reclaiming genres as American traditions, Sundance was also an entry point for foreign films. The selling of Spanish cinema on the international market was largely predicated upon the presence of sex and stars for such ingredients had recently proven themselves attractive to American audiences with the $3.8

million take of Almodóvar's *¡Átame!* (*Tie Me Up! Tie Me Down!*, 1989)
and the comparative successes of films with a sexual charge such
as *Amantes* (*Lovers*, 1991), *Jamón, jamón* (1992) and *Belle époque*
(1992), which had carried off the Oscar for Best Foreign Language
Film. Alongside this success, Spanish production companies with
knowledge of European film funding, its loopholes and tax breaks, had
begun to pool pre-Euro currencies with their counterparts in France,
Germany and the UK, where Channel Four was a viable force, to
produce what were sometimes referred to as Europuddings. Although
second-guessing of a potentially worldwide audience for arthouse and
subtitled films was difficult on any level above the most salaciously
generic, Sogetel suspected that *La ardilla roja* had crossover appeal for
the film had an exciting, sexy plot and its director had an attractive,
possibly unique, visual flair that would suit a bankable star.

La ardilla roja tells of a suicidal ex-rocker called J who takes advantage
of Sofía's amnesia to convince her she is his adoring girlfriend Elisa.
They journey to the Red Squirrel campsite but are followed by Sofía's
vengeful husband Félix, who confronts them and is killed while Sofía,
who has always faked her amnesia, escapes to Madrid, where she is
finally reunited with a genuinely lovestruck J. Medem had written his
first draft of *La ardilla roja* while awaiting callbacks from producers for
the script of *Vacas*, and moving straight onto pre-production of *La
ardilla roja* so soon after the release of *Vacas* was exhausting for him,
his cast and crew, most of whom returned to work as if they had never
disbanded. The rookie in the team was the actor Nancho Novo, whose
casting as J had occurred after Medem watched countless tapes of
young actors being interviewed by his assistant, Txarli Llorente. Again,
while watching all those talking-heads, Medem's television screen
became a mirror in which he sought his own reflection. Popular actors
were considered, including Antonio Banderas, but Medem still did not
settle on the actor to play his namesake (at least as far as the solitary
initial J identifies him as such) until Novo's tape turned up, offering
Medem five hours of the actor's reflections on life and death, love and
hate, sex, rock 'n' roll and, crucially, motorbikes. Carmelo Gómez
describes Novo as the perfect actor for Medem:

> He sings, he's got a great sense of humour and he's got this dark side.
> He's a rocker, and that's just perfect for Julio, because Julio has always
> hung onto that part of his adolescence. Nancho's a romantic rocker, who
> can't help falling in love with things, just like Julio. On the one hand,
> they have this rascally side, and on the other, this wild romanticism. [15]

Novo was born in La Coruña, Galicia just a month before Medem in 1958 and asserts there is plenty more symmetry with his writer-director. Like Medem, Novo studied medicine, at least until dropping out against his parents ambitions for his career. He enrolled in Madrid's School of Dramatic Art at the age of twenty-one and began acting professionally during his second year of studies, when he bagged a minor role in *El juego más divertido* (1987) alongside Victoria Abril. In 1992, whilst appearing in Madrid's María Guerrero Theatre under the direction of Manuel Gutiérrez Aragón, Novo heard that the director of *Vacas* was in search of 'a rocker type' [6] for his second film, so called the production company Bailando con la Luna. Medem's response was enthusiastic but tempered by what he calls 'a lot of pressure to cast Antonio Banderas' [5]. Casting Banderas as J would have clinched a more expansive budget and distribution deal for *La ardilla roja*, especially because J was remarkably similar to his Ricky in *¡Átame!*, another romantic rocker who kidnaps a woman to love him. But comparisons were ultimately avoided because the 2 million peseta wage for Novo meant he was far cheaper for the role than the 25 million Banderas. 'Besides, it had to be Nancho. The character he played was him. Although, putting it that way, it was Julio too', says Carmelo Gómez, who would himself substitute Banderas in *Tierra* [15]. Novo agrees: 'I identified with J but I also identified J with Julio and watched Julio closely in order to play him' [6].

Medem's avoidance of casting stars, even when it countermanded the wishes of his backers, suggests an indication of the autonomy that he identified as an essential factor in developing his auteurism, for his use of unknowns ensured greater creative control. Gómez, it should be remembered, had only played bit parts in films prior to *Vacas* and Suárez was a jobbing actress, while actors such as Fele Martínez, Najwa Nimri and Tristán Ulloa were only slightly better known than complete novices such as Novo in *La ardilla roja*, Silke in *Tierra*, Paz Vega in *Lucía y el sexo* and Bebe in *Caótica Ana*. To the extent that Gómez and Suárez became stars thanks to appearing in Medem's first three films, it is of note that their eventual stardom was perhaps a factor in their being removed from *Lucía y el sexo* after its initial pre-production. While Alejandro Amenábar has worked well with Nicole Kidman and Javier Bardem, Álex de la Iglesia has collaborated with Bardem and Carmen Maura and Almodóvar has relished the challenge of directing actors as unique and forceful as Maura and Bardem, Victoria Abril, Marisa Paredes and Gael García Bernal, Medem has employed actors whose inexperience and gratitude for the role makes them arguably more malleable and submissive to his working methods. Just as Gómez had become such a powerful screen presence by the time of *Tierra* that his own screen persona outgrew the confines of imitating Medem, with whom he clashed repeatedly, so it seems that the challenge of controlling actors of the calibre of Abril and Bardem, who would never limit themselves to imitations of their writer-director, is something that Medem has avoided. Even Suárez, who inspired *La ardilla roja*, would be so constrained by her role in *Tierra* that her working relationship with Medem ended and was only briefly revisited in the early days of *Lucía y el sexo* until personal differences that (Suárez claims had much to do with Medem feeling betrayed at her making films for other directors) scuppered their professional and, to some extent, personal reconciliation.

Nevertheless, Medem admits he wrote *La ardilla roja* thinking of Suárez, 'although I hardly knew her at the time' [5]. Suárez's Sofía is another imagined female made real by the emotion invested in her by men, first by Medem's writing of the character and, secondly, by his protagonist J, who takes advantage of her amnesia stemming from an accident following her escape from her psychotic husband, Félix, to turn her into an adoring girlfriend named Elisa. Medem had even sought Suárez's collaboration in creating Sofía while shooting *Vacas*. As he recalls: 'I wrote *La ardilla roja* from J's perspective, but she gave me lots of ideas and when I wrote the final draft Sofía was a fully mature character because I'd been so inspired by her' [5]. Sofía, Elisa and Emma are thus like Russian dolls, with each incarnation inspiring a particular male: Sofía's Félix, Elisa's J and Emma's Julio. Within the ideal of Elisa is the fearful but resilient Sofía and inside Sofía is Emma. As Suárez recalled:

> I loved playing her because I believed in Sofía. There were many similarities to me. I'd describe her as a person, as a woman, who is absolutely feminine, with all the primary characteristics of a woman. She's an idealised woman, a kind of symbol. The representation of the female as Sofía is flirtatious, seductive, playful; she's a liar, quick-witted with sharp reflexes. She's capable of using any kind strategy to inveigle the person in front of her. [14]

The fifth draft of the script for *La ardilla roja* is dated 6 August 1992 in San Sebastian and its plain red cover conceals a description of the film that warns of a convoluted plot: 'Juego intrigante en torno al machismo en clave de comedia mágica a través de una historia de amor que nace de la mentira y crece por el misterio y el deseo' (Medem 1992: 3) (A game of intrigue about machismo in the style of a magical comedy mixed with a love story that starts with a lie and grows through mystery and desire). Writes Friedrich Nietzsche of people like J: 'The liar is a person who uses the valid designations, the words, in order to make something which is unreal appear to be real' (Nietzsche 1873). Thereafter, the potential for confusion from so many lies, protracted deceptions and juxtaposed subjectivities is so evident that on the back of a following page Medem has already unmasked the squirrel: 'La ardilla hace de conciencia contra los excesos de la mentira establecida, machista' (Medem 1992: s.n.) (The squirrel is the conscience for the excesses of the established, chauvinist lie). As the tone of the script darkens, he scribbles notes upon its themes: 'Las relaciones entre la verdad y la mentira son relativas como entre el bien y el mal. Por otra parte, la mentira es una de las formas más sutiles de indicar la dirección de la verdad. También crea humor' (Medem 1992: s.n.) (The relationship between truth and lies is relative, like that between good and evil. Moreover, lying is one of the most subtle ways of showing the truth. It's also funny). And a few pages from the end, when he is sure of how it all will turn out, he offers this binding definition of the film: 'Es una burla, una broma irónica sobre la virilidad' (Medem 1992: s.n.) (It's a gibe, an ironic joke about virility).

The only major difference between this draft and the film is an excised sequence at the campsite in which Sofía and fellow camper Carmen (María Barranco) take advantage of the absence of Carmen's husband Antón (Karra Elejalde) to go shopping in a nearby village. There they get drunk and Carmen flirts with a musician called Ternero. Meanwhile, back at the campsite, the girl with blue hair remembers J from his time as singer in Las Moscas (The Flies) and invites him to the village festival where, coincidentally, a Las Moscas tribute band will be playing. When she returns, an inebriated Sofía berates J for lying to her but ends her diatribe by fellating him. That evening in the village festival, Sofía is told the story of J's emotional breakdown following his break-up with band member Elisa by Nicola, an ex-member of the real Las Moscas who now fronts the tribute band, which plays the song *Elisa* as a drunken Sofía sways along and, in her mind, hears J's voice. This sequence, if it had not been deleted, would have had curious consequences for the plot. Carmen's fling with Ternero would have added guilt to her anguish at the lateness of Antón's return at the film's climax; but, more importantly, the relationship between J and Sofía becomes less romantic than sado-masochistic as the tensions of their rôle-playing and tale-telling are here more psycho-sexually perverse than in the finished film where they translate into an allegory of seduction and romance. Moreover, the scene reveals the scheming of his characters too early for any credible chance of romance and the accusations of chauvinism directed at the film on its release would have been more justified by Sofía's seemingly willing, masochistic victimhood. One other change occurs after the death of Félix and has J's ex-girlfriend Elisa calling the apartment-bound J from Lisbon (the city where Sofía hopes to have been born) and provoking a solemn closure to their relationship that would have distracted J from his quest for Sofía, which is subsequently completed by J's staring at the photograph of himself with Elisa in Madrid's Plaza de España and spotting Sofía in the background, alone without Félix in a picture that does not spring to life.

What the excision of all these scenes attests to is the struggle to make J an attractive and sympathetic character. As an emotional coward, J conforms to an archetype in Medem's films, though scribblings on the fly-pages of this shooting script reveal the endeavour to redeem him. For example, when Salvador explains the whole plot to J – 'Sofía has never had amnesia' – J was to have slammed the desk and shouted, '¡Se va a enterar!' (She's going to pay for this!), but in the film he simply asks for the keys to Salvador's car. Medem's most obvious deflection of audience antipathy away from J is achieved by shifting his more despicable traits onto Antón (Karra Elejalde), the brutish, unfaithful *taxista*. Even so, Medem has attempted to limit this damage by writing himself an urgent memo: '¡Tenemos que trabajar la simpatía de Antón! ¡Tenemos que perdonar a Antón! Es el estereotipo de machista ibérico, ¡pero humano!' (Medem 1992: s.n.) (We have to work at making Anton more sympathetic! We have to pardon Antón! He's the stereotype of the Iberian chauvinist, but he's human!). Nevertheless, Antón remains a decoy for the hostility that should be directed at J, who himself remains a character that Medem tries to justify in self-defence:

> *La ardilla roja* is a parable against machismo, and it bothers me deeply that some have turned it on its head and called me *machista* (chauvinist) for having made it. The fact that J is *machista* doesn't make me one too. Not even J is *machista* in the worst sense. He's a representation of it. He's a metaphor for machismo, but as a person, he loves and respects Sofía. [5]

Even though he lies to her, kidnaps and manipulates her into loving him, at least physically?

> J is *machista* in this dark moment in his life because he doesn't know what else to do. In the beginning he's flirting with death, but he's useless at that too and can't commit suicide. Then Sofia appears in his life and he's swept along by circumstances, caught up in what I call a moral rape, which is taking advantage of someone, appropriating the life of another person. From that point on, what I'm talking about is machismo and, in a certain way, the machismo of women too, because she lets herself be deceived and uses it to her own advantage. It is a *machista* situation, but it arises from them both. There's no tyranny when one is the tyrant and the other allows herself to be tyrannised. [5]

But doesn't this excuse a person you have described as a moral rapist and make Sofía one as well?

> It's a game. This is the feminine guile of the famous squirrel. That's his lie and she knows it. It's her, evidently, who makes you think that he's not actually in control. She plays this sinuous game of seduction, of letting herself be deceived, but she's the one who does the most deceiving. The one who truly controls the farce is her. [5]

Medem's defence of *La ardilla roja* is practised but protracted. The metaphorical reading is something of a smokescreen for the subtle switching of victimhood from what he sees as the lying, deceiving and opportunist Sofía to the loving, respectful J, while the 'the one who truly controls the farce' is not Sofía but, of course, the film's writer-director. This control is essential to auteurist ambitions and it is therefore pertinent that Medem's casts and crews all insist that Medem rarely says exactly what he wants while filming, prompting them to guess until their director seems happy that the reality they have created resembles his fantasy. This relationship is therefore somewhat similar to J giving the amnesiac Sofía the bare details of their story together and expecting her to embellish her rôle as his adoring girlfriend to his liking. Gómez and Suárez both attest that Medem most often expresses his vision through abstract similes and impenetrable metaphors: 'Pull a face like a rollercoaster', is one they remember from *Vacas* with affection and stupor [15 and 16]. Stills photographer Teresa Asisi adds that Medem 'never tells you what he wants or explains anything. You have to imagine what he wants and give him what you can. And if that's not what he has in mind, he's not going to tell you directly. There'll just be another take. And then another' [18]. In his defence, Medem admits that he is difficult:

> I have to trust people a lot. There are things I can't explain because they
> have to discover that territory for themselves and if I explain everything,
> I limit them. Sometimes with the cast and crew I have to demand that
> trust. I explain things up to a point, and then there are things that I'm not
> going to explain, and we discover them together. [5]

Medem's belief in collaboration is akin to dropping his cast and crew into a maze he has built and expecting them to find their way back to him. He may grow to trust them and rely on their abilities to escape, but there is only ever one exit and that is the one facing him. A more generous overview might suggest that in allowing his cast and crew to 'discover the territory' of things he cannot explain, Medem provokes them into developing the mindset of his protagonists, for, as the saying goes, one has to think like a monkey to catch one. The freedom of this collaborative venture is still illusory, however, because the target of the actors' endeavour is never a methodical creation of an original character but the paradoxical triumph of surrendering to their writer-director's vision. Medem argues that his cast must understand the subjective truths of their fabricated characters by endowing them with genuine emotion, which echoes the Romantic imperative to achieve a self-created identity that is as relevant to Basque nationalists as it is to characters like Sofía and Lucía in *Lucía y el sexo*, but the danger exists that a sense of self may be thwarted by a physical inability to embody this perfected being, whether it be the Basque Country's conflict with the mythical notion of itself or the incapability of actors to understand or perform characters that, in turn, aspire to the sentimental and carnal dream so common to Medem's films of an ideal, responsive lover. In this respect, however, the closeness of Suárez and Novo to the characters they played in *La ardilla roja* seems like particularly foolproof insurance. Suárez especially was so close to her character that her emotional investment in the part that she had inspired led her to provoke and demand changes to the script at the read-through stage, causing Medem, for perhaps the only time, to adapt his script as the actress manoeuvred Sofía out of the realm of male fantasy and into the reality of a credible modern Spanish female. Gómez, meanwhile, quickly surmised that his character Félix was 'the dark side of J. He's in love too but it's driven him mad' [15]; but convincing Novo, the terrified novice, that he could measure up to Gómez's actorly understanding of their characters' symmetry and duality was a more difficult task and he was overwhelmed in rehearsals, only settling into the rôle when Suárez bullied him into overcoming his sense of inadequacy and repulsion for a character that Medem had described to him as 'a moral rapist' [5 and 6].

Vacas had been well received at the Berlin Film Festival but the objective for *La ardilla roja*, which was shot in nine weeks on a budget of 200 million pesetas, was Cannes. The beach scenes were filmed in San Sebastian, the lake was the Pantano de San Juan near the village of San Martín de Valdeiglesias about 60km north of Madrid, where Medem now owns a house, and the campsite was erected in Madrid's Casa de Campo, a large country park to the west of the city that contains the zoo where Sofía is finally discovered to work. Sofía's nightmare was shot in the barren lands of Usanos in the province of Guadalajara and the photograph that springs to life in J's apartment was taken in Madrid's Plaza de España. Suárez recalls the filming as hectic and draining:

> *Vacas* was delightful, but *La ardilla roja* was a much harder shoot. Besides, I was pregnant while filming, so I was very sensitive and very irritable. I'm the kind of person who gets lost with too much verbiage and Julio is the kind of person who likes to communicate with rhetoric, maybe because he always feels that nobody understands him. So yes, there were moments of tension between director and actress, even times when I told him it was best not to explain things because I didn't have a clue what he was talking about. [14]

An example of the confusion caused by Medem's demand for a blurring of reality and fantasy that even disconcerted his cast is Novo's recollection that 'Julio told me, "Emma and you have to really fall in love"' [6]. Novo replied that he was already in love with someone else, but Medem insisted that he transfer what he felt onto Suárez. The actors settled on a long-standing friendship. Further confusion was caused by *La ardilla roja* being filmed largely out of sequence, which greatly disturbed Suárez's balancing act of Sofía and Elisa's duality: 'I had to pretend to have amnesia and not know what the film was about at the same time as I had to make the film knowing all the lies I was telling' [14]. Cohesion was nevertherless maintained by cinematographer Gonzálo Fernández Berridi who had shot Medem's short films *Patas en la cabeza*, *Las seis en punta* and *Martín* and would work with him again on *Los amantes del Círculo Polar*. He designed a fresh, natural look for *La ardilla roja* that effected a realistic contrast to the subjectivities of the protagonists and the range of flamboyant point-of-view shots underwater, inside juke-boxes and from the perspective of the squirrel. Indeed, it was this playful emphasis on juxtaposed subjectivities that signalled the originality of the film and garnered it the Youth and Audience Awards at the Cannes Film Festival 1993, where it featured in the new directors' season.

From three generations of Irigibel versus Mendiluze in *Vacas* to J versus Sofía, Ángel against his angel in *Tierra*, Otto and Ana in *Los amantes del Círculo Polar*, Lorenzo and Lucía in *Lucía y el sexo* and all the myriad interviewees in *La pelota vasca*, Medem's protagonists all stake a claim on truth through their subjectivity. *La ardilla roja* renders the courtship of two free-wheeling fabulists through such point-of-view shots, whereby Medem's sensual way with a sinister premise allows a couple's fantasies of perfect partners to become real through their emotional investment in their subjective views of each other. Juxtaposed subjectivities can create an odd rhythm to a narrative that is traversed by zigzagging from one character's viewpoint to the next, but balance is provided by the third leg of the tripod: the paradox of the subjective/objective camera that Medem hitches to the gaze of cows in *Vacas* and squirrels here. Audiences can never be certain if J is sadistic or romantic or whether Sofía knows more than she lets on, nor whether Ángel is sane or insane, whether Lucía is herself or Lorenzo's re-imagining of Elena, or whether all the politicians, journalists and activists of *La pelota vasca* are telling the truth, but this does not create an image of Medem as unreliable narrator. Rather, it positions him as the only secure point of reference in the quagmire of competing subjectivities, wherein the symmetry imposed by editing creates not a bias but a balance in the tensions between such seeming antagonists as men and women, loss and longing, love and hate, separatists and centralists. This kind of subjectivity was the primary factor in Pier Paulo Pasolini's recognition of a new poetic cinema that 'entails immersion of the filmmaker in the experience of the subject who possesses some clear affinity with the auteur' (Orr 1988: 3). In privileging the subjective camera in his films, Medem ascribes to memory, emotion and imagination as a corrective to an otherwise compromised history and makes these instances key to an understanding of his narrative structures and aesthetics. In other words, Medem employs subjective camerawork because to him it is more truthful.

Pasolini argued that the interior monologue of modernist fiction was equivalent to free indirect subjectivity in the cinema, but Medem's assumption of subjectivities is more dream-like, especially when attributed to objects and animals, and therefore corresponds more avidly to the contention illustrated by the cinema of Tarkovsky, for example, that it is not narrative-based literature but poetry that is linked to the cinema by dreams. Surrealism and its free association of imagery are open to interpretation by psychoanalysis, which awards equal status to objects, persons, landscape, memory, fantasy and dreams in order to decipher reality, just as Medem's oneiric assumptions of subjectivities amount to poetic dream-flights that are contained by the objective imposition of symmetry in the editing that is another determining characteristic of his auteurism. In extending his control of the filmmaking process, Medem's decision to reassemble much of his cast and crew included working again with the editor María Elena Sáinz de Rozas and the composer Alberto Iglesias, whose score not only ratchets up the suspense and sexual tension in loving imitation of Bernard Herrmann but also revels in the ridiculousness of making visible an invisible squirrel.

Iglesias, who describes Medem's 'poetic world [as] very unstable' [16], began by expressing the speed, agility and invisibility of the squirrel by scraping at strings and moved on through Puccini, Prokofiev and Ravel to arrive at a score that identifies characters by themes and interweaves them. He clarifies:

> In *La ardilla roja* all the structural elements submit to a lack of rationalism. Matching a theme to a character is very easy, you know, a character appears and it sets off the violins; but here I thought I might try other associations, because although I associated an instrument or melody with a character, there are moments when the character doesn't appear but the music does. That's a very interesting use of empty space. Then, perhaps, the same melody is repeated in association with one character and then with another: maybe it's the melody that unites them. *La ardilla roja* is a film where I didn't want to immediately establish relationships between the characters and the music. I wanted those associations to make sense at the end. [16]

At least Medem, his cast, crew and composer all agreed that the end of *La ardilla roja* should be romantic, partly because, as Suárez explains:

> The most important part of the film is the process these characters go through in order to discover the truth. The funny thing is that J and Sofía

are both lying, but they don't know the other one is. I like these games with truth and lies a lot, because at heart it's what us actors do: we turn a lie into something real and to do so we have to believe in the lie and become it. This is what I've always loved about acting: knowing that I'm capable of inventing a lie and believing it and defending it. That's what the cinema is all about. That's what *La ardilla roja* is all about. [14]

The defence, tag and marketing of the romanticism of *La ardilla roja* may be distractingly superficial, however, for although at first glance the film seems frivolous, superficial and absurd, its playful, sensual and suspenseful textures only disguise an underlying trauma that is both individual and national. As many critics of contemporary Spanish cinema have lamented, the new filmmakers of the 1980s and 1990s appeared to deal very rarely with pressing social and political issues and it was not until the next decade and Bollaín's *Te doy mis ojos* (*Take My Eyes*, 2003) about spousal abuse and León de Aranoa's *Los lunes al sol* (*Mondays in the Sun*, 2002) about unemployment, that the conscience of this generation was properly recognised. Yet prior to this recent occasion of social realist films, filmmakers such as Álex de la Iglesia and Pedro Almodóvar had hidden their no less profound social and political commentary beneath the scuff-proof gloss of genres. Iglesia's heavy metal horror *El día de la bestia* (*The Day of the Beast*, 1995) followed a priest's battle to save a rampantly consumerist Madrid from satanic forces who dress, drive and detest the poor just like stereotypical supporters of the ruling Partido Popular, while Almodóvar's *Kika* (1993) only looked, acted and behaved like a farce in order to deliver a stinging, prophetic and 'serious critique of the role of the communications media' (Jordan and Morgan-Tamosunas 1998: 83). *La ardilla roja* is another example of a film with a surprisingly bitter twist on contemporary Spanish society and politics, as its narrative disguises a metaphorical critique of national disguise and a conspiracy of lies that recalls the metaphorical cinema of dissident filmmakers during the dictatorship.

Although *La ardilla roja* pretends to be a romantic comedy, in form and narrative it actually suggests that post-dictatorship Spain and more specifically the Basque Country have assumed a socio-political disguise of progress that hides simmering resentment and trauma, just as Sofía pretends to be Elisa in order to escape her violent past and can hide everything but the fear that gives her goosebumps. Like Vacas, *La ardilla roja* is concerned with national, regional and individual constructions of identity and the threatening legacy of the dictatorship.

It even begins with an explicit political statement that hides in plain
sight, literally drowning in its own symbolism as the credits play over
a submerged forest of whitened, bone-like trees; for, like a miniaturised
scientist in a science-fiction film, Medem begins his Surrealist film
inside Sofía's subconscious as indicated in the song by Las Moscas:
'Sueño que vivo dentro de ti' (I dream I live inside you). The metaphorical relationship between Sofía and water will be made explicit in her
surname Fuentes (meaning fountain or source of water) and the slow
dissolves from her skin to the surface of the lake. This continues the
affinity between females and nature in *Vacas*, but it also illustrates
Surrealist beliefs that the hidden depths of her subconscious are where
the real Sofía exists. That Sofía is later revealed to be a champion
swimmer who can hold her breath underwater far longer than J, for
example, merely demonstrates how much more meaningful and
profound for her is her immersion in the lie of their relationship. Yet
what is most crucial to an understanding of *La ardilla roja* as allegory
for the evolution of post-dictatorship Spain and the parallel struggle for
self-determination of previously oppressed sections of society such as
women and geographical areas such as the Basque Country is that
Sofía's subconscious should be represented metaphorically as these
murky but specific waters. The female and the Basque Country are
two victims of Francoist oppression and its legacy that are conjoined
in the persona of Sofía and therefore present in the symbolism of
the lake; for the dead trees prove that this is not a natural lake but one
that has been artificially created by the flooding of a previously verdant
valley. The imagery therefore brings to mind the Development Plans
that were instigated by Franco during the 1950s, when the government
initiated practical measures to prevent summer droughts and provide
enough water for the growing towns and cities by diverting rivers to
flood valley areas north of Madrid and form reservoirs, including the
Pantano de San Juan in 1955, where *La ardilla roja* was filmed. The
plan went ahead with scant attention to the plight of those whose
homes, farms and livelihood would soon be underwater, drowning
farmland and forests in the campaign of modernisation undertaken
by the regime. The credit sequence of *La ardilla roja* therefore
symbolises not only Sofía's subconscious, where fear and traumatic
memories lie buried, but also the affined, forgotten suffering of
the land and its inhabitants under Franco. An awareness that Sofía
carries the combined weight of symbolism for many identities lost to
dictatorial oppression, whether national (rural Spain), regional (The

Basque Country) or social (women), is essential to appreciate the allegorical nature of a film that, like its lead character, pretends it is a fantasy in order to deal with reality.

The immediate context of this reality is identified as Basque by a tilt down onto the back of J on the promenade above the beach of Medem's birthplace of San Sebastian. Indeed, from the back this J could stand for Julio as easily as the initial itself. J's first word – 'shit' – foretells the film's final, more literal comment from the squirrel, while the juxtaposition of subjectivities that provides the dominant visual motif of the film begins with a shot from J's perspective of the crashing waves below him that is countered by Sofía's helmeted view of her motorbike as it careers out of control and crashes through the railing. Although her approach is shown in long shot, her fall was staged by dropping the bike and a following camera from a crane above the beach, thereby creating the impression that Sofía had fallen straight down from the night sky. The allusion is both timeless and contemporary, for her heavenly descent is both mythical and allusive to the kind of common cynicism reflected in the title of the self-help bestseller that contends men and women hail from different planets (Gray 2002). J hurries down the slipway towards her crumpled body as the hand-held camerawork and lunar texture of the beach consolidate the other-worldliness that is complemented by her biker suit and helmet creating the impression of a crashed astronaut. J immediately takes advantage of her amnesia to fabulate his selfish version of events, but his subjective view of an upside-down Sofía is countered by a shot from inside Sofía's helmet: a narrow view of J through the visor that switches the frame to cinemascope and suggests how Sofía might take to this myth-making with even greater aplomb because she sees in such a cinematic way. Moreover, J's description of her as a fish out of water inadvertently identifies this moment as Sofía's potential escape from the watery subconscious of the credits.

J's imagining of a history for himself and Sofía erases his condition as cowardly victim of a broken heart and involves the projection of male desires that recalls the transformation of Judy (Kim Novak) into Madeleine (also Kim Novak) by Scotty (James Stewart) in *Vertigo* (1958) (Stone 1998); but unlike the ultimately deadly plight of Judy, it allows Sofía to escape her conditioning as sexual object and victim of machismo. More than this, however, her paradoxical liberation through being kidnapped by a fantasist reflects histories of nation-building in Spain because this traumatised, female victim of machismo is analogous to the feminised Basque Country that is depicted as suffering the oneiric nationalism of males in *Vacas*. This deployment of the female as symbol also relates to the tradition of her suffering in the metaphorical cinema of the dictatorship, when filmmakers unable to illustrate the plight of victims of Francoism such as political opponents, regional identities and a wide range of disenfranchised minorities used a female protagonist instead as symbol of more generalised oppression. *Calle mayor* (1956) and *Ana y los lobos* (1972) exploited the fact that a suffering female protagonist was institutionalised in Francoist culture and law, being central to the cult of the Virgin Mary in Catholicism and even upheld in the Civil Code, which forbade women from holding a passport or driving licence without the permission of their husbands and outlawed divorce, contraception and abortion (Gacto 1988: 32). The oppression of female autonomy and identity was thus a legal imposition under Francoism and its legacy of obeisance has extended far into democratic Spain. In response, *La ardilla roja* revitalises this tradition of symbolism by intricately positing Sofía as metaphor for the post-Franco struggle of regions, minorities and marginalised sections of society to acquire autonomy, independence and self-determination.

In her few moments of genuine amnesia on the beach, when Sofía is so wiped clean of any notion of her former identity that she cannot even recall the colour of her eyes, she experiences genuine escape from her past and subsequently chooses to prolong it by faking amnesia when her memories come flooding back in the ambulance. Thus she goes along with the identity that is handily imposed upon her by J, who ironically becomes the victim of her deception. He tells the brown-eyed Sofía she has 'blue eyes that entangle' but fails to realise that it is he who is entangled by her. As Sofía falls asleep from concussion in the ambulance, the slow fade to black can be read as entry into the dream-state that she desires: 'My eyes are entangled in dreams.' Thereafter the temptation to read the entire film as the dream-flight of Sofía is both pressing and evocative, for this interpretation reveals a troubled and symbolic woman who has taken the opportunity of (democratic) freedom to extemporise a rôle-play of her dilemma in order to liberate herself from the (dictatorial) legacy. This makes the identification of Félix and J as similarly metaphorical much more explicit: Félix is the dark, violent, patriarchal, oppressive and dictatorial past that still threatens the stability of contemporary Spain, while J may be democratic but he still upholds many of the retrograde traditions of

Félix, especially his oppressive treatment of women, which is parodied in the pop video in which he wears 'prehistoric' skins (although it can't be easy to shake off four decades of conditioning). The good news is that J, being a metaphor for democracy, is capable of change, his 'prodigious reflexes' offer ample evidence of that. All J has to do is ditch the conditioning that makes him think he can still treat Sofía in this way, repent, and he will be redeemed by the love of a woman he has learnt to treat as equal. Thus shall *La ardilla roja* reveal itself as a metaphysical, allegorical narrative about the transcendental movement of modern Spain from the nightmare reality of the dictatorship to the realised dream of democracy, as well as a metaphorical illustration of the emergence and self-determination of the contemporary Basque Country and a complementary examination of the struggle for independence of Spanish women.

This allegorical reading of *La ardilla roja* as illustration of the dangers of a Spanish and Basque extremism that (as in *Vacas*) is founded upon

3 The performance of Basque origins by J (Nancho Novo) and Las Moscas in *La ardilla roja*

the intertwined precepts of machismo and nationalism is underlined by J identifying San Sebastian by its Basque name of Donosti and his giving Carmen the made-up address of Calle Euskal Herria, which literally means 'the street of the land of the Basque speakers', for this is the Basque nationalist term for the linguistically-determined myth of the utopian Basque Country and the fact that J gives this as his false address is a notably pointed comment on such dogmatism. Just as J's nickname has nothing to do with his real name of Alberto and might therefore be said to ultimately stand for nothing at all, so the nationalist term for the Basque homeland has nothing to do with the real Basque Country, where only a fraction of the people speak Euskera, and in practical terms may stand for just as little. In addition, the challenge to gender conditioning of *La ardilla roja* extends to the inclusion of two homosexual couples (Salvador and Luis Alfonso and the lesbian campsite workers) whose apparent equality and success seems due to the exclusion of the retrograde, chauvinist male, thereby indicating how J might be redeemed by an affined negation of the more extreme aspects of his machismo. This in turn suggests how the resolution of conflict in the Basque Country, whose mythology, as illustrated in *Vacas*, is founded on suffering femininity and sacrificial maternity, might be achieved by a lessening of the destructive, aggressive, possessive traits of the male.

   The rôle-playing of both J and Sofía that ironically culminates in true romance is a game of transcendence that is enjoyed by several characters in a film full of replicas, simulacrum and imitations. Sofía's brother pretends to be a woman 'alone in the darkness, sad and neglected' and the song he dedicates to the object of his affection, Luis Alfonso, is *Let There Be Love* by Nat King Cole, who sings in Spanish. The cyclical nature of imitation is further illustrated by both Félix and Carmen singing along in Spanglish to this song played on a radio programme called *La vida y la muerte* (Life and Death), which only enhances the cyclical connotations. In addition, the symmetry between females and cows that is explored in *Vacas* is rendered here as a direct kinship between Sofía and the red squirrel that is invisible to men (at least until J earns the right to see it at the end), for Sofía also wishes to be invisible to men and so disguises herself as Elisa, again until J earns the right to truly see her at the end. This kinship is made explicit in the scene of J asleep in his apartment, when a pan across the photograph of J and Elisa in a forest is overlaid with the commentary from a television documentary on squirrels that intrudes on J's subconscious and helps to warp his reality into the peculiar formations of his dream. Sofía's rapid breathing from the beach accompanies the subjectivity of the squirrel that the documentary describes as 'crafty, nimble as flies, liars, elusive but strategically so, sinuous and able to carry out their plans behind the backs of men', thus indicating that the Sofía-squirrel chimera is more than a match for the J-fly. Moreover, Sofía's sly grin and knowing greeting – 'Hello, J, I'm your amnesiac girlfriend, remember?' – when she appears in J's dream-forest confirms that it is she who controls his fantasy. Clues to how Sofía's escape from Félix is analogous to Spain's transition from dictatorship to democracy are scattered in the dialogue with reappearing words and phrases indicating how the film's true concern is the subconscious trauma of Sofía. Already in the scene at the beach, for example, J says things ('*Vaya*, you're a girl' and 'say a place') that will be repeated by Félix in Sofía's nightmare. But just as words and phrases enter Sofía's subconscious and are recycled in her dreams, the crucial importance of Sofía's greeting in this dream is that, although it originates in the subconscious of J, she later repeats it in the real world when J regains consciousness after being hit on the head by a pine cone. That characters and phrases from reality reappear in our dreams is quite usual, but how can a phrase from J's dream reappear in the real world? The answer lies in the recognition of the metaphysical journey between reality and fantasy as a two-way street that allows for an almost classically mythological aspect to the plot of *La ardilla roja*: Sofía could even be Aphrodite, whose seasons in the Underworld as prisoner-wife of a patriarchal Hades (Félix) are balanced by her time above ground with Adonis (J).

J and Sofía move from the reality of their encounter to the fantasy of a relationship that they both fabricate without the other knowing and Sofía's admission upon waking in the hospital that she too has had a dream but will not tell J its content provides evidence of her equal metaphysical ambition. It also suggests a link with the Spanish mystics of the Middle Ages, Saint Teresa of Avila and Saint John of the Cross, whose erotically charged poetry employed the metaphysical strategy of stepping from the real to the unreal in order to express the struggle between spiritual longing and physical desire. Transcendence was always frustratingly out of reach for the saints, but for Sofía and Jota it is a possibility. As J invents a life story in answer to Sofía's questions it is clear that this 'couple of champions' (as Carmen describes them) are equally matched, for J shares, albeit unwittingly, the task of fabricating the fantasy with Sofía, whose playful rebuttals accept only what is good about the life he invents for her. An apartment at the beach is fine, but when J consigns this professional zoologist to the drudge of a shoe shop, she rebels, prompting him to close down his imaginary shop and put her on the dole instead, thereby conjuring a period of appropriate limbo from her unemployment that is more amenable to her. This strategy of juxtaposed subjectivities is then extended visually in J's packing of the t-shirt emblazoned with his own face, perhaps in case his point of view ever needs reinforcing.

Like the invention of a fantastically detailed alibi from the clutter in his interrogator's office by Verbal Klimt (Kevin Spacey) in *The Usual Suspects* (1995), J builds his fantasy from such stimuli as the painting in his apartment of the couple by the side of the lake, which is the exact image that he urges Sofía to imagine when describing their forthcoming trip, and the *sirena* (siren) of the ambulance that will be echoed in his nicknaming of Sofía *sirena* (mermaid). Yet J's inspired interweaving of conscious and subconscious threads is almost undone by the hospital psychologist, whose analysis of Sofía reveals a hint of her trauma, as well as a plethora of in-jokes that attest to the affined projection of Medem's self into his films. Start with Sofía, which is the name of one of Medem's sisters, flicking through photographs of the backs of people and naming them automatically as if in some Surrealist parlour game, quickly, without thinking: 'Ana', she says, then 'Julio', thereby identifying Medem's other sister, who worked as choreographer on the film, and Medem himself, of course, whose physical similarities to both J (whose real name is revealed, bizarrely, as Alberto, same as one of Medem's brothers) and Félix are referenced in a photograph that recalls the film's first shot of J: except, as the psychologist admonishes, the subject is a woman. 'Well, Julia then', says Sofía, prompting an intriguing corollary that Medem might be represented by a woman in this photograph and, therefore, the female in this film about fluid identities.

A sense of identity is normally based upon memories of the self, but what of identities whose founding memories are false? *La ardilla roja* contends that an identity based on false memories can still be validated by emotion, for just as the artificial relationship between J and Sofía will be authenticated by their mutual investment of emotion in each other, so too might the radical Basque nationalist's relationship to the myth of a utopian Basque Country be substantiated by the campaign for its existence. In developing this notion, Medem juxtaposes the motorway journey of his couple away from the Basque Country with a parody of the mythic sense of Basque origins that they are leaving behind in the video-clip of Las Moscas. The prehistoric costuming of the band members parodies the beliefs disguised as historical fact of many Basque academics and politicians who claim pre-historical, genetic, linguistic and even musical reasons to justify the separatism of the Basques. Las Moscas play traditional Basque instruments such as the *txalaparta*, thus signifying what Jo Labanyi has described as 'the "back to roots" strain in Basque nationalism [thereby illustrating how] the plot of the film undermines the notion of the need for a "myth of origins" by insisting on the advantages of feigned amnesia' (1995: 405). Yet this is not just a Basque phenomenon, for these advantages also resulted from the mutual agreement between political extremes during the period of Spain's transition to democracy to forget the conflicts of the past: a period and attitude of feigned amnesia termed *la desmemoria* that was not a fantasy, but a ruse whose political and historical pragmatism was vital to the reconfiguration of Spain's identity in the aftermath of the dictatorship. In secretly agreeing to their own *desmemoria*, J and Sofía may actually be illustrating their nation's past.

Often in films written and directed by Medem, characters that wish to escape the past such as J and Sofía, Ángel in *Tierra*, Otto in *Los amantes del Círculo Polar* and Lucía in *Lucía y el sexo* redefine themselves in more heroic or romantic moulds. J becomes all sorts of things including a champion runner, Sofía becomes Elisa, Ángel dresses up as an astronaut and takes on the alien forces of beetles, Otto becomes a pilot, Lucía takes off to explore an island and several of the speakers in *La pelota vasca* align themselves with majestic notions of nationhood. Their use of fantasy as a refuge is only temporary, however, for although J and Sofía, Otto and Lucía create new lives for themselves that should respond more satisfyingly to their imaginative visions of themselves, they are inevitably confounded by the illusion. Even the ideals of Basque or Spanish nationhood that inspire contrary speakers in *La pelota vasca* are, to a certain extent, unworkable fantasies that have made a solution to the Basque conflict impossible. Thereafter, a refusal to let go or compromise on the fantasy seen in Félix and some Basque extremists prompts recourse to violence. Moreover, when these characters fail in their desire to achieve an emotional utopia they can end up looking back at false ideals and proclaiming them to be nostalgic visions. As some Basque nationalist extremists fall into this trap, so too do J and Sofía, who both become dependent on the false memories that they embellish.

The benefits of *desmemoria* are added to by J's kidnapping of Sofía, which relieves her of her condition as traumatised victim of a violent marriage because it immerses her in a therapeutical rôle-play that allows her to redefine herself, just as the show-off boyishness of J's detailing his catching of the helmet in a slow-motion replay illustrates his similarly healthy regression. 'This helmet smells of you', he tells her, thereby confirming their gradual exchange of immediate senses and emotions in place of the memories that they are both, in effect, conspiring to preclude. Indeed, their latent collusion is confirmed when Sofía mistakenly signs herself into the campsite under her real name and, although both she and J notice, neither of them makes any comment, just like the political parties of the transition. This allegory of modern Spain's transition from dictatorship to democracy becomes explicit in the microcosmic campsite, which contains representatives of various gender relations within 'a context of parody and performance' (Smith 1996: 129) that is mostly filmed in the flatly lit mid-shots and close-ups of a television soap or situation comedy. The traditional family unit is symbolised by the bullish Antón and his mousey wife Carmen, J and Sofía are the newlyweds and the children offer caricatures of them all in games that recall the incestuous family tree of *Vacas*: 'This is your grandfather because he's the father of your mother and your father'. Indeed, intertextuality is emphasised by Ane Sánchez playing Cristina, the name of the character she shared with Suárez in *Vacas*, and, incidentally, there are more personal resonances here too: Cristina's brother is named Alberto (J's real name and the name of Medem's brother) and like J and Medem, Alberto is a champion athlete, while Ana (the name of Medem's sister who isn't Sofía) is the daughter of Begoña, the widow with the German boyfriend called Otto, which is the name of Medem's real-life uncle, the pilot who will play a key rôle in *Los amantes del Círculo Polar*.

This tangled web of metaphorical, allegorical and personal threads 'invite[s] the spectator to reflect on the ways in which we construct our notions of self, cultural heritage and national identity, which can be seen as potentially fanciful, always provisional and subject to trans-formation' (Jordan and Morgan-Tamosunas 1998: 101). Furthermore, the rules of the game can be advantageously changed, a strategy made clear to J and Sofía when they are woken by Cristina explaining the rules of her family rôle-play to Ana; and if rules can be changed so can reality. Sofía can boast of her swimming prowess and then prove it in competition with Alberto, just as J can claim prodigious reflexes and subsequently pass Sofía's test by catching a glass that she nudges off the table. Together they can even detail their sexual preferences over dinner and then act them out fulfillingly. This ruse reflects the belief of many Basque writers and linguists that the 'telling' of something calls it into existence, just as the Basque writer Bernardo Atxaga called the contemporary Basque Country into existence by writing of it in the Basque language of Euskera (Jones 2006). Yet, although 'within each little narrative (each spiralling lie on the part of both [J and Sofía]) the characters experience their improvised roles as authentic' (Smith 1996: 134), the metaphysical adventuring of these characters is betrayed by their baser instincts. As Félix tracks them to the campsite, thereby emerging from Sofía's subconscious, her fear is registered by close-ups of her gooseflesh and the camera's approach to the edge of the water that symbolises her inner self. Her mix of fear and conscience provokes a moral quandary that prompts her to ask J if they are good people, and when he fails to give an answer she provides her own by pulling down his t-shirt so that his portrait grimaces. Soon, lies so dominate the relationships at the campsite that it seems all but Antón lose sight of a minimum of truth: 'Look here, no cheating. This doesn't lie', he boasts, tapping his speedometer.

Disturbed and exhausted by the escalation of his lie, J distances himself from the macho posturing of Antón and Alberto by expressing disinterest in their speeding and swimming, though Sofía ably takes up the challenge and bests the boy in her natural element by swimming underwater. Machismo may meet its match in Sofía, but the romantic side of performative mating rituals is also indulged when the kiss between J and Sofía is echoed in that of the two cooked fish. Sofía, at this point, appears to be taking charge, while J shows signs of turning into a sensitive new man whose more brutish sexual fantasies are replaced by the liberation of more nurturing desires: 'What I like most of all is to cook for you, to care for you, just having you around.' Subsequently, the past and present, myth and reality, truth and lie all mix when Sofía and J, who sings of a 'bird of blue steel' in his song *Elisa*, confuse the reality of Sofía playing Elisa with the fantasy of her flight in the old song by Las Moscas in which Lufthansa provides both the vehicle of her sexual freedom and a nod to the Germanic origins of Medem that are also referenced in Sofía not only discovering she can speak German but also belting out Annchen's aria from *Der Freischütz* in the shower.

Der Freischütz (1821) is a sylvan romantic opera in three acts composed by Carl Maria Von Weber and is an affined tale of star-crossed lovers, evil spells and invisible woodland creatures. Intertextuality is heightened by the fact that its first performance initiated the 'release of German operatic art from its bondage to Italian and French influences and [was] the first decisive triumph of the Romantic movement in German music and the enthusiastic acceptance by the German people of a form of art peculiarly its own, based on its own nature and characteristics' (IUDLP 2004a: 5). This triumph of Romanticism and self-determination against 'bondage' to other influences and based on uniquely personal qualities clearly resonates in *La ardilla roja*, while Sofía's rendition of Annchen's aria 'Kommt ein schlanker bursch gezogen' (Along Comes a Tall Young Lad with a Rifle) gives the game away to J, or it would if he understood German.

> Let a gallant youth come towards me,
> Be he golden-haired or dark.
> Eyes that flash as he regards me,
> Him my captive I will mark.
> Him my captive I will mark.
> Yes, him my captive I will mark!
> Eyes bent down to earth for shyness,
> As befits a modest maid.
> With a stolen look of slyness,
> Yet may everything be said. (IUDLP 2004b)

However, J only grows more frustrated by his failure to control the fantasy and struggles to discredit it by telling Sofía that the squirrel tracks are from rats and that the lake and trees are artificial, man-made like her. 'You're so naive. Everything here is a lie', he tells her, only for the film's plot to be performed in miniature before them by Cristina fooling Alberto into thinking he has her hypnotised; but not only does the far more naive J not twig the analogy, he then asks Alberto if he could do the same with Sofía and the equally ignorant Alberto replies, 'well, if she's willing . . .'. Ironically, however, Sofía's hypnotic trance is real this time and her irrational ramblings allow Félix to emerge fully from her subconscious, bursting into her brother's apartment with all the weight of the past that he can muster, while, crucial to an understanding of the film's simmering political allegory, a television

4 Sofía (Emma Suárez) and Cristina (Ane Sánchez) watching the squirrel watching them in *La ardilla roja*

documentary on the Carlist Wars is kept in aural range and visual frame throughout the scene because, as *Vacas* shows, for many Basques the origins of the modern Basque conflict originated in these civil wars that therefore make a provocative connection with Félix.

As Félix emerges from Sofía's past, J's self-pitying retreat from machismo seems a particularly ill-timed strategy, and when he answers Antón's statement that women lack the balls to drive well by stating 'I've no balls either' it falls to Sofía to reconstruct a male whose deconstructed machismo has culminated in his auto-castration. Testing his resolve, she taunts him by saying 'he only knows how to fuck, cook and lie', which are, as Smith has recognised, 'the domestic, sexual and discursive roles traditionally assigned to women' (1996: 138); whereupon J literally puts the brake on his enmasculation by unsubtly erecting the motorbike in a spectacularly phallic wheelie. The fact that Sofía is mightily turned on by this display suggests that a sensitive new man is all well and good, but a bit of the caveman is also desirable.

Thereafter, Sofía collaborates greedily on the upkeep of their lie. Wiping her plate of J's cooking (just as Lucía will do of Lorenzo's in *Lucía y el sexo*), she demands more details of his fantasy. 'Suddenly you'll say, "I was born in San Sebastian"', says J in something of a premonition of Medem's return to his Basque roots with *La pelota vasca*. In return, Sofía immerses him in her world by teaching him to hold his breath underwater. Making real the lie of their fulfilling and equitable relationship pushes Sofía beyond the reach of the past ('I don't remember anything and I don't want to') and is based upon her validation of their emotional investment in each other: 'Do you love me? I know you do.'

Sofía subsequently turns machismo against its perpetrators, daring Alberto to follow through on feebly slapping her bottom before vengefully grabbing his hand and feeding it down the back of her jeans until she bites his fingers with her labia: an explicit representation of Freud's concept of *vagina dentate*, which holds that men's fear of women is prompted by the vagina's concealment of teeth. However, her desperate attempts at protecting a fantasy of herself that is close to becoming a reality take her close to the edge of insanity and when Félix erupts through the radio with an appeal for information about his deranged wife, Sofía's devastating self-doubt is only assuaged by J's feat of extemporisation about her escape from a psychotic husband that impresses all but the squirrel, which clocks him with a pine cone. 'Hello, J, I'm your amnesiac girlfriend, remember?' says Sofía, repeating the line from his earlier dream; but the masquerade is clearly crumbling and when a shot of the sleeping Sofía's skin dissolves into the reservoir that symbolises her nightmare-filled subconscious, there emerges a drowning Félix: 'Sofía, I need you to breathe, without you I lack air.' Her nightmare of a barren, windswept terrain regurgitates many details and phrases from previous scenes in the film, including her repetition of Antón's counting one-two-three, Félix's revival of J's comments to her on the beach ('Who are you?' and '*Vaya*, you're a girl!') and Antón's rage at the campsite ('I'll leave your face looking like a sack of potatoes!'). Above all else, there is the phallic knockout punch with which Félix flattens J that is a counterplot rebuttal to Sofía's *vagina dentate*. That the rôle-play is over is subsequently confirmed by Antón when he slaps Alberto for kissing his sister Cristina in their 'mothers and fathers' rôle-play: 'Let that be the last time I see you playing that game!'

The surfacing of Félix from Sofía's subconscious is rendered with an appropriately expressionist finesse that shatters the televisual bliss of the campsite. The dramatic score, low camera angles, distorted close-ups and reaction shots attest to the noirish horror of Félix emerging through the washing line that suggests Sofía's traditionally subservient past. She escapes on her motorbike, prompting the dream-feat of J's impossible clamber into Félix's speeding car (achieved by having the car speed past Novo while his stand-in, who was already on the back of the car, grabbed the window), while the duality of Félix and J and their juxtaposition as metaphors for the dictatorship and democratic Spain is made apparent in their brief, surprisingly peaceful, transitional co-existence in the speeding car before it careers over a cliff. Félix drowns in the reservoir that symbolises Sofía's subconscious, like a bad memory that she has finally managed to overcome, while J, who is not shown escaping, remains in watery limbo in fulfilment of his song: 'I dream I live inside you.' He prowls his apartment until he is inspired by the resurgence from his own subconscious of the coincidence of having seen Sofía many years previously while having his photograph taken with Elisa in Madrid's Plaza de España and the photograph springs to life as the seemingly telepathic Sofía tells him to check with her brother, Salvador Fuentes, whose name means 'source of salvation', and whose explanation of the plot prompts a montage of key events that clarifies J's gullibility. Sofía Fuentes (whose name means 'source of wisdom') works in a zoo and cares for the red squirrel in a forest enclosure in the heart of Madrid, wherein this modern Adam and Eve symbolise new hope for gender relations in democratic Spain and the possibility of attaining autonomy, equality and understanding.

Finally, it becomes apparent that *La ardilla roja* is a modern-day, improved final chapter or sequel-of-sorts to *Vacas*. *La ardilla roja* was written in the week of Medem's despair between hawking the script for *Vacas* and receiving the callback from Fernando de Garcillán and it is apparent that Medem responded to the apparent lack of commercial viability of *Vacas* by replaying its themes and characters in a more contemporary and commercial setting, for *La ardilla roja* is a condensed and linear recycling and resolution of the narrative strategies and characters of *Vacas*. J is Manuel, Ignacio and Peru Irigibel compacted into one person. He begins as a coward (Manuel), a disgrace to himself and the dogma of machismo being unable to even pluck up the courage to kill himself, then turns arrogantly chauvinist (Ignacio) as the personification of every chauvinist stereotype when transforming Sofía into his adoring girlfriend, but finally ends up a sensitive new man (Peru), an emotional artist in touch with his feminine side but still able to call on his machismo when it counts. The symmetry continues with J's doppelgänger, the insanely *machista* Félix, who combines the proud machismo of Carmelo Mendiluze and the violent psychosis of his son Juan. The death of Félix therefore completes the equation by repeating the lack of a third generation of Mendiluze to conflict with Peru. This allows J, like Peru, to unify all the inherited elements of the Irigibels and Mendiluces into one progressive and balanced whole. Sofía, meanwhile, like the females in *Vacas*, still suffers the burden of symbolising the Basque Country, for J's remodelling of her as the perfect girlfriend is akin to Basque nationalists' imagining of a utopian motherland and beneath the glossy, absurd disguise of *La ardilla roja* lies another complex and painful examination of the process by which identity is acquired. Nevertheless, Sofía may still offer hope for the realisation of an autonomous, independent Basque Country that, unlike her, is yet to emerge from a history of frustrated ambitions, violence and lies.

Ignoring its political resonance, *La ardilla roja* was mostly dismissed as frivolous by Spanish critics when it opened in Spain on 21 April 1993, a few weeks before the ruling Socialist party (PSOE) won the general election with support from the independent Catalan party (CiU) but lost its overall majority in the Spanish parliament. Come August and President Felipe González would have to follow through on his part of the deal by ceding 15% of direct taxes to Catalonia and other autonomous communities including the Basque Country. It was a time of seismic shifts in the social and political landscape of Spain that were nonetheless reflected in films such as *La ardilla roja*, the sour diatribe against media corporations and reality television that was *Kika* (1993) and the flailing parody of machismo and capitalism that was *Huevos de oro* (*Golden Balls*, 1993), three of fifty Spanish films released that year, all of which were dwarfed by the box-office of the escapist *Jurassic Park* (1993). *La ardilla roja* did become a minor domestic sleeper hit, however, thanks to youthful word of mouth and awards from the festivals of Cannes, Denver and Gerárdmer that were boasted of in posters for the film that hailed a new Spanish auteur. Its domestic gross was the equivalent of € 478,223 from 178,228 spectators (Sogecine 2004), but as with *Vacas* it was the foreign trajectory of the film that confirmed the wisdom of Sogetel's investment for, as Fernando de Garcillán claims, *La ardilla roja* 'showed us the value of foreign markets and of investing in a director like Medem' [9].

La ardilla roja may have gone begging for an American distributor, but it was sold to ancillary markets in twenty-seven other countries, including all of Europe, New Zealand, Australia, Hong Kong and Cuba. Most international distributors copied the Spanish poster and used a wide shot from Sofía's dream, though the UK's Metro-Tartan went for Sofía in the eye of the jukebox, the French chose a frame of foliage around Sofía, J and, bizarrely, the young Alberto, and the poster for Germany, where it took € 45,530, offered an enigmatic close-up of Sofía and J kissing underwater. Stanley Kubrick liked it enough to purchase his personal celluloid copy from Medem and enthuse about it to Steven Spielberg, who offered Medem the Banderas-starring *The Mask of Zorro* and the female lead subsequently played by Catherine Zeta-Jones to Emma Suárez, both of whom turned him down.

The 35-year-old Medem was nominated for the Youth Prize from the European Film Awards and, when the Spanish award season came around in 1994, memories of the early hostile reviews were softened by the Luis Buñuel Award for Cinematographic Creation of the Year, the Ondas prize for Best Spanish film, a Spanish Film Academy Award for Alberto Iglesias (plus nominations for Suárez and Barranco) and the Catalan Sant Jordi awards for Best Spanish Film and Best Spanish Actress for Emma Suárez. In contrast to the rush between *Vacas* and *La ardilla roja*, Medem would take three years to script, ready, shoot and release *Tierra* in 1996, and there were times when he re-considered Spielberg's offer and the opportunity of working in Hollywood. Like Pedro Almodóvar, he has so far resisted but surely imagined taking meetings with executives enthused by his visual style, hoping to fluff up their generic product with some vaguely European flair. Julio Medem's *The Mask of Zorro* might have been quasi-mythic, sexy and romantic, perhaps even a touch more authentically Hispanic, but it would have been just make-believe, nothing at all like *La ardilla roja*. In rejecting the compromise that came with a Hollywood contract, Medem had his feet set firmly on the ground and his eyes set determinedly on *Tierra*.

5

That part of you that died: *Tierra* (1996)

Just as the autonomous Basque government of the 1980s had subsidised Basque filmmakers such as Imanol Uribe, Daniel Calparsoro and Julio Medem as a means of creating a credible notion of Basque cinema, so in the 1990s did Sogetel (renamed Sogecine in 1997) invest in projects that might realise the company's ambitions for international success. This strategy was predicated on the auteurist credentials of filmmakers such as Álex de la Iglesia (*El día de la bestia* [1995], *Perdita Durango* [1997]), Fernando Trueba (*Two Much* [1995]), Vicente Aranda (*Libertarias* [1996]), Alejandro Amenábar (*Abre los ojos* [1997]) and Julio Medem, whose *La ardilla roja* had encountered critical success, at least beyond Spain, and thereby convinced Sogetel to double Medem's budget for his next film *Tierra* to 380 million pesetas, which was partly raised by employing a French sound unit as part of a co-production agreement that gave access to funding from the European Union.

Since the 1960s, the name and reputation of a film director had been a marketable commodity on the international arthouse and festival circuit, where critics raised on auteurist cinema have a great deal of influence. However, although Sogetel provided generous budgets on an understanding of reciprocal collaboration and compromise, the risk of endowing film directors with the kind of creative freedom, however pressurised and limited, that came from financial empowerment and a consequently consecrated sense of auteurism was that films written and directed by them might become halls of mirrors offering reflections of their own reflections on politics, history and philosophy. The risk was arguably illustrated by *Tierra*'s resistance to explanation in its poster. The Spanish single-sheet was an abstract print of red earth against a blue sky and tumbling black letters above a lightning-like tree stump, while later publicity employed a collage of scenes around Mari gazing at Ángel through his fumigator's helmet. Nevertheless, rationalisation of its content became a lost cause for a film that stubbornly added to its foreignness by keeping its Spanish title in all foreign territories except Australia. In Spain, meanwhile, *Tierra* premiered on 24 May 1996 during the aftermath of the national elections that were won without an outright majority by the centre-right Partido Popular following a stability deal with moderate Catalan and Basque nationalists. From 226,174 domestic spectators, it took the equivalent of only € 717,729 (Sogecine 2004) and failed to enter that year's domestic top ten, which was led by *Two Much* (1995). It was sold to most of northern and western Europe, South America and new markets such as Singapore and Macao, but still did not attract American distribution despite its many festival screenings. It won nothing at Cannes, but did gain awards for its music and special effects as well as the best actor and actress awards for Carmelo Gómez and Emma Suárez from the Spanish Film Academy, which had included their performances in *Tierra* in their composite nominations for *Tu nombre envenena mis sueños* (1996) and *El perro del hortelano* (1996).

Although the doubling of his budget allowed Medem access to digital effects and expert cinematographer Javier Aguirresarobe, this came with constant reminders attached of Sogetel's expectations for a marketable auteurist work. The risk that the naturally introverted Medem might become a solipsistic auteur, whose creativity would be stymied by repetition, self-indulgence and the second-guessing of his own artistry, did not seem relevant to the financing of *Tierra*, however, because Medem's obsessions with existentialism, symmetry and identity on a personal and national level had been so well disguised by style and metaphor in the Cannes prize-winning *La ardilla roja* that the story, theme and setting of *Tierra*, about a man named Ángel who, while fumigating the vineyards of Cariñena, is bedevilled by his conscience in the guise of his identical guardian angel, seemed original and always marketable.

In fact, the backing of *Tierra* as an auteurist work prompted Medem to fabricate *Tierra* as a suitably assertive illustration of the philosphical concerns that had underpinned his formation as a film-maker and been implied in *Vacas* and *La ardilla roja*. Chief amongst these influences was the nineteenth-century German philosopher Friedrich Nietzsche, whose *The Birth of Tragedy* (1993) is claimed by

Medem as the source of his own filmmaking compulsion to differentiate between what he describes as 'the Dionysian, which is irrationality, passion and instinct, which has a lot to do with the memory of the species and the ego described by Freud, and the Apollonian, which is structured and realised, which is the centred self' [5]. Nietzsche may be seen as one of the first existentialist philosophers, whose work was based upon the notion of questioning socially dominant doctrines and structures such as traditional morality and Christianity by exploring an atheistic view that non-rational forces reside at the foundation of all creativity and of reality itself. In *The Birth of Tragedy*, Nietzsche attempts to justify life on aesthetic grounds in response to his own belief that human existence is meaningless because it has no specific purpose. He discusses the angst of Shakespeare's Hamlet, a precursor of Medem's Ángel in *Tierra*, whose 'To be or not to be' Nietzsche takes to express not the multitude of options that paralyse him, but the knowledge that whatever Hamlet decides is ultimately meaningless (Nietzsche 1993: 30–40).

Nietzsche goes on to dismiss religious attempts to deliver a moral or ethical justification for life by claiming that humans console themselves with images and dreams and that religions only substitute one illusion for another. This, says Nietzsche, is soothing, structured Apollonian art, whereas the Dionysian is spontaneous and non-rational, provoking the dismissal of illusory identities and the release of the true Self, which renders it clearly relevant to Surrealism. Apollonian and Dionysian inspirations together evoke and signify the duality of art as a juxtaposition of rationalised images and irrational impulses, a concept that Medem professes to adhere to in fictions that commonly present human interaction in terms of non-rational forces, such as coincidence, fate, instinctive impulses and passion, which are balanced by the structure, mise en scène, framing and editing of films that are themselves the product of rational, carefully calibrated measurements and intellectual rationalisations of images and their relationships to each other. In addition, Medem claims it is his adherence to a belief in non-rational creativity that inspires his technique of developing scripts by assuming the first-person subjectivity of his characters and 'writing feverishly without brakes' [5], leaving his Apollonian side to provide the structure of the script in rewrites.

Medem also professes to favour writing above filming and editing for, if an auteur is the person who makes the most decisions during the entire filmmaking process, it is here that he has complete control:

> I prefer to write. I feel freer. Once the script is written and filming begins there is a massive commitment to many other people, to the budget, to the schedule and to the time and work of all these people. Of course, that's why I write, but, even so, writing is the creative process that makes me happiest. [5]

In successively assuming the subjectivities of his characters Medem believes that he attains an intimate kind of truth, though the risk is that he only imposes his subjectivity on all his characters rather than conceiving of them in anything approaching opposition to his own beliefs and prejudices. With Lorenzo in *Lucía y el sexo*, for example, the risk of his inhabiting a character with whom he shared the omnipotence of authorship resulted in this initially minor character graduating through eight versions of the script to become the dominant perspective on events.

In the case of *Tierra*, moreover, the effect of Sogetel's communication by economic means of its trust in Medem's auteurism must be appreciated for its corroboration of Medem's belief that true artistry resulted from the artistic transference of his personal experiences into his writing, which in turn ensured his emotional investment in the filming. Moreover, the common elements of multiple, juxtaposed subjectivities and fateful symmetries in films written and directed by Medem all point to the fact that, following Nietzsche, he believes that this kind of truth is:

> A movable host of metaphors, metonyms, and anthropomorphisms [. . .] a sum of human relations which have been poetically and rhetorically intensified, transferred, and embellished, and which, after long usage, seem to a people to be fixed, canonical, and binding. Truths are illusions which we have forgotten are illusions. (Nietzsche 1873).

Thus, in explaining his rejection of Christian faith and Basque nationalism, Medem expresses the view that truth is only the invention of fixed conventions for practical purposes, especially those of security and consistency. The rhetoric of Basque nationalism and the Catholic Church in Spain, for example, are truths because they impose order, meaning and self-worth, but this only suggests that truth, like Alicia Medem's Clecla, J's Sofía and Ángel's angel in *Tierra*, is an imaginary friend.

Contextual analysis of *Tierra* reveals that truth was also hard to come by in mid-1990s Spain when, although living memory of the Spanish Civil War was dwindling, Spaniards and foreign observers alike looked on democracy as a peeling dressing on an open wound of political and social unrest. The Socialist Workers' Party (PSOE) was re-elected in 1993, thanks partly to distracting public attention from its internal corruption scandals by exploiting extant fears of a dictatorship that had ended eighteen years before, but in an atmosphere of imminent crisis, the Spanish National Bank vowed to restructure an economy laid low by rampant speculation, insider trading and the *cultura del pelotazo* (get-rich-quick culture) that dominated the banks and big businesses that were so slickly represented by characters such as the flamboyant *über*-yuppie Mario Conde and the ex-governor of the Spanish National Bank, Mariano Rubio, both of whom would be imprisoned the following year. But reform was slow and one-day general strikes by the main unions in January 1994 revealed the extent of public distress at the social fissures. While themes of duality dominate in any land to have suffered a Civil War, the Capitalism that came with democracy and was always bound to result in social divisions between the haves and the have-nots made mid-1990s Spain a battleground between the fucked and the fuck-yous. It is therefore pertinent that it was within this period of social and political conflict that Medem made *Tierra*.

The pre-production pressures felt by Medem were exacerbated not only by the burden of living up to the Cannes consecration of his auteurship that had been sanctioned by Sogetel, but by the fact that his marriage of eighteen years was falling apart. Nevertheless, the status of auteur that was assigned by festival prizes and the doubling of his budget seemed to confirm that 'the distinguishable personality of the director [was] a criterion of value [and that] the way a film looks and moves should have some relationship to the way a director thinks and feels' (Sarris 1992: 586), prompting Medem to write several drafts of a script that illustrated an existential conundrum by reference to his own personal dilemma. He began by reworking *Mari en la tierra*, the script he had written in 1987 about the legend of a highly-sexed Basque elf who preys on travellers, seducing them into her cave, where she submits them to a variety of sexual tortures. The elfin Mari became a leather-clad biker, an urban nymph who wrought sexual havoc among the men she encountered; but, due to assuming the subjectivity of other characters and identifying with the male protagonist, *Tierra* became more the story of Ángel, who meets Mari when he journeys from the Basque Country to Cariñena in order to exterminate a plague of beetles that is making the region's wine taste earthy. This Ángel is plagued by déjà vu, existential despair and an excess of conscience, which is represented in the meddling presence of his identical angel; though he may, of course, just be mad. Inadvertently, Ángel disrupts the rural community when his emotional and carnal desires are split between the sensual and nurturing Ángela and the sexual, free-spirit that is Mari, whose brother Alberto is in love with Ángela while she has frequent flings with Ángela's husband Patricio. Convoluted but sprightly, the plot turns on Ángel's deliberations about freedom of choice and destiny and involves him in a chaste romance with Ángela, who wants to be more sexual, and a lustful fling with Mari, who wants to be more romantic. Eventually, he leaves with the latter.

The third draft of the script is dated 13 February 1995, has a black cover bearing a photograph of the film's red landscape, and begins with a quote from Blaise Pascal's *Pensées* written in 1670, a collection of hundreds of notes intended for a book that counters Nietzsche by presenting a rational defence of Christianity and has as its running theme the duality of man, who is both noble and corrupt: 'Si fuera por el espacio, el universo me rodearía y se me tragaría como un átomo, pero por el pensamiento yo abrazo el mundo' (Medem 1995: 2) (By space the universe encompasses and swallows me up like an atom; by thought I comprehend the world). Scribbled on the facing page, Medem diagnoses Ángel's condition as 'el conflicto entre su ego secreto, complejo e interno y otro más sencillo y físico' (Medem 1995: s.n.) (the conflict between his internal, complex and secret ego and another, more physical and simple). He explains Ángel's duality in terms of 'earth or cosmos, sanity or madness, sex-love or love-sex, Mari or Ángela' and adds that 'we are an insignificant species, lost somewhere in the middle of immensity and eternity. Our size and the paths our lives take are absolutely ridiculed by the laws that rule the cosmos' (Medem 1995: s.n.). Although this reeks of a stoner's eureka, Ángel's ultimate rejection of mysticism, metaphysics, cosmos, madness, love-sex and Ángela reflected what Nietzsche identified as Hamlet's frustration at the indecision that comes from an awareness of all points of view and Medem's awareness that by assuming the subjectivity of all characters in their writing, including that of Ángela, he had become more conscious of the effect his marriage problems were having on his wife, who had inspired her. Indeed, as Gómez observes, '*Tierra* is Julio's particular paranoia and has everything to do with the contradictions in his life' [15].

To offset this, the subjectivity of Ángel, with whom Medem as writer-director most identifies (as he would with Lorenzo in *Lucía y el sexo*) became absolute and god-like, 'seeing space from the earth and vice versa' [5]. But Ángel is a Nietzschean lab-rat just as K is Kafka's in *The Trial*, for Medem charged the (also) 35-year-old Ángel with resolving a mid-life crisis in a way that might assist his creator's own personal situation. Thus, Medem justifies Ángel's effect on others by overstating his martyrdom, claiming that 'his desirable physicality is at odds with his tender, unloved core' [5]. In addition, directing Carmelo Gómez to make Ángel 'make everything he says sound really important' [5] reflects an overcompensating attitude that comes from both the character's existential inferiority complex and the writer-director's identification with the rôle. Medem's diagnosis of Ángel's 'suffering' justifies his choice of Mari over Ángela, whom Medem blames for her own abandonment, stating 'she deserves a more intense life, but her submissive character hasn't left her with any opportunities' [5] and this foreshortening of female subjectivity reflects the fact that in developing *Tierra* from *Mari en la tierra* Medem had built up the subjectivity of the male protagonist with whom he identified and reduced that of Mari, only to later rework Mari's subjectivity in diary form in order to prepare Silke for her role (later published as *Mari en la tierra: diario de un personaje* by Planeta in 1997). Ángel's subjectivity consequently dominates the film and assumes the prerogative of resolving the conflict that is centred upon the duality of physicality and spirituality that is illustrated by him being both the terrenal Ángel and his celestial angel. And just as Sofía managed to resolve her duality by choosing between two men in *La ardilla roja*, so Ángel chooses between two women in *Tierra*.

Ideas of fractious duality based upon his reading of Nietzsche schematised Medem's thinking when he rewrote several drafts of the script in search of a rigid structure that would contain his spontaneously generated characters, thereby illustrating a philosophical struggle to resolve the conflicts that are essential for balance and unity in Greek tragedy and have symmetry as their aesthetic by-product, with Apollonian rationality, reason, culture and brains on one side and Dionysian irrationality, instinct, primitivity and loins on the other. This leads to what Paul Julian Smith has described as 'the dichotomy, then, of physical and metaphorical, abstract and concrete [that] will be played out by repeated patterns of splitting and doubling, on the one hand, and fusion and identification, on the other' (2000: 149). By these means, *Tierra* explores the duality of Ángel, a conflicted individual who falls to Earth at a mythic crossroads midway between all these opposites, 'half-way between the atoms and the stars' as his angel says. Furthermore, as this conflict within a divided self is such a recurring theme in films written and directed by Medem, so it should be noted that duality is also a malleable concept of Spanishness that has been used to explain the Spanish Civil War, the intensification of social and political divisions during the dictatorship and the fundamental divisions that resurfaced under the recent presidency of José María Aznar. The duality of Spain was evoked by the poet Antonio Machado in his *Proverbios y Cantares* when he wrote of 'una España que muere/y otra España que bosteza' (one Spain that dies/and another Spain that yawns) as well as historians such as the Portuguese Fidelino de Figueiredo, author of *As dues Espanhas* (*The Two Spains*, 1932) and Santos Juliá, author of *Historias de las dos Españas* (*History of the Two Spains*, 2004). Medem construes and constructs these metaphorically-charged notions of duality as symmetries that are rendered by juxtaposed subjectivities and resolved in the heterosexual couplings that form the happy endings of *Vacas*, *La ardilla roja*, *Tierra*, (Ana's half of) *Los amantes del Círculo Polar* and (the happy middle of) *Lucía y el sexo*. However, just as Williamson argues for 'a residually Romantic notion that true subjectivity is to be found in the incomple-tion of the self [. . .] and an oscillation between sexual polarities, not bisexuality in any fixated form, but a continuous androgynous deferral of identity, the intermediate's space of desire' (1999: 122), so Medem adheres to this Romantic notion of the incomplete self by situating his male protagonists, cowards all, in constant flux between concepts of masculinity that are burdened with social, political and mythic baggage. Manuel, Ignacio and Peru Irigibel reflect generational oscillations between mythic and progressive ideas of masculinity in the Basque Country in *Vacas*, while J in *La ardilla roja* embodies Spain's transition from dictatorship to democracy by switching his polarity from sexist abuser to that of sensitive 'new man'. Duality is structurally determined in *Los amantes del Círculo Polar* by the oscillating subjectivities of soulmates, while in *La pelota vasca* the notion of multifarious competing subjectivities builds a polyphonic dialogue out of almost all sides in the conflict over the Basque Country in which the documentary's structural equation based on symmetry posits the brief and controversial mirage of a balance to the differences onscreen.

    Tierra develops this oscillation in the split subjectivities of Ángel and his angel that are appropriated by subjective camerawork and divided in the editing between two women who are rendered as polar opposites. The space between Ángela and Mari is where indecision is located for Ángel, who finally resolves his deferral of identity in a coupling with Mari, who is a cliché of male heterosexual desire, a masquerade of femininity that disguises and displaces Ángel's own doubts about his identity that he anchors voyeuristically by means of his sexual attraction to Mari. However, Ángel is effectively denied the affirmation of his heterosexual identity by Mari's demand that he withhold his orgasm, which suggests the distance between desire and object that signifies 'control of the image and its loss' (Doane 1992: 762) as well as the idea that irony is a determining feature of Romanticism, which inspires us to overcome the paradox that true subjectivity is found in the incompletion of the self by obliging us to make up for this lack by acting upon the desire for symmetry. However, the illusion of symmetry that Ángel finds in Mari's masquerade of simplicity is merely an illusion of himself as a man defined by basic masculine urges that exists in opposition to his true complexity and is duly thwarted by his proximity to her in the sex act, for, as Doane states, 'this body so close, so excessive, prevents the woman from assuming a position similar to the man's in relation to signifying systems' (1992: 763).

The spatial and sexual pairing of Ángel with Mari in *Tierra* was also a practical consideration that relates to an audience's positioning within related theories of spectatorship, because Medem wrote the script with specific Spanish film stars in mind: 'I wrote Ángel for Antonio Banderas and Mari for Penélope Cruz' [5]. The stellar pairing of Banderas and Cruz was an objective shared by many Spanish filmmakers during the 1990s, though even Pedro Almodóvar, who to some extent nurtured their screen personas, has so far failed to unite them. In 1994, pre-production on *Días contados* (1994) was held up by negotiations to secure them as its leads and when negotiations failed Carmelo Gómez stepped in to play the lead of an ETA terrorist opposite Ruth Gabriel and, incidentally, provide a performance of fearful rage and lost innocence. Medem served on the jury in the San Sebastian Film Festival when Gómez won the prize for best actor for this rôle. Shortly thereafter Banderas rejected the rôle of Ángel in *Tierra* to work instead with Fernando Trueba and the producer Andrés Vicente Gómez of Lola Films, who were determined to break America with Banderas as the star of *Two Much* (1995). Entering the international and American markets was thus a common objective of the larger Spanish film companies, and when Sogetel and Canal Plus announced

fifteen features including *Tierra*, *Libertarias* (1996) and *Tu nombre
envenena mis sueños* (1996) at the San Sebastian Film Festival in 1995
it was with a keen eye on foreign markets. *Tierra*, it seemed, had appeal
for both arthouse and mainstream audiences that was based on the
reputation of its director, an anticipation of sensual imagery, an offbeat
narrative and an attractive cast, even without Banderas. The producer
Fernando de Garcillán admits that he had expected *Tierra* to recoup
75% of its production costs in the international market alone. In fact,
Tierra was deliberately not pre-sold, which increased both the
possibility of profit and, as it turned out, the possibility of loss.

Banderas as Ángel, like Banderas as J in *La ardilla roja*, is not easy
to imagine in place of Gómez and Novo respectively, though Medem
also had problems persuading Gómez, who had already been cast as
Patricio, to take the lead. Gómez recalls that 'Banderas left to make
Two Much and Julio turned back to his usual actors. The part of Ángel
had been bounced all over the place and I was very reticent to accept it'
[5]. At the time he was also acting opposite Emma Suárez on *El perro
del hortelano* (1996) directed by Pilar Miró, so Medem tested the singer
Miguel Bosé, who had appeared in *Tacones lejanos* (*High Heels*, 1991),
and the dancer Nacho Duato before coming back to Gómez, who, says
Medem, 'insisted he wasn't Ángel but Patricio [Ángela's farmer
husband] because his father also had a tractor' [5]. Medem worked
hard to convince Gómez that his physicality and earthiness made
him perfect for the rôle over two weeks of read-throughs, but Gómez
claimed not to understand the script. Medem made him watch
Krzysztof Kieślowski's spiritually disquieting *La Double vie de
Véronique* (1991) about two physically identical young women who are
capable of feeling the suffering of each other as preparation for the
character of Ángel, but when this failed he deduced the problem was
'Carmelo doesn't believe in duality, symmetry or balance' [5]. Tensions
increased to the point at which Gómez stabbed the script with his
penknife during a read-through and left. However, as Gómez recalls:

> I returned the next day with a hundred million questions and tried again,
> but the same thing, and the next day a hundred million more. What finally
> gave me a way into the character was the birth of my daughter. I used to
> take the script everywhere with me, even when I took my daughter to the
> park in her pram. And one day, I was just watching her, and I saw such
> a fragile creature, who just by looking back at me brought out this
> immense feeling of tenderness. She was an angel. And suddenly I knew
> who was Ángel. [15]

The cast was then constructed around Gómez beginning with Silke, who had acted in *Hola, ¿estás sola?* (1985) directed by Iciar Bollaín and on which Medem had collaborated on the script. Suárez was the introverted and self-disciplined Ángela and Karra Elejalde, who was initially due to play Alberto to Gómez's Patricio and Banderas's Ángel, became Patricio, leaving the easy-going Alberto (which was J's real name after all) free for Nancho Novo. Also returning were Txema Blasco as Ángela's father Tomás and Ane Sánchez as her daughter, the physical similarities between her and Suárez becoming even more pronounced since they had shared the rôle of Cristina in *Vacas*. There was also the coincidence (much to the delight of Medem) of Sánchez's reunion with cinematographer Javier Aguirresarobe, who had once shot a live birth for a documentary on hospitals, for that baby had been her. Pre-production stuttered through various delays, but Medem took this as an opportunity to refine his script through rehearsals:

> I told my actors we were going to rehearse from the inside out. I said, 'I'm going to take you by the hand to the centre of your character, we'll go together, and once we're there, I'm going to leave you. Then I'll watch you from outside and ask you to make your own way out alone'. [5]

Cast rehearsals of characters that were largely shaped by occurrences in Medem's own life also signified a method of protracted self-analysis that made almost tangible 'these moves from reality to fiction' [5] that Medem claims are essential to his films and are achieved in collaboration with his actors.

> In the beginning, I don't tell my actors anything. I just tell them a story that I'd like to be able to tell, but not all of it, because I don't want to. I tell them enough to stimulate them, but I want the characters to belong to them. I like it when each actor or actress finds something of their own human quality in their character. [5]

Again, however, the risk that the cast might develop their characters in a different manner to that intended by Medem is pre-empted in his withholding of information, which makes them correct their mistakes until his increasing pleasure in their performances coincides with their gradual resemblance to his notion of the characters. This was especially infuriating to the classically-trained Gómez:

> I suffered a lot on *Tierra*. Julio didn't understand that you have to explain the film to an actor. Not explaining things makes an actor very dependent on him. In order for the character to emerge you have to try lots of things and it's very frustrating because you're always pending his reaction. [15]

Pending Medem's reaction made the actor slip into the 'mirror-mode' that Medem had also assumed when casting Gómez and Novo in *Vacas* and *La ardilla roja* respectively, by which the actors returned to their director something akin to the reflection that he himself identified in his protagonists. According to Lacan, this process is essential to the creation of an identity, for an infant lacking motor control and any sense of completeness fails to recognise the seeming unity of its own reflection in a mirror and only forms a notion of its own identity by the substitute mirror of another's face, thereby noting the corresponding sense of completeness that results from the correlation between its own actions and the nodding, smiling face of its mother (Lacan 1991). Consequently, the infant creates a notion of its own identity by responding to the emotional needs of the parent, just as Gómez's need for approval and direction was only met when his performance of Ángel's identity conformed to the reflection that Medem sought, if only subconsciously, in his actor.

'In many shots in *Tierra* I speak like he speaks. I imitated his voice, his accent and his intonation', says Gómez [15]. Indeed, the imitation became more intense during filming when it became clear to the cast that Ángel's choice of lusting Mari over trusting Ángela reflected Medem's personal complications at the time of its production, for just as Ángel ends the film with an attempt to resolve his tortuous duality by taking off with the younger, adoring Mari and leaving the trusting, maternal Ángela in the dubious care of his angel, so did *Tierra* mark Medem's separation from Lola, his wife of eighteen years and the mother of Peru and Alicia, and the beginning of his relationship with Montse Sanz, assistant art director on *Tierra*. The influence of this break-up on the plot and resolution of *Tierra* was inevitable for an auteurist-minded Medem, who has dedicated each of his films to family members, for these poetic dedications suggest the personal resonances of each film: *Vacas*, written while unemployed and living in a house in the Basque mountains, is dedicated to Lola, who supported him; *La ardilla roja* is dedicated to their daughter Alicia and *Tierra* to their son Peru; *Los amantes del Círculo Polar* is dedicated to his estranged father, whose recent death informed the film to such an extent that the reconciliation Medem might have sought is withheld by the final dedication being obliterated by a blizzard, and *Lucía y el sexo* is dedicated to Medem's sister Ana, who inspired her namesake in *Los amantes del Círculo Polar*, a character whose death was followed by that of the real-life Ana during the filming of *Lucía y el sexo*. It is not in-jokery that prompts Medem's actors to imitate him onscreen, for Suárez too based Ángela on Medem's estranged wife Lola, but that their adoption of certain gestures and phrases testifies to these insiders' awareness of their writer-director's projection of his Self and his experiences into their Others. For Gómez, the task of performing a rôle that seemed to him partly this schematic Nietzschean lab-rat and partly the alter ego of his writer-director was especially frustrating, to the extent that he justifies the broad strokes of the film in terms of its antipathy to naturalism, 'where the smaller a thing is, the more real it seems, until we can no longer play with fiction' [15].

Gómez is an unlikely alter ego for Medem, however, who is physically more like Novo; but, as Chris Perriam expertly describes him, Gómez is exactly what Medem's archetype of the cowardly male aspires to:

> Gómez very markedly incarnates for his audience a solid yet sensitive virility; his intellectual and philosophically inflected performance style constructs intense effects, variously, of closeness to land and region, of plain, magnetic manliness, and of a psyche and identity troubled by doubt and desires but able to overcome the former and to fulfil the latter. (2003: 71)

Not only does Gómez not believe in duality, he also comes from such a rigid academic and theatrical training that when asked to differentiate between his rôles as Ángel and angel in *Tierra* he provides a simple breakdown of their differences that undermines the existential complications expounded by Medem and, indeed, the characters themselves. Says Gómez: 'I think Ángel's angel is the bad guy because he's the one who causes the confusion. He's the angel of a thousand contradictions, while Ángel, who has a thousand problems, is the one who truly suffers from the thousand doubts thrown up by these contradictions' [15]. For Gómez, this polarisation of his rôles meant that:

> Ángel and his angel are like the great characters from the classics who represent the concept of good and evil. Ángel has these two sides that are pulling him apart, because on the one hand he's a man in love with a woman and he'd like to settle down and enjoy his commitments, but he's not able to, not at the moment, because he's busy with these big, existential problems that are so contradictory. That's why he's so intense about everything, because he has this serious, massive, internal problem that he's unable to resolve. [15]

This problem is nothing less than the cosmic weight of responsibility brought on by awareness of his place at the centre of chaos theory, as if the proverbial butterfly were somehow aware of the typhoon that might be caused by its fluttering wings and is frozen by its conscience, thereby falling to Earth just like Ángel. In *Tierra*, however, the infinite choices thrown up by all these contradictions, doubts and imaginings come down to a simple election between two women: Ángela or Mari. Mari wins out at the film's conclusion, which provides a tenuous and temporary balance, but mostly suggests irritation with solipsism and a reaction against the existentialist headache, whereby Ángel accepts being insignificant and enjoys the lack of consequence to his actions. Dionysus therefore triumphs over Apollo in a classically-minded conflict that plays to morbid introspection due to Medem's characteristic transformation of the physical terrain into a psychological landscape that stretches from the furthest star to the smallest atom, while, at the centre of this universe, like a spoke in a great cosmic wheel, is the subjectivity of Ángel, who professes to live in 'un mundo a la altura de los ojos' (a world at eye-level). This world is clearly that of Medem, dubbed 'the cineaste of subjectivity' (2000: 146) by Paul Julian Smith, who describes Medem's tendency to utilise subjective camerawork and sound as a means to express what 'can be defined, briefly, as the cohabitation of self and other, man and machine, in the cinematic apparatus' (2000: 146). However, this emphasis on subjectivity also attests to Medem's projection of his Self into the films that he writes and directs. As he describes:

> When you create people and characters, you gradually create, over time, a very powerful place that you can return to quite easily. It's a place where other characters exist and you can imagine them all very well. It's very close to being this other parallel world of duality into which you can project yourself into characters that have come from inside you. There's a part of you that they take with them and pull on, and that's where this great tension is created around your duality. [5]

In an interview in 1997 on the occasion of the film's premiere on the pay-TV channel Canal Plus, Medem stated that *Tierra* was so personal he had decided not to watch it again for a long time (Anon 1997). All this invites an objective comparison of Medem and Ángel to which Medem now responds: 'You only have to see *Tierra*. Like Ángel there was a part of me that was searching for something else without my wanting it to. During *Tierra* I met Montse because I also had this need.

Later I saw a psychiatrist who told me, "You've already written your answer!"' [5].

During the writing of *Tierra* Medem was distracted by the idea of making a complementary film of *Mari en la tierra* in black and white on 16mm to show events from Mari's point of view, though this was vetoed by concerns of scheduling and cost. Nevertheless, this objective can still be achieved by reading *Mari en la tierra* in a book published by Planeta (Medem 1997) that matches it back to back and upside down with the script for *Tierra*. Medem dedicates the film's script to Silke, 'más hermosa que en la imaginación' (Medem 1997: 7) (more beautiful than imagined), but 'Mari' dedicates 'her' diary to Ángela, 'la mujer más hermosa de la tierra' (Medem 1997: 15) (the most beautiful woman on Earth). Although the film has them as suspicious rivals, Mari's diary reveals that she and Ángela actually share a friendship based on mutual admiration and it is regretful that this female perspective was elbowed aside by the single and solipsistic male subjectivity of the film. This imbalance is most acutely felt at *Tierra*'s ending, when Ángel's abandonment of Ángela in favour of Mari seems like the self-serving action of a male with a mid-life crisis, whereas Mari's diary makes it clear that the choice of partner actually belonged to Ángela, who was also waiting outside Ángel's hospital room but chose not to enter, pushing Mari in instead (Medem 1997: 149). But this scene is missing from the film, along with the friendship, solidarity, mutual admiration and good-natured envy that exists between the women. Instead, *Tierra*'s oscillating subjectivity is between a man and his angel (both played by Gómez), who objectify Mari and Ángela respectively, which contrasts dramatically with the balance of male and female subjectivities on either side of *Tierra* in *La ardilla roja* and *Los amantes del Círculo Polar*. The character that suffers most from this foreshortening is Suárez's Ángela, partly because she is a less spontaneous, more melancholic figure than Sofía in *La ardilla roja*, but also because the amount of screen-time and close-ups given to the leather and midriff charms of Silke seem, by comparison, a rather superficial obsession rendered by the cliché of Ángel's objectifying subjectivity (see Mulvey 1992: 746–57).

On the other hand, Ángela's soulfulness, shared enthusiasm for the taste of the earthy wine and name alone indicates that she is Ángel's soulmate; but the debate that largely divided and dissatisfied audiences is also unresolved in the minds of the film's cast and crew. Medem says that 'Ángel chooses the way out that isn't exactly love, sure, but it's an option that still promises a lot of love' [5] and claims the relationship between him and Mari will last because 'just as Ángela wants to be more sexual, Mari wants to fall in love, and she and Ángel both start down their chosen paths at the moment when they meet' [5]. However, this interpretation liberates Ángel from his conscience by excusing him from all responsibility because the final choice of partner is not his. Medem counters that Ángel was going to leave anyway and it just so happens that Mari leaves with him: 'When Ángel's in hospital, if Ángela had appeared instead of Mari, I'm sure he'd have been equally delighted' [5]. But although Mari's diary tells us she was there, in the film we do not see Ángela outside the hospital room, so Medem's argument is again skewed to justifying the actions of a male with whom he identifies and is identified, who idealises both Ángel and Mari from a chauvinist point of view that has Mari representing youth and disinhibition in opposition to Ángela, the suffering, cuckolded widow who gets on with her household duties and sacrifices her sexuality while Ángel gets on with exploring his. Suárez concurs: 'The thing is, Julio puts women on a pedestal and tends to mythologise them. When he writes female characters you notice this, whatever type of woman it is, you notice they are always a bit above you' [14]. Gómez, however, admits to an enduring state of bafflement:

> I've no idea why Ángela doesn't enter the hospital room. Following an actor's logic, I suppose Ángel would go with Ángela and not Mari. So why does he go with Mari? Well, she represents youth, going out drinking, getting drunk, riding motorbikes. I think the most surprising thing is that Ángel says 'I'm sorry' to Ángela when she's so cute in the bar, when Emma is so ripe for a cuddle, and suddenly he says, 'I'm going with this other one, the one who plays billiards and wears leather, the flashy one, the nymphomaniac'. [15]

Perhaps it is Mari's missing perspective on events, her sidelined diary and unmade film, that means *Tierra* lacks the female subjectivity of *La ardilla roja*, *Los amantes del Círculo Polar* and at least the intention of it in *Lucía y el sexo* that would balance that of Ángel, providing narrative equilibrium, symmetry and even consensus amongst Medem and his cast, while also perhaps resolving what Paul Julian Smith sees as the central concern of *Tierra*, that is 'the reconciliation of the subjective and the intersubjective in an ideal of differentiation without isolation and unity without violence' (2000: 149). Gómez explains that the original approach to Mari was that 'she was a nymphomaniac, but with a lot of problems just like Ángel, and it was more obvious then that they were soulmates' [15]. The Mari of the film, however, responds to the projected fantasies of middle-aged males by embodying them in a superficial manner that limits her to symbolising sex and the potential of adolescence. In addition, the fact that she is supposedly looking for love is just as much of a male fantasy as her leather-clad antics with a snooker cue, while her wish to escape her enslavery to orgasms suggests censorship of exuberant female sexuality. In short, *Tierra* is imbalanced and contradictory, which testifies somewhat to Medem's frame of mind at the time of its making. That the three years of production of *Tierra* ran in parallel with the break-up of his marriage and the beginning of his new relationship with a younger woman was bound to affect the film in some way, especially when the status of auteur almost demands the interpretation and performance of Self by a writer-director. Like adjudging whether auteurism fits Medem or if Medem fits theories of auteurism, it is also possible that Medem's identification with the character and mid-life crisis of Ángel ('half-way between the atoms and the stars') provoked or at least contributed to the problems in his own life. In concluding discussion of *Tierra*, Medem once more justifies, even invites the comparison:

Ángela could be a wonderful woman with whom to share life because she's prepared to share the complexity of Ángel, but nevertheless there's a part of him, as a person, as a man, that goes with the more physical woman and that's how he gets rid of his complicated conscience. That's how he can leave his angel behind. However, losing Ángela, who could very well be the love of his life, is the price that Ángel must pay for his freedom, to make himself lighter, to escape from this excess of conscience; because, at heart, he does this out of fear, a fear of death, a fear of feeling himself so small before the laws of the cosmos, out of knowing that his existence is limited in time and that he's going to die. [5]

The filming of *Tierra* in the vineyards of Cariñena was delayed through autumn into winter, when the red earth was rock hard and the cornfield had to be rented so that the farmer would ignore its harvesting. Emma Suárez stayed in a house with her children to deliberately separate herself from the intense camaraderie of the production unit in order, she says, not to jeopardise the detachment of her character, but most cast and crew lived in a roadside hotel that doubled as production offices and included a makeshift editing suite and screening room. Editing on location allowed Iván Aledo to screen rushes to the cast and crew, though he recalls 'this made Julio very nervous because he only likes to see things when they're finished' [12]. Stills photographer Teresa Asisi recalls 'a very hard, very cold shoot' [18] during which the relationship between Medem and Montse Sanz leaked into common knowledge amongst the cast and crew who found the parallels with the film they were making so unavoidable that, for some, the final question of whether Ángel should choose Mari over Ángela became answerable by observation of Medem.

Meanwhile, challenges to these presumptions of Medem's absolute auteurism included his indecision about the film's conclusion, his creative disagreements with Gómez and his deferral to the figure of cinematographer Javier Aguirresarobe. Born in the Basque province of Guipuzkoa in 1948, Aguirresarobe graduated from Madrid's Official Film School in 1973 and was one of the key figures in Basque filmmaking of the democracy, filming many short documentaries in the *Ikuska* series and collaborating with the director Imanol Uribe on *El proceso de Burgos* (1979), *La fuga de Segovia* (1981), *La muerte de Mikel* (1983) and *Días contados* (1995). Says Aguirresarobe: 'The films I made with Uribe are the ones that Medem had in mind when he wrote about the new Basque cinema, accepting them or not, just being convinced that this could be a new cinema' [8]. Medem had asked Aguirresarobe to shoot *Vacas* but previous commitments made collaboration impossible until *Tierra*, though it is clear that in wanting to work with him on *Vacas* and actually securing his talent for *Tierra* Medem was consciously situating the films he made in the line of the aforementioned 'New Basque Cinema'.

Aguirresarobe says it was the script of *Tierra* that convinced him: 'For us cinematographers the script is like a window through which you begin to see the film you're going to make. And Julio's scripts are transparent. I don't mean easy, I mean dynamic, so that you can work quickly because the light and the colour are very specific' [8]. Indeed, the descriptions in the script for *Tierra* are as enthusiastic about red as Teresa Asisi recalls was its writer: 'The only thing Julio said was "Reds! Everything red! You have to show how red the earth is!"' [18]. Aguirresarobe was similarly enthralled:

> When I get a script, I think first of the colour, texture and contrast and I identified completely with *Tierra*, with the space, with the immense plains and red earth, with the character, with the imagery, with the philosophy that the film expressed. I asked Julio in what month he'd been

born and he told me October. Me too. That's why everything was so
familiar to me. [8]

Being born in autumn, when everything else is dying, is perhaps a
requisite for sensitivity to notions of duality, especially when that
autumn is Basque. Aguirresarobe claims that Ángel is very much a
Basque character 'if only for the bipolarity' [8]. Indeed, if Ángel is not
quite schizophrenic, he does embody the idea of the interior conflict
of the Basque Country that is illustrated in *Vacas*, *Aitor* and *La pelota
vasca* and more metaphorically in *La ardilla roja* and *Tierra*. As with all
of Medem's films, moreover, it is essential to track the references to
Basque culture in *Tierra* for their incidents of social, historical and
political relevance. To begin, Ángel's surname is Bengoetxea and he
hails from Bilbao. That his over-excitable imagination was diagnosed
as madness and involved his incarceration in a psychiatric hospital
might therefore be understood as a comment on the treatment meted
out to Basques who dare to act upon their imaginations in demanding
such things as an independent homeland. In this respect, Paul Julian
Smith makes the case for considering *Tierra* in the context of Basque
postnationalism for the manner in which the film disentangles
'nationality from the land (and language) with which it is so frequently
fused' (Smith 2000: 150). Ángel's falling to Earth (and Spanish earth
at that, for he journeys from the Bilbao to Cariñena) may indeed be
read as Medem's irritation with exclusivising notions of a linguistically
and geographically determined identity for the Basques. Just like
Ángel, it seems, Basque nationalists might be expected to take a stand
for something other than impossible dreams of nationhood, while the
film's suggestion that madness might just be another's subjectivity
makes Basque nationalist obsessions with the criteria of nationality
analogous to Ángel's enslavement to a fantastic sense of his own
identity.

A further indication that *Tierra* was conceived in the line of a new
Basque cinema that Medem had intended with *Vacas* and *La ardilla
roja*, one that was deliberately self-reflexive in its questioning of
Basqueness and subversive in its challenges to conventions, was the
continued collaboration with the composer Alberto Iglesias, who like
Aguirresarobe had developed his craft in the new Basque cinema and
worked on a number of films directed by Imanol Uribe. Medem
oversaw fourteen versions of *Tierra* during its four months of editing
by Iván Aledo and another month for the sound mix and the music. For
Tierra Iglesias sought 'an empty, sombre and deep noise that wouldn't

terrify the audience' [16] that relates to the ideas of space, absence and lack that dominate Basque art and sculpture. He experimented with recordings of draining water and ended up with a multi-layered electronic sound that was marked by juxtapositions that illustrated the theme of duality and was recorded in London with an orchestra with a large string section. Iglesias remembers:

> I liked the contrasts. The score says one thing and then suddenly says the opposite. It's a giddy way to compose because you're exposed to the most unconscious impulses. In the cinema this gives rise to a score in which the music is not saying the same thing as the image and in *Tierra* this has a lot to do with the contrast between the music and the narrative of which it is a part. For example, there's a love scene between Ángel and Mari and the music never quite manages to be romantic. [16]

Indeed, what hope is there for Ángel and Mari when even the music doesn't think they should be together?

Actually, it is in this very juxtaposition of music and image that the meaning of *Tierra* is found, for what is suggested is the search for a match that relates to the changing of partners by Mari, Ángel, Ángela, Patricio and Alberto. In turn, this *ronde* that comes to a head around a breakfast table in *Tierra* reflects the difficulty of reconciling the doubts that increase as one grows older with the options available and thus an expanding awareness of one's duality. It also suggests that, in contrast to the indecision of Hamlet that is a consequence of fear at making the right decision, if the imagination grows exponentially to embrace other less obvious or less morally sanctioned options, someone like Ángel might escape the trappings of duality such as doppelgängers and déjà vu, as well as his more specific dilemma, that half of him matches up to one woman while his other half connects with another. Nietzsche may have mused upon 'how miserable, how shadowy and transient, how aimless and arbitrary the human intellect looks within nature' (Nietzsche 1873), but it is the arbitrary decision taken by an aimless Ángel that liberates him from Hamlet's stagnant questioning. Ultimately one might not agree with Ángel's choice of Mari over Ángela, but at least it cures his delusions of divinity, eradicates his abstraction and refocusses his subjectivity on practical matters rather than the imaginary, which is something that extremist Basque radicals who obsess about a mythic Basque Country might learn from in their claims to favour progression in their conflicted nation. In this respect, ironically, it may be Gómez who understands *Tierra* best:

Maybe it would all make sense if Ángel were to end up alone, frozen by
so many doubts. It would be more realistic, sure, and consequently more
boring. But it's much more interesting that Ángel takes the next step into
the void and deals with his paranoia. [15]

This step into the void is rendered visually and aurally in the film's
first shot from Ángel's point of view of hurtling towards Earth as if
he were Milton's Satan or Kubrick's star-child. The voice of his
conscience, meanwhile, juxtaposes the spectacle by acting like a
diffident tour-guide, pointing out the expanse of space and time and
identifying the barely supportable sound as anguish. The direction of
the fall nonetheless recalls the opening of Nietzsche's *On Truth and
Lies in a Nonmoral Sense* ('Once upon a time, in some out of the way
corner of that universe which is dispersed into numberless twinkling
solar systems, there was a star upon which clever beasts invented
knowing' [Nietzsche 1873]) and therefore ironically denies the
insignificance of Earth's inhabitants. Bursting through clouds, the
camera twists above a patchwork of red fields, the speed of descent
lessens and the autumnal season is highlighted in the crumpled tree
stumps of vineyards. The camera does not stop at this mid-point
between the stars and the atoms, however, but dives beneath the earth
to find it hollowed by the plague of beetles that Ángel has come to
eradicate, a computer-generated example of which scurries past as the
voice of Ángel's conscience alerts us to their ability to make the wine
taste earthy. Finally, the camera resurfaces in a rainstorm and follows
sodden tyre tracks to a tree that is blown apart by an animated bolt
of lightning. All this trickery and special effects is the opposite of
complexity, however, for it is a journey to simplicity that resembles
a cosmic prank in which Medem splits his protagonist into the
bewildered human Ángel and his possessive, meddling angel and sets
them squabbling over women.

Tierra is Kubrick by way of Lubitsch, though pulling the wings off
angels is a trick that finds Medem in the more immediate company of
Frank Capra, whose *It's a Wonderful Life* (1946) has the angel Clarence
sent to convince a suicidal George Bailey (James Stewart) that the world
would be a better place with him in it, and Wim Wenders, whose angel
Damiel (Bruno Ganz) in *Der himmel über Berlin* (*Wings of Desire*,
1987) searches for humanity in Berlin and finds it in the love of a
trapeze artist. The Ángel of *Tierra* is on a similar search for meaning
and fulfilment, but is thwarted by his conscience in the guise of his
teasing angel, who tells him, 'I'm that part of you that died and I'm

speaking to you from the cosmos.' But in answer to his half-dead angel, the half-alive Ángel takes up the mission to resolve his duality and so rallies to the task of eradicating a plague of beetles in the vineyards of Cariñena that might also end the plague of doubts that impedes his functioning on this Earth. His aim of simplicity involves a lightening of his morbid introspection and a silencing of his solipsism, a respite from psychoanalysis and relief from an addiction to over-complicating matters. Instead, he seeks the freedom of gut reactions, choices unburdened by guilt, and the simple goals of everyday fulfilment instead of having to consider the infinite possibilties of each action. Unlike the proverbial dancing centipede stymied by the question of which foot he begins with, Ángel just wants to not mind. But this is not a simple matter: similar indecision and conscientiousness affects the Jesus Christ of Kazantzakis's novel *The Last Temptation of Christ* when he is faced with the option of a family life and elects to give up the role of messiah for the more fulfilling job of carpenter. Indeed, the opening of *Tierra* allows for the film's analysis in terms of its religious parallels, but this is just a trap that Medem baits with such imagery as Ángel hoisting a lost lamb upon his shoulders and resuscitating the shepherd hit by lightning while delivering a treatise on life after death. Beneath the burns, however, is the comic actor Pepe Viyuela, who appeared on the Spanish television game show *Un, dos tres* (1993–95)

5 Ángel (Carmelo Gómez) as the good shepherd in *Tierra*

in the guise of village idiot. *Tierra* is a joke told backwards, with this punchline at the start and, thereafter, a long preamble to an uncertain warm-up.

Serious religious parallels to Ángel's actions should also be avoided because, peculiarly for a Spanish filmmaker, Medem has yet to include religion in his dramas, even ignoring the rôle of Catholicism in Basque history and politics in *Vacas*, preferring instead the more Buddhist understanding of reincarnation in *Vacas, Tierra, Los amantes del Círculo Polar, Lucía y el sexo* and *Caótica Ana*. The universe traversed by Ángel is not ordered and therefore not that of any Christian God. As in *El espíritu de la colmena* (1973), directed by Víctor Erice, which includes teasing allusions to Christian iconography and the Christ-like appearances and capabilities of strangers in a strange land such as the *maqui* befriended by the infant Ana, Ángel's Christ-like qualities should be appreciated for their juxtaposition with his actual nature. Further discredit to any Christian interpretation of *Tierra* is also signalled by Ángel's fumigation firm being named Urtzi, a Basque word meaning both sky and a Thor-like god which effects an immediate juxtaposition of Ángel with Mari, who is the goddess of earth and fire. Basque mythology holds that Mari dwells in a cave like that of her brother Alberto's bar in *Tierra* (which Medem calls La Letxe Basterretxe in reference to Azkona's silent Basque melodrama *El mayorazgo de Basterretxe* (1928) and the script *La leche Basterretxe* that he wrote prior to *Vacas*) and another contrast with Christianity is provided by the Gypsy clan that aids Ángel in his mission, for although Spanish Gypsies are commonly assumed to be profoundly religious, they are actually 'irreligious, adopting the going faith as it suits them, in the hopes of [. . .] reaping whatever benefits membership might bring [as] they have no need of the religions of other nations' (Fonseca 1996: 48). Instead, Gypsies are superstitious, believers in a spontaneous, pantheistic culture that is both of this earth and, by dint of their nomadism, paradoxically unrooted. Ángel is noticeably without guile or racism in his respectful dealings with the Gypsies, who he hires to help fumigate the land, yet he is as unable to locate himself within their beliefs and consequent social and familial structure as he is within a dominant Christianity. 'Don't you see that I'm all alone?' he asks them. 'Your problem is you're mad', they reply, a diagnosis compounded by that of the security guard from the Bilbao psychiatric hospital, who reminds Ángel of the head-butt he once dealt him in an effort to quieten the voices in his head.

However, *Tierra* contends that madness may be just another's subjectivity and although the allusions to duality are suggestive of some kind of universal balance that might be adversely affected by Ángel's actions, this hall of mirrors is all in his tortured mind. Note, for example, when he calls at Patricio's farm and Tomás (Txema Blasco) opens the glass door, for not only is Ángel literally confronted with his own reflection in the door but, thanks to intertextuality, with the actor who played his aged self in *Vacas*. This may be important, but it is also very possible that it means nothing at all. It is Ángel's aim to cure himself of such chaos theory, not position himself as the instigator of an infinite number of emotional, psychological and physical disasters, nor become the caretaker of any higher belief system. The challenge to be inconsequential is what he has set himself and when the infinite possible choices faced by Ángel are polarised around a simple election of female (Ángela or Mari?) he recognises an opportunity to act by choosing a side, as it were, thereby shattering the condition of fearing himself to exist at the absolute centre of a universe that he is conscience-bound to keep symmetrical by his inaction.

Luis Buñuel, who would have relished this particular exterminating Ángel, famously tired of critical readings of every filmic detail. Others relished the attention, like Alfred Hitchcock, who was so flattered by the auteurist compliments of François Truffaut that he took to second-guessing his own mise en scène in favour of its symbolism. David Lynch, a frequent point of comparison with Medem, similarly packs his screen with portent, chops up his narratives and strikes an enigmatic pose in speaking and writing about his own films in full knowledge that the Surrealist qualities of *Mulholland Drive* (2001), for example, and so the auteurist qualities of his directing, are enhanced by this very process. Medem may be as intrigued and delighted by the cult of the auteur and its resultant creative freedom as Quentin Tarantino, but, unlike the director of *Pulp Fiction* (1994), he claims he is indebted not to pop and exploitation culture but to such influences as New German Cinema, Basque art and literature, Nietzsche, Freud and magical realism, all of which drive him to explore the psychology of his characters as much as their actions. The paradox of *Tierra* is that it is an introspective parable on a mythic scale about the greatest themes of life and death and love and sex, whose protagonist is heartily sick of such twaddle.

Until the moment of his final decision, Ángel cannot move outside the limits imposed by his conscience in the guise of his angel, who

insists upon interjecting unhelpful comments, correcting his lies, and
telling him what to think. As Ángel enters Patricio's homestead,
Medem cuts to a hand-held camera that moves around the kitchen
table. Subjective camerawork might be expected by an audience aware
of Medem's previous films, but a headcount confirms the stray
anonymity of this subjectivity and it is only when Ángel reacts to his
angel's censure of his lying that the source of the subjectivity is
determined. As always with Medem, subjective sight and sound (for
only Ángel hears his angel) illustrates the psyche of a character and a
determinant perspective on events. However, Ángela is constructed by
the oscillating subjectivities of Ángel and his angel, whose juxtaposition
of her strength and fragility might attest to a split personality that is in
two minds about this woman. Paradoxically, however, these subjective
shots from both angles (or angels) make her so much more of a multi-
sided character that it ultimately complicates audience response to
Ángel's resolution of his dilemma by choosing Mari instead of her.
In contrast to Ángela, who is beautiful, soulful, sensual, nurturing,
mature, forgiving, loving, intelligent and desirous of sexual adventure,
the nymphomaniac Mari, who is rendered almost exclusively through
the subjectivity of Ángel and barely glanced at by his angel, is 'the only
character subject to sexual objectification' (Smith 2000: 157). Thus, on

6 Ángela (Emma Suárez) comes between Ángel (Carmelo Gómez) and his
angel (Gómez) in *Tierra*

top of excising Mari's subjectivity at script stage and the cancelling of *Mari en la tierra*, the representation of Mari in *Tierra* is limited to her objectification as what Patricio describes as 'a savage, pure sex.' Nevertheless, the simplicity that she represents is precisely what most attracts Ángel, who hopes her superficiality might prove contagious.

Medem's use of the subjective camera invokes the power to make concrete and unite the forces and object of love in a way that André Breton claimed was deficient in books because 'nothing in them can render the seduction or distress of a glance' (Breton 2000: 74). The representation of the glance on film delighted the Surrealists, who adored what Breton called 'the priceless giddiness' that existed in the feeling of sight (Breton 2000: 74). Subjectivity was there in the silent films adored by the Surrealists, in which the pan, the close-up, mise en scène and editing represented the glance at a spot of blood on a handkerchief, a glimpse of a gun being lifted out of its holster or the furtive look between lovers. More than anything, love in the Surrealist sense resonated in this process of abstraction because the Surrealists believed that what is real exists only in its abstraction, in its diminution, in how it is perceived. Medem himself once exlaimed: 'I'm a mountaineer of imaginary mountains! Of mountains that I don't even have to see! Because, whether they exist or not, I invent them, and they exist because I climb them' [2]. Because a Surrealist sense of an object's reality, like the Romantic perception of its beauty, exists only in the eye of the beholder, Ángel's choice of Mari over Ángela must therefore be recognised as a Surrealist act; for it is a spontaneous and illogical action that answers to nothing but the priceless giddiness of its own high. Love, like truth, is an imaginary friend.

In moving towards this final act, Ángel is empowered by the Surrealist details that surround him to resolve 'the undecidability of the film' (Perriam 2003: 73). Coincidences, déjà vu and juxtapositions as absurd as that of the high-tech fumigation of one cornfield and the primordial boar hunt through another are the exceptions that prove the universe is without order, divinity or consequence. The fact that Ángela's daughter named Ángela has a schoolteacher called Federico, which Ángel says is the name of the father he never knew, and therefore, as she says, might even *be* his father, is ridiculous enough to be true and is certainly Surreal. Similarly, Ángel chats to a woman named Cristina (the name of Suárez and Ane Sánchez's character in *Vacas*) who claims to have a son who looks just like him and a husband who bears his name and she therefore may even be a premonition of

Ángela grown old beside him. Yet instead of imbuing these exceptions to a disordered universe with meaning, Ángel struggles to laugh them off. The ultimate irony is that Ángel's choice of Mari over Ángela is so illogical that several viewings of *Tierra* reveal it as inevitable, for to read *Tierra* as Surrealist is to enjoy its contradictions instead of suffering them.

An associated element of Ángel's contradictory character is that, although he professes to be hopelessly deep, he often speaks without thinking, accusing the Gypsy children of stealing the wages and tactlessly asking Ángela about Mari. Another is that his flights of excessive and excitable imagination are intensified when frustrated by reality: for example, during a phone conversation he asks Ángela to describe what she is wearing ('I want to imagine you') but her cold-water reply ('a blue robe, nothing unusual') does little to dim his ardour or that of his angel, who appears beside Ángela in her kitchen to kiss her. These undecidable contradictions are best represented in the fumigation scene when a mid-shot of Ángel turns Mari and Ángela, who are standing apart on a hill behind him, into bad and good angels on his shoulders. This centring of Ángel continues with Mari's placing him between her lovers, Patricio and Manuel, in the boar hunt ('put yourself between them, they don't get on') and only adds to his anguish at having to maintain the mid-point in every universal or personal conflict. Shooting Patricio is Ángel's desperate attempt at wrecking the balance of a system that imprisons him at its centre, though Patricio's subsequent death by lightning that, it is suggested, may have come from the mythologically-aware Mari, is a clear sign that Ángel has met his match in this bossy nymphomaniac. When he tells her it only needs one person to fumigate, for instance, she answers 'even half a person is enough', thereby implying that she understands his duality and can resolve it. Ángel and Mari play up to the characteristics of their mythological namesakes as a form of courtship and when they do consummate their desire for each other, their union is achieved without orgasm or even genitalia, as befits the sex life of angels.

Tierra is a comedy of errors in which the biggest mistake is to take everything too seriously, just like Ángel. However, the representation of the landscape and references to the borders that define the territory do challenge the ambiguity or 'undecidability' of *Tierra* that begins with its title, which appears twice during the credit sequence. Whether it refers to the planet or the beetle-infested ground beneath Ángel's feet is undetermined, which allows for the film to be read as both a universal fable of existential angst, as a satirical treatise on the Basque-Spanish divide, and as a localised examination of personal and romantic tribulations. However, because Nietzsche denies the Aristotelian concept of tragedy as a means of vicarious experience that culminates in catharsis, whereby an audience is morally educated, informed and improved by what they have seen, it is not appropriate to expect such a resolution of *Tierra*. Instead, as an illustration of Nietzsche's belief that audiences should be made to understand that even the noblest physical existence is inconsequential, Ángel pre-emptively denudes himself of complexity, consigns all his anguish to his subconscious and is finally empowered to make a simple choice without fear of consequences: a fling with Mari over an entire lifetime with Ángela. It may be that this solution to Ángel's complexity is only temporary, for though he jettisons his conscience by leaving his angel behind with Ángela, he also predicts the plague will return to the vineyards. For now, however, the decision represents Ángel's liberation from the stasis of an infinite number of metaphysical considerations by the kick-start of accepting the pleasures of inconsequentiality. Never mind that sex with Mari turns out to be purposefully and literally anti-climactic, the new Ángel is the one subsequently empowered to define himself by a spontaneous response to his car: 'This car's not for me. That's very clear to me.' Nietzsche's justification of existence as an aesthetic phenomenon is extreme but just as valid as any moral reason to live and a lot more fun than the miserable response of existentialists to the absurdity of life. So yes to Mari, no to the car and, as Alberto says, first breakfast and then we'll see about the rest. 'At the end, everything is much simpler than I'd thought. So I'm going to stop being so complicated', concludes Ángel, last seen heading for the beach with a nymphomaniac.

6

A question of love: *Los amantes del Círculo Polar* (1998)

Spanish film audiences grew during the decade of the 1990s along with the number of private television channels and new cinemas, 982 of which had opened by its end (ICAA 2003). However, so did the average cost of film production, prompting Spanish companies to seek foreign investors and co-production partners with their sights on the pan-European multiplex audiences and the favours of such American distributors as Miramax and Fine Line. By the mid 1990s, however, an impending crisis in the Spanish film industry was blamed on a government set on eroding subsidies and abandoning a system of screen quotas by which a percentage of domestic screens were reserved for Spanish films instead of waiting in line while Hollywood busted blocks. Sogecine (previously Sogetel) responded by promoting homegrown auteurs such as Medem and Alejandro Amenábar, because, as the managing director Fernando Bovaira explains, 'auteurist cinema is the surest bet in the international market, though success requires understanding and a common objective and requires mediation between artistry and the market' [17]. Nevertheless, the relative commercial and critical disappointment of *Tierra* in 1996 illustrated the risks of investing heavily in films that depended upon an indefinable international audience for its profits and arguably steered Sogecine into a period of uncertainty in which some attempts at combining conventional generic pleasures with arthouse aspirations in an international market disappointed, such as the Mexican-Spanish-American co-production *Perdita Durango* (1997) directed by Álex de la Iglesia, and some excelled, such as the French-Spanish-Italian co-production *Abre los ojos* (*Open Your Eyes*, 1997) directed by Alejandro Amenábar.

The perception of *Tierra*'s failure following its unrewarded screening at Cannes in May 1996 came on top of Medem's distress at the death of his father a week earlier and prompted his move to his brother's apartment in Paris following the annulment of his marriage, where he took to writing and emerged with two scripts, one about hate called *Aitz: viaje al fondo del mar* (*Aitz: Voyage to the Bottom of the Sea*) that he would rework four years later as *Aitor* (which in turn would beget *La pelota vasca*) and one about love called *Los amantes del Círculo Polar* that he claims was 'based on my feelings of having disappointed myself, of being furious with myself and with love too' [5]. Proving that Ángel's dedication to simplicity was but a temporary resolution, these scripts were an ironic postscript to *Tierra*; for reconciled duality was split again between *Aitz*, which unnerved Medem by drawing out his capacity to hate in his characteristic assumption of the subjectivity of its protagonists in their writing, and *Los amantes del Círculo Polar*, which Medem claims conversely revitalised his capacity to love.

Los amantes del Círculo Polar tells of soulmates Otto and Ana, who have the fortune to meet at a moment of emotional need and the misfortune to become step-siblings when they do. Both are in search of eternal love as a refuge from grief over the loss of a parent and their beliefs about fate form a private world in which each sees the other at its centre. The much-travelled script on file in Alicia Produce has a postcard of the Arctic Circle on its cover amidst a collage of photographs from the filming that includes one of Medem's son Peru amidst reindeers. Its pages are crinkled from drying out after shooting in snow and the artificial downpour of the scenes outside the school. This shooting script, which follows the rewriting of several early drafts that included the death of Otto, begins with Medem's introductory notes to himself on how the story occurs within the circles of the eyes of his protagonists. Thereafter the 'world at eye-level' of *Tierra* goes global in the prominence awarded the midnight sun 'that moves silently around you in a circle in an instant and is the reflection of your face' (Medem 1998: 3) and symbolises both the film's cyclical narrative structure and its theme of eternal love. The idea originated in Medem's observation of the phenomena when he took *Vacas* to Finland's Festival of the Midnight Sun in 1992, when he claims to have sat at the top of a hill and watched the midnight sun move around him, experiencing 'the sensation that my entire life was very far away from me, that it was behind me in a sense. It was as if I couldn't move forward from there, from where I was, towards the sun. Being there with the midnight sun evaporated all sense of time' (Stone 2001: 178).

Like Ángel in *Tierra*, therefore, half-way between the atoms and the stars, Medem situated himself at the centre of his own Ptolemaic universe in the writing of the character of Ana, who makes her vigil on the same spot in expectation of 'the coincidence of her life' on 24 June, the night of Saint John, the summer solstice that Spaniards celebrate in pagan rather than Catholic ways with bonfires that symbolise the burning of the past. The allusion, which also features prominently in *El espíritu de la colmena* (1973), is one of very few to faith in the films written and directed by Medem, whose atheism in *Los amantes del Círculo Polar* may be compared and contrasted with Krzysztof Kieślowski's bleakly anarchic *Dekalog*, which illustrates the Christian Ten Commandments with paradoxical tales of human disassociation and loss, because it offers the coincidence of love being reciprocated as proof of lives worth living. The connections between *Los amantes del Círculo Polar* and the work of Kieślowski, who Medem venerates, are suggested in its northern European setting, which Triana Toribio takes as evidence of the 'Europeanization' of Spanish cinema (2003: 150), and confirmed in the more specific influences that follow that of *La Double vie de Véronique* (1991) on *Tierra* and include the invocation of the imagination as release from grief in *Trois couleurs: bleu* (*Three Colours: Blue*, 1993), the symbolically rich treatise on male-female equality and sexuality in *Trzy kolory: bialy* (*Three Colours: White*, 1994) and the resolution based on coincidences of *Trois couleurs: rouge* (*Three Colours: Red*, 1994).

Like Kieślowski, who was eventually located at the heart of European arthouse cinema but began making films 'outside mainstream Central European aesthetics [within a] highly politicised culture, where political choices were of greater importance than aesthetic ones' (Haltof 2004: xi), Medem makes it clear in his early critical writings that he aspired to an auteur-driven, politicised 'New Basque Cinema' that would be located at the edge of European cinema and be distinguised from mainstream Spanish cinema by a balance and interaction of personal, aesthetic and political choices. The exclusive contextualisation of Medem within contemporary Spanish cinema and its canon in academic and critical studies at the expense of his Basqueness and to the detriment of an appreciation of Basque cinema is equivocal at best and at worst recalls the Francoist dictatorship's reinscription at the centre of its culture of what were rightly expressions of identity that were marginalised from Spanish society. For example, although flamenco was mostly the cultural property of the Gypsies, it was censoriously diluted of its nihilist content to be presented as indigenous and attractive Spanish folksong (see Stone 2004b). Similarly, the regime allowed the films of dissident filmmakers such as Carlos Saura and Elías Querejeta to compete in foreign film festivals, be classified as 'of special interest' and play in domestic arthouse cinemas as evidence of its tolerance. In recent years, Pedro Almodóvar has been celebrated for his opposite strategy of relocating symbols of the dictatorship, such as the Civil Guard and the *bolero*, at the heart of a more anarchic democratic Spain, but the traditions and conventions of Basque cinema to which Medem subscribes are more about maintaining a peripheral stance that tallies with ideas of aesthetic as well as political separatism. Núria Triana Toribio states that 'Julio Medem's cinema can be understood as an instrument by which the discourse that locates the Spanishness of Spanish cinema in high art and the intellectual traditions of the country is maintained' (2003: 149), but such a typical view ignores the Basqueness of Basque cinema and its relevance to films that are often located erroneously within Spanish cinema and, indeed, often confused with its Spanishness. Basque cinema, unlike Catalan cinema, was not defined by its spoken language but by its metaphorical visual grammar. Documentaries such as *Pelotari* (1964) and *Ama lur* (1968) imitated the staccato rhythms and abrasive consonants of the forbidden Basque language of Euskera in their camerawork and editing, which provided for the rapid juxtaposition of awkwardly angled shots. At the same time, Basque cinema has been defined by its concern with the rôle of the landscape in the historical, political and social formation of the Basque Country, as well as its shaping of the indigenous humans. Like the Basque art of Jorge Oteiza, Eduardo Chillida, Vicente Ameztoy and Daniel Vázquez Díaz, whose *Alegría del País Vasco* (*Joy of the Basque Country*, 1920) hangs in Madrid's Reina Sofía Museum of Modern Art and depicts a Cubist rendering of a tumbling Basque landscape, Basque cinema is concerned with physical space as the absence of something that is yearned for, which is often interpreted as independence or a separate identity. This definition allows for the contextualisation in an analysis of Basque art and culture of films produced by the Basque Elías Querejeta such as *Tasio* (1984), which is set in Navarre and directed by the Navarrense Montxo Armendáriz, and *El espíritu de la colmena* (1973), which is set near Segovia and directed by the Navarrense Víctor Erice, for both films reflect a concern with the isolation of their human figures in relation to vast natural spaces that is a world apart from the usually intense claustrophobia of Spanish films with a rural setting such as *La caza* (*The Hunt*, 1965) and *Furtivos* (*Poachers*, 1975) and plays such as Federico García Lorca's *Bodas de sangre* (*Blood Wedding*).

The films written and directed by Julio Medem should therefore be recognised for their Basqueness prior to the argument that 'his films often directly engage with questions of Spanishness, of the nature of modern national identities, and the places of those identities in a wider European network' (Triana Toribio 2003: 149). Indeed, locating Medem exclusively in Spanish national cinema diminishes his relevance to Basque cinema, which is evident in such aesthetic considerations as the juxtaposition of subjectivities and strangely angled shots that resonate with the grammar of Basque documentaries, the emphasis on natural spaces and the isolation of the individual within those spaces that is common to Basque art, and the emphasis on internal and external exile that is endemic to characters such as Manuel, Ignacio and Peru Irigibel in *Vacas*, J and Sofia in *La ardilla roja*, Ángel in *Tierra*, Otto and Ana in *Los amantes del Círculo Polar*, Lucía *et al* in *Lucía y el sexo* and the majority of speakers in *La pelota vasca*, who Medem purposefully situates in a variety of natural settings. The isolation of characters in natural landscapes suggests both internal and external exile and relates to conflicting ideas of the Basque Country as being both within Spain and beyond it, as well as to the condition of a variety of Basques themselves, who may find themselves exiled physically from Spain or the Basque Country because of contrary political beliefs or fear (such as those fleeing extortion, harassment and violence in both directions) and at the same time exiled internally by their exclusion from the hegemony in the Basque Country or elsewhere.

The notion of exile is often associated with postcolonialism, which, because of the importance awarded racial identity in postcolonial studies, makes for a highly polemical approach to studies of the Basque Country. Just as it may be argued that the Basque Country has been colonised by Spain and more specifically the dictatorship of Franco, so it may be construed that it warrants the liberty awarded Cuba, which is otherwise accepted as Spain's last true colony, at the end of the nineteenth century. On the other hand, when exile is considered in the terms expressed by Edward Said in his essay *Reflections on Exile*

(2000: 173–86), the concept of exile that permeates Basque art, literature and film may be appreciated as a deeply felt condition of the mind that is shared by those who experience and express estrangement from their roots as well as a critical distance from all cultural identities. This dysphoric opposition to the rigid beliefs of the colonizer and those of the colonised, especially when tainted on either side by euphoric nationalism, makes exile a moral condition. Thus, the geographical displacement of characters such as the aforementioned characters in the films directed by Medem illustrates this concern with achieving a position of objective morality that must be outside the Basque Country in order that its Otherness may be recognised in contrast to Spain and, at the same time, that the concept of Basqueness may be separated from the extremist Basque nationalism with which it is unfortunately so associated. Just as the refuges of France and America function as ideas of the world beyond the Basque Country in *Vacas*, so the campsite in *La ardilla roja* and the vineyards of Cariñena in *Tierra* allow for resolutions of identity beyond the influence of the politics of national identity. The symbolism of characters such as Sofía and Ángel may provide metaphorical commentary on the condition of the Basque Country, but the final affirmation of identity embodied by Cristina, Sofía and Ángel also complies with Said's appreciation of any formerly colonised people's struggles for justice and a voice that is validated in their cultural expression of identity, rather than by political or violent means.

The extreme distance around the globe travelled by Otto and Ana, who are reunited by the Arctic Circle, is symbolic of Medem's desire to experience a physical and psychological understanding of Otherness that will allow for moral objectivity. Thus, the striking incongruity of the Finnish landscape in the context of Spanish cinema awards metaphorical status of Otherness to Finland that affines it with the polemical Otherness of the Basque Country. Consequently, just as the Spanishness of Otto and Ana, who grow up in Madrid, is contrasted with the inescapable roots and resolution of their condition that they find in Finland, so the ill-fitting contextualisation within Spanish cinema of Medem must be understood and countered by reference to his Basque origins and the intentions expressed in his critical writings that emerge by aesthetic and thematic means in his films. For example, the chapters of *Los amantes del círculo polar* are structured in an oppositional framework based upon the alternating subjectivities of Otto and Ana that is redolent of the tradition of radical and meaningful juxtaposition in the cinema of the Basque Country, whose history is also referenced in specific details such as the prominence given Germany's official apology for the bombing of the Basque town of Gernika during the Spanish Civil War that Olga describes on her television news programme and is represented in oneiric flashbacks to Otto's ancestors during the bombing. Although Medem's characters seek objective truth through exile, the influence and legacy of the Basque Country is never far away, which clearly also relates to Medem's leaving the Basque Country at an early age and returning there as a student and novice filmmaker, whose increasing assumption of his Basqueness culminated in the premiere of *La pelota vasca* (and the birth of his daughter Ana the morning after) in San Sebastian in 2003.

The process first identified by Santaolalla (1998: 331–7) of Medem's distancing from the Basque Country also allows for his gradual settling in the midst of European arthouse cinema that begins with Cristina and Peru fleeing to France in *Vacas* and continues with the situating of Finland as the object of desire in *Los amantes del Círculo Polar*, which allows for an auteurist investigation of the northern European aspect of Medem's genealogy and his use of a setting and aesthetic choices that set the film apart in Spanish cinema but within a romanticised notion of politicised but personal auteurist cinema in northern Europe that includes the Swedish director Ingmar Bergman, the Danish Carl Theodor Dreyer, who Querejeta identified as having 'showed us [Basques] how to contemplate reality' (Stone 2001: 4), Medem's revered New German Cinema and the Polish Krzysztof Kieślowski. In discussing *Los amantes del Círculo Polar* Medem follows Kieślowski, who 'following the great European auteurs from the 1960s and 1970s [. . .] often stressed the semi-autobiographical nature of his films' and once pronounced 'I turn the camera on myself in all my films' (Haltof 2004: 147). This strategy, which contributed to Kieślowski becoming one of the most popular and respected European directors, is evident in the writing of *Los amantes del Círculo Polar*, which Medem says began where his own life had stopped after *Tierra* with the end of his marriage and the death of his father; that is, with the break-up of two families: one from death and one from divorce. He wrote the script according to his favoured technique of assuming the subjectivity of first one protagonist and then the other, and gave his father's death to Ana (the name of his real-life sister) and his divorce to Otto's father, Álvaro (the name of his real-life brother) in order to attempt a working-through of his personal condition by a process of projection and empathy.

As confused by death as her other namesake in *El espíritu de la colmena*, the infant Ana (Sara Valiente) runs from her grieving mother and, quite by chance, finds herself in the position of being chased by Otto (Peru Medem), who is running after a ball, a set-up that was suggested in a story by the postmodern Spanish novelist Ray Loriga, in which a boy who likes chasing girls meets a girl who likes being chased. The perfect coincidence of their encounter is deemed inevitable by Ana, who takes Otto to be her reincarnated father, but their relationship is exploited by Otto's father Álvaro (Nancho Novo) and Ana's mother Olga (Maru Valdivielso), who begin a relationship based on the convenience of child-care but soon marry, thereby bringing Otto and Ana together in an unnatural and restrictive relationship. Pushed together during puberty, Otto and Ana effect a pretence of mutual animosity that Olga later blames for her separation from Álvaro. Paradoxes abound as Otto and Ana are lost to each other in order to save themselves the pain of ever losing one another, until Ana, who uses frivolity as a defence and pretends that coincidences amuse her while suspecting her life depends upon them, determines to test her faith in destiny by positioning herself beside a lake on the Arctic Circle and waiting for 'the coincidence of her life': Otto's bailing out of his doomed plane and parachuting into the trees on the opposite shore. As Edward Said declared that 'there are things to be learned: he or she must

7 Ana (Najwa Nimri) waiting for the coincidence of her life in *Los amantes del Círculo Polar*

cultivate a scrupulous (not indulgent or sulky) subjectivity' (Said 2002: 184), so Medem explains the meaning of *Los amantes del Círculo Polar*:

> My idea was to write a love story told by each of its protagonists from their subjectivity and bias and always emotionally determined by the life of the other. That's to say, for each person, the only thing that matters is what they feel for the other. [5]

Unfortunately, Ana leaves the lake before Otto lands and he has to follow her to a nearby village, where, because the juxtaposed subjectivities of Ana and Otto constitute alternating chapters that retell events with voiceovers that allow for different interpretations of their story, either Otto sees her knocked down by a bus and killed, or they are reunited in an apartment.

Crucial to the engineering of this cyclical narrative based upon the juxtaposition of interpretations of events as if Otto and Ana were journeying around opposite sides of the same circle, were the palindromes of their names and in the titles of their respective chapters by Medem, whose own surname can be read the same backwards and forwards. The oscillating subjectivities provided Medem with chapters, symmetry, an accumulative consideration of duality in the tale of a boy and girl who are both eternally united and forever separated, and the potential for drastically different interpretations of the same ending. The script visits Otto and Ana aged eight in 1980, thirteen in 1985, eighteen in 1990 and twenty-five in 1997 and, apart from that very first coincidence of Otto running after Ana in the park and their very last encounter on the roadside in Rovaniemi, finds them going in different directions. Otto, a pessimistic fabulist, heads into the future like a test-pilot, always expecting the gasoline to run out, while Ana, a practical optimist, retreats into the past, expecting to find a proven resource of love based on the past romances that have resulted in her birth. Heart versus head: where Otto is impetuous, bewildered and prone to panic from an excess of imagination, Ana is pragmatic, reasonable and focussed in her use of hers. Both are endowed with one half of the condition of duality that so bedevilled Ángel in *Tierra*, but whereas Otto flees from suffering, Ana turns pain to her advantage by escaping to the Arctic Circle and conjuring an imaginative world as a cure for her suffering, in which neither her father, nor love, nor even herself will ever die. As in the beginning, so in the end, Ana runs to make a metaphysical fantasy come true.

The film's budget was set at 400 million pesetas following co-production agreements between Sogecine and Le Studio Canal Plus, which would manage international sales and entry into the American market thanks to a distribution deal with Fine Line Features. In the margins of the shooting script, Medem describes his story as 'una fábula de pasión [con] una atmósfera de gran presión emocional' (Medem 1998: s.n.) (a passionate fable with an atmosphere of great emotional tension). In contrast, he also notes that any colours are to be neutralised by filters so that the controlled, schematic coolness of the film's structure will offset the passionate, romantic intensity of the characters that is symbolised in the bright red cushion-heart that Otto gives to Ana, a unique moment of intense colour that reveals a glimpse of the passions that burn within this superficially icy film. The film's cold colours, or rather the lack of them, reflect the void that dominates Basque art, while the filling of this lack of colour by the red heart illustrates the view that the Basque void, which suggests the lack of a true identity that is caused and maintained by hate, can only be filled by love. Working with cinematographer Kalo F. Berridi, who had previously shot *La ardilla roja* as well as the short films *Las seis en punta*, *Martín* and *Patas en la cabeza* (which has a similar structural conceit), Medem designed the film to have a preponderance of close-ups and blurry backgrounds and no warm lights or colours, wherein even his protagonists' clothes were intentionally dull and bland:

> I was aiming for romanticism through suspense, much like a psychological thriller that's based upon destiny, like film noir. We achieved this cold, blue light that's so extreme in places like Finland. That was like our contrast with the rest of the world. Everyone goes towards the colour and the light, while Otto and Ana do the complete opposite. [5]

Also crucial to the film, and a notable advance in Medem's writing, was the structural, philosophical and thematic integration of a female subjectivity that balanced that of the male. In *Vacas* the females had suffered the status of cows without the privilege of providing their perspective on events, while the authenticity of Sofía's view of events in *La ardilla roja* was only discernible in retrospect from the vantage point of knowing the twist in the tale. *Tierra* had neglected the female frame of mind altogether; but *Los amantes del Círculo Polar* has it in perfect half-measure, for Ana is a protagonist who does not depend upon the male gaze for validation at the same time as she embodies the paradox of being observed half the time from the point of view of Otto.

Unlike Otto, whose character is shaped by the imaginary world that marks his ethics, inspires his conduct and maintains his distance from reality, Ana pragmatically interprets events to shore up her faith in destiny: 'I could tell you the story of my life by linking coincidences', she says. Otto, meanwhile, sees in his infatuation with Ana the chance to disprove his father's assertion that all things die including love. Although their parents' marriage skews destiny by adding false but insistent tones of incest to their relationship, the need for secrecy only intensifies the taboo. Following Otto's abandonment of his mother, however, who shortly thereafter dies, Otto's guilt estranges him from Ana and he becomes an air mail pilot whose route takes in the Arctic Circle, while Ana, who believes she can tempt fate by placing herself in the path of coincidences, determines to close the circle that will end in their reunion in the appropriately named Finland or, as she writes as the return address on her letter, 'Fin-Landia': a land of cinematic endings. Except, as the oscillating subjectivity of their respective chapters grows more distant, the lovers lose sight and knowledge of each other and their interwoven narrative begins to fray like plaited hair, allowing for split ends to the film in which Ana and Otto first meet and embrace in Ana's version of events, and, in Otto's version, the circle is closed by Otto's being reflected for a second in the dilating pupils of the dying Ana. Even so, it is the death of Ana that one remembers rather than her rising to embrace Otto, perhaps because unlike the embrace that is filmed in mid-shot, this tragic and poetic second ending is based upon the Surrealist exaltation of film for its representation of the glance. It also recalls *Romeo + Juliet* (1996) directed by Baz Luhrmann, which improves on Shakespeare by allowing the dying Romeo (Leonardo DiCaprio) and the reviving Juliet (Claire Danes) to catch sight of each other in passing on their opposite journeys between life to death.

Says Medem:

> *Los amantes del Círculo Polar* is a love story and nothing else. It starts with a secret love, which is very contained, and ends at the other extreme, with eternal love, which can never die, can never run out, can never end, not ever. It's a love story powered by idealism. It idealises itself in order to create this moment in the future, in the Arctic Circle, where there's nowhere left to go, where the circle closes and the lovers go to live their romantic zenith. [5]

But this notion of eternal love effects a striking contrast with *Tierra*, which celebrates the immediacy of a fling. Medem locates an explanation of this contradiction in terms that, as for Kieślowski, stress the semi-autobiographical nature of his films:

> When I made *Los amantes del Círculo Polar* I was out of love. Better said, I was living the absence of love, which isn't cold, it's very intense, it's very passionate. You suffer a lot. As with death, so with love. The absence of someone is like their death. Tragedies return you to life, because you're living a part of yourself that's very vivid and very human. This love that we feel for the missing person gets greater. It makes us feel the immense value of being human and we love feeling that way. [5]

It still contrasts with *Tierra*, however, which ultimately celebrates the insignificance of being human. Medem answers:

> No, the opposite of *Los amantes del Círculo Polar* and *Tierra* is when you don't feel anything at all. I believe that's the worst that can happen to you. [5]

It may be noted here that Medem maintains an excellent relationship with his first wife, Lola Barrera, who painted the portrait of the reindeer that plays a crucial role in *Los amantes del Círculo Polar*, and they share the welfare and upbringing of their son Peru, who plays the child Otto in *Los amantes del Círculo Polar*, and their daughter Alicia, who incidentally has Down's Syndrome and inspired the name of her father's production company, Alicia Produce. Medem's second daughter was born to Montse Sanz in 2003 and named Ana after Medem's sister, who died during the filming of *Lucía y el sexo* and inspired both the Ana of *Los amantes del Círculo Polar* and the protagonist of *Caótica Ana* . Medem says of his sister and her namesakes that they 'exist in this world but belong to another' [5]. Key to her representation in *Los amantes del Círculo Polar* was the casting of Najwa Nimri (Pamplona, 1972) whose gender and Basque-Arabian extraction had already illustrated complex themes of Otherness in the Basque Country in the films of her then husband Daniel Calparsoro: *Salto al vacío* (*Jump into the* Void, 1995) in which she played an androgynous Basque punk, *A ciegas* (1996) in which she played an ETA terrorist, and *Pasajes* (1997) in which she essayed lesbianism. The theories of Otherness that explain Nimri's suitability for such rôles posit identity in terms of becoming, as a state of instability and transition in which the subject is haunted by images of the ideal, the Other, self-image and alter ego. However, whereas this kind of analysis throws up active/masculine and passive/feminine oppositions, Nimri does not conform to such stereotypes but rather personifies their instability and transition. As an actress she should probably be assigned a place in the language of filmmaking that corresponds to a gender or racial identity, but her characters are wholly contrary to the idealised femininity and desirable Spanishness of, say, Penélope Cruz (literally so in *Abre los ojos* (1998) in which Nimri plays the nightmare to Cruz's dream-woman). Yet Nimri's Otherness is not due to her being both Basque and Arabian, but the fact that she is *neither* Basque *nor* Arabian, for her transitional being negates nationalism and its assertion of belonging and instead illustrates what Edward Said described as 'the perilous territory of non-belonging' (2000: 177). Her Ana, like her Elena in *Lucía y el sexo*, chooses estrangement from Spain and even makes a fetish of exile: as Ana seeks solitude and coincidence on the shores of an Arctic lake, so Elena finds solace and sense to life on the floating island of an out-of-season Formentera. Nimri personifies that which Edward Said called 'the unhealable rift forced between a human being and a native place, between the self and its true home' (1994: 137) and is therefore an ideal muse for imaginative reflections on Otherness by Medem, whose fictions are invariably concerned with the fact that 'much of the exile's life is taken up with compensating for disorienting loss by creating a new world to rule, [although] the exile's new world, logically enough, is unnatural and its unreality resembles fiction' (Said 2000: 181). In addition, the meaning Nimri brought to the film was personal, for she reminded Medem of the neighbour with whom he had been hopelessly infatuated as a boy and, it must be said, bears some resemblance to Medem's partner Montse Sanz (who can be glimpsed in the film two seats behind Otto on the bus to school, while Medem is seated further back in a red jacket). Meaning is also present in the film's intertextuality with *El espíritu de la colmena* (1973) and *Cría cuervos* (*Raise Ravens*, 1975), whose infant heroines are also called Ana, and in the film's autobiographical elements, which include echoes of Medem as a child filming secretly at night with his sister Ana, and are most explicit in Medem's casting of his son Peru as the youngest Otto.

Medem claims to have based Otto on his son without actually considering Peru for the part. In fact, he worked backwards in his casting after first deciding on Nimri and Fele Martínez as the adult Otto, hoping to align some resemblance in his younger actors. It was only while auditioning actresses for the part of the infant Ana with Peru helping out by reading the part of Otto that Medem was convinced to cast him in that rôle. Thus it fell to Nancho Novo as Álvaro to assume

the paternal rôle of Medem, though only after a long period of fruit-
lessly auditioning older actors did Medem grant Novo a complicated
make-up test that added a credible couple of decades to the actor. Novo:
'I remember seeing myself made up as an old man and feeling such
deep pain and pity. The truth is I reminded myself of my father, who
had died that same year' [6]. Nevertheless, Medem's attempt to cast a
different actor probably failed because he was again seeking his own
reflection in an actor who would not only assume the rôle of father
to his own son, but also (in the sense that the infant Otto is closely
modelled on the infant Medem) assume the rôle of Medem's own
recently deceased father. Indeed, the most emotional relationship in
the film is arguably not that between Otto and Ana but that between
father and son, for, although Medem's themes of symmetry and duality
are conjoined in the reconciliations that take place between Germany
and the Basque Country in the official apology for the bombing of
Gernika that Olga describes on her television news programme and the
final reunions of Otto and Ana, the most poignant reunion is that
which takes place between the regretful Álvaro and the recalcitrant
Otto, especially bearing in mind the death of Medem's own father
shortly after completing *Tierra*.

Novo attests that his experience, observation and understanding of
an older, more troubled Medem informed the way he played Álvaro,
while Medem agrees that the personal connections he saw in his
characters and sought in his actors were most evident in Otto (through
the performance of his own son) and in Álvaro, who represents both
Medem (as the father of Peru) and his father (in terms of Medem's
identification with Otto):

> In a way I was that boy and that father. When the father and son are in
> the car, for example, and the father's telling his son that he's going to
> separate from his mother because nothing lasts in life, not even love,
> there was I, split between them. I understand that boy because I have
> been, and still am, that child who believes in eternal love. [5]

To lessen the potential trauma, Medem filmed Novo separately from
his son and constructed the dialogue in the editing:

> I didn't want Peru to be there, because that's not how I would have liked
> to have heard such a thing, that that's how love ends. I'm a romantic and
> Álvaro says it in a way that sounds like a punishment. [5]

Like its casting, *Los amantes del Círculo Polar* was filmed in reverse
chronological order, beginning in Finland and ending with a recreation

of Madrid in the early 1980s. Having filmed the death of Ana, however, the journey back to childhood prompted Medem to harshen his attitude to Álvaro and Olga as if blaming them for the already-filmed tragedy of their children: 'It's more like a marriage of convenience, of hardly any passion between them', says Medem, who filmed scenes so that 'the children turn their backs on their parents. If the parents are there, they're out of focus' [5]. A lucky snowfall cut the travel budget by allowing the sledding scene to be shot in the mountains just north of Madrid, but it took seven months of editing by Iván Aledo until the film could be completed with Alberto Iglesias's music. In tune with the space, lack and longing that characterises Basque art, Iglesias says he likes his score for its silences rather than its sounds:

> I like minimalist music very much. It's one of my greatest influences and that's why I like silence so much, because silence is a sound. Silence has a powerful emotional effect. There are silences for breathing or for glancing to one side and silences that provoke a change in the way you listen, because they change the density of the piece. [16]

Iglesias sought transparency in the thematic framework of a score that he tried to weave out of the plaited subjectivities of Otto and Ana. The main instrument he used was not indigenous to Finland but a Turkish oboe called a *mei* which was played by Javier Paxariño and this replication of folk music through alien instruments echoed his provocative recreation of Basque themes through Spanish instruments on *Vacas*. Iglesias has no time for nationalism in music: 'I simply thought it would be interesting to use an instrument that evokes the idea of distance and the *mei* sounds like a man talking to a far-off mountain. Maybe his love is far away, and that's what the film is saying' [16].

For *Los amantes del Círculo Polar* Sogecine imported the American ruse of test-screenings to Spain and worked hard at encapsulating the film in posters that included early drafts of a blue heart wrapped in barbed wire on a white background and a collage of circling planes around the heads of the adolescent Ana and Otto. A studio mid-shot won out, however, of a dreamy Otto leaning back onto Ana, who stared out at the observer: a stark image that was softened for American audiences by being rendered in incongruously lush colours, while the much starker Spanish one-sheet flipped the image so that Ana's stare came first. It also edged the photograph with the technical data of a filmstrip, a ruse picked up for the quad British poster favoured by Medem, which offered a single contact strip of photographs of Nimri and Martínez smiling and touching heads, thereby offering a unique but welcome focus on the film's romance rather than its tragedy. Ninety-four domestic copies reached 752,396 spectators and took € 2,827,371, more than two million more than *Tierra* (Sogecine 2004). It played in almost fifty foreign territories including the UK, Canada and the USA and featured in thirty international film festivals, including Sundance and Venice, where it was nominated for the Golden Lion alongside *Lola rennt* (*Run, Lola, Run*, 1998), as well as Athens, where it won the Audience Award.

The international trajectory of *Los amantes del Círculo Polar* inspired critical comparisons with the work of Krzysztof Kieslowski, Atom Egoyan, Tom Tykwer and Wong Kar Wai and notions that Otto and Ana were representative protagonists of a postmodernist cinema, where the link between the actions of humans and the world they inhabit is weak and the consequences of those actions are often arbitrary. The link can be strengthened, however, by a subjective understanding of love, which empowers characters to existential leaps of faith that allow them some rôle in the construction of the narratives that enfold them, where past, present and future are shuffled by the interaction of memory, thought and action. The protagonists of the films written and directed by Medem are all in flux, fleeing from stifling myths and resulting wars in *Vacas*, a violent marriage in *La ardilla roja*, a conscience plagued by existentialist doubts in *Tierra*, the end of love in *Los amantes del Círculo Polar* and the death of a loved one in *Lucía y el sexo*; but like the protagonists of Kieślowski's *Trois couleurs: rouge*, Egoyan's *Exotica* (1994), Tykwer's *Lola rennt* and Wong Kar Wai's *2046* (2004), Medem expresses a stubborn optimism that fantasies might be realised by investing emotionally in them. This begins with the infant Otto thumping his father when he tells him that 'everything runs out, even love' and with Ana refusing to believe her mother when told that her father is dead. Running from miserable fatalism, Otto and Ana reach a metaphysical plane where Ana's father has not died, but is alive inside Otto, and Otto's parents have not separated, but are rejoined in his efforts at being a go-between and substitute for his father in romantic memories of his mother.

Prior to this meeting of like-minded infants, however, their adult fates have already been determined in the film's credit sequence, which emerges out of a blizzard accompanied by the song *Sinitaivas* (Blue

Sky) by Olavi Virta and the Harmony Sisters, a Finnish tango classic from the 1950s that expresses a melancholic longing and sorrow that is affined with the dominant theme of the void or lack in Basque culture and induces nostalgic sentiments that uncover what lies buried beneath the snowstorm of the credits: a crashed plane and a fade into a disorienting montage of the film's final scene of Ana's tragic death. The cold whites and blues of this beginning/ending contrast with the muddy warmth of *Tierra* and suggest the contemplative and regretful maturity of a film that reclaims the responsibilities that Ángel discarded at the end of *Tierra*. As the infant Otto and Ana embrace their recourse to the imagination, so Medem essays a metaphysical tale where life and death is the ultimate duality and love and imagination form the bridge between them.

Rarely has the deathly pall of midwinter been so vividly captured on film as in the bleached whites and grey-blues of the schoolyard where the children meet. A crane-mounted camera provides the first of several overhead shots that symbolise the enduring guardianship of those who have died, such as Ana's father, whose car, her mother tells her, ran out of petrol just as he was overtaking and left him facing an oncoming truck. Trying to turn back time to a moment when her father was alive, Ana runs from reality with only her imagination and stubbornness to protect her, and entirely by coincidence finds herself being chased by a boy who is trying to catch a football and is equally surprised to be in the position of chasing her. Their subjective views of each other are juxtaposed as low angle steadicam shots that provide a vivid sense of what it feels like to be small and scared by an adult world, though this montage is also juxtaposed with the nostalgic voiceovers of the adult Ana and Otto, which evoke the sense that this was the moment that the world shrank to exclude everyone but each other. Ana copes with the death of her father by imagining him reincarnated in Otto, while Otto just falls hopelessly and hopefully in love. 'Where do girls run to?' wonders the adult Otto in voiceover before reflecting upon his own running by replaying the narrative in his mind and imagining three of an infinite number of other footballs that would never have led him to Ana. If the ball had been kicked straighter, or if he had run a fraction later, or if he had saved the ball in the goalmouth, for example, there would be no more film.

By combining juxtapositions of the visual and aural subjectivities of Otto and Ana as infants and as adults in this single sequence, the rules and structure of the film's fractured narrative are established in a manner that may be compared with the post modernist ploys of Kieślowski's *La Double vie de Véronique* (*The Double Life of Veronica*, 1991) and Michael Haneke's *Code inconnu* (*Code Unknown*, 2000), which both explore the interconnectedness of people who are doomed never to meet, as well as with *Lola rennt*, which details Lola's apprenticeship to the repetition of events, Pedro Almodóvar's *La mala educación* (*Bad Education*, 2004), which switches subjectivities for several versions of several stories, and *Memento* (2000), which presents a jigsaw narrative from the viewpoint of a protagonist who is clinically incapable of ever seeing the big picture. *Los amantes del Círculo Polar* provides a similar challenge to an audience of assembling its narrative and exists in a parallel fractal universe which may be ordered according to either Otto's belief that life is an unbroken circle or Ana's conviction that it is a chain of coincidences. The juxtaposition of the visual and aural subjectivities of Otto and Ana moves the narrative between spaces and places as well as five different time periods (the four ages of the lovers and the 1936 bombing of Gernika) that illustrate the protagonists' conflicting reflections on events. Yet, for all the many escape routes from the death of love that the lovers test, including physical distance, memory and their imaginations, Otto and Ana both struggle against the notion expounded by Álvaro that empirical experience of love is part of life's inexorable movement towards death: 'Everything that is born dies. Love too. It's good that life goes in cycles.' Nevertheless, Álvaro's recourse to homily is dismissed by his son, seconds before the second of several crashes in the film throws Otto against the dashboard. 'Forgive me, it's not my fault', says Álvaro, but Otto matches his father's guilt at driving badly and possibly killing him to that of killing love by leaving his mother and smacks him hard across the face.

In addressing the mythic nature of eternal love, the film also connects with other resonant myths, for Ana's obsession with Otto and the dead father that she sees within him illustrates both the Electra complex, which describes the sexual attachment of a female child to her father, and the Electra paradox, whereby one may know something to be true of an object according to one description but not according to another. In the original myth, Electra, daughter of Agamemnon and Clytemnestra, persuades her brother Orestes to avenge her father's murder by killing her mother and her mother's lover. In psychoanalytical practice, the myth gives its name to a daughter's fixation on her father and may be applied to Ana's repossession of her father through

Otto. The Electra paradox, moreover, relates to Electra's knowing that Orestes was the man before her but not that the man before her was Orestes, for Ana knows that Otto is her brother (by their step-parents' marriage) and is not her brother (by their lack of true sibling blood and their romantic love for each other), while also believing that this boy is Otto (on the outside) and is not Otto (on the inside, where he is her father). Consequently, recognition of what is known is intensional – that is to say, incapable of explanation solely in terms of empirical data and requiring an explanation of its meaning by reference to such phenomena as faith or metaphysics. Consequently, Ana's relationship with Otto can only be explained by recourse to the belief system that is expressed by her visual and aural subjectivity that also structures her existence in her half of the film's dedicated chapter headings.

Similarly, in yet another juxtaposition, Otto represents the Oedipal complex, by which a group of emotions arising from the desire of a male child are focussed on the mother. Again, the original myth deals in mistaken identity, with Oedipus, son of the king and queen of Thebes, unwittingly killing his father and marrying his mother with whom he subsequently has four children. In *Los amantes del Círculo Polar* Otto suffers his parents' separation and attempts to compensate his mother by assuming the romantic role in their relationship, telling her he loves her and taking her on what he refers to as a mystery 'date'. But he also rejects her by moving out and going to live with his father in order to be closer to Ana. Consequently, when Otto's mother dies 'from too much love' it is unclear whether it was for Otto or for Álvaro, thus exacerbating the guilt that prompts Otto to separate himself from Ana. Because the original myth ends with Oedipus putting out his own eyes when the truth of his relationship with his mother is revealed, it indicates a belief system that is ratified by sight, and when that belief system is proven to be erroneous, so sight, which is the basis of its beliefs, must be destroyed. Thus the film's final chapter 'Otto in the eyes of Ana', with its final shot of Otto reflected in the eyes of the dying Ana, relates to the blinding of characters whose juxtaposed subjectivities, voiceovers and chapters provide the structure of a film that, like their subjective experiences of life and love, must end.

As a child, however, Otto has hope that love will not end and writes 'a question of love, too lovely for the handwriting of a boy' on a fleet of paper planes that he launches into the schoolyard. Medem claims not to remember what was written on this paper and suggests that the Surrealist act is best completed by the projection of one's own question onto the planes. However, one might safely assume that Otto's question is something akin to asking whether love can be eternal. As Otto walks to his waiting father, he sees that Ana exploits his romantic gesture for mischievous match-making by telling her mother that it comes from Álvaro, thereby engineering the coincidence of a relationship between their parents that will bring her and Otto together. Ana's early triumph at helping fate along by the deployment of her imagination is rewarded by her being granted the first eponymously-titled chapter, 'Ana', which begins at the film's end by the Arctic lake but turns back time to her running from her father's death and falling in front of Otto. Thereafter, the children develop a pretence of mutual antipathy, sitting silently in the family car as a series of wipe cuts illustrates the changing fortunes of the family. The model of car improves with news of Álvaro's promotion and Olga switches to the driving seat when Álvaro's work obliges him to forego the routine of the school run. Ana and Otto also age until the repression of their Oedipal and Electra complexes is ended when a change comes suddenly with Olga crashing into a bus and the masterful edit by which Otto and Ana's infant selves are thrown forwards and fall back into their adolescent, hormone-driven embodiment by the teenage Víctor Hugo Oliviera and Kristel Díaz. Ana's bare thigh falls on Otto's hand and the two of them are empowered to overcome their respective complexes by recognising each other as individuals rather than as substitutes for the parent that each of them lack. Finding herself listening to Otto for the very first time, Ana knows she has overcome the death of her father and resolves to fall in love, though their relationship is now complicated by sex.

Oblivious to the sexual attraction between Otto and Ana, however, Álvaro attempts to capture the appearance of a family unit in a photographic portrait but is betrayed by the unmanned objectivity of the timed camera, which he sets up in the manner of the aged Manuel attempting his portrait of unified Basqueness in *Vacas*. As with Manuel's fallacious *tableau vivant*, however, the camera captures details that invalidate the myth: Ana slips Otto a note – 'I'll wait for you tonight in my room' – that can be seen crumpled in Otto's hand, thereby giving the lie to the family portrait and the myth of unity.

Photographs play a crucial role in Medem's films. In addition to Manuel's portrait of mythic Basqueness and Peru Irigibel's work as photojournalist in *Vacas*, there are the three pictures that spring to life in *La ardilla roja* (the psychologist's photo of the back of Félix, the

8 Ana (Sara Valiente) meets Otto (Peru Medem) in *Los amantes del Círculo Polar*

picture of Las Moscas on the record cover and the shot pinned to the wall in J's apartment of him with Elisa that reveals Félix and Sofía) and the collage of Polaroids that illustrates Lorenzo and Lucía blurring into each other in *Lucía y el sexo*. This use of photographs effects a tension between their practical and objective purpose of recording times and places, and their emotive, subjective and conflictive function as instruments of memory. Manuel manufactures an image of Basque purity and unity out of his fractured family in *Vacas*, while Peru Irigibel later offers up his camera as an instrument of hagiography when he pacifies the Carlist officers by offering to take their portraits. As in the photographic session afforded J's group Las Moscas in *La ardilla roja*, the camera constructs a pastiche of mythic Basqueness that is thwarted by the irony of Romantic unity being rendered by divided elements, for the portraits of Carlist officers that might indicate progressive Basqueness are truly evidence of a destructive Civil War, while the shot of Las Moscas, like that which Manuel takes of his family in *Vacas*, conjures an illusion of unity from the moment when J's relationship with Elisa foundered on promises of a romantic trip that would never happen. In *Lucía y el sexo* the collage of body parts suggests a jigsaw that might, when constructed, reveal only Lorenzo, for whom sex with Lucía is an imaginative act. With similar irony, in *Los amantes del Círculo Polar*, Álvaro's photograph records his family's division rather than its unity, for when the photograph is later seen from the subjectivity of Otto, it features not the adolescent Ana and Otto who posed for it but their adult selves played by Najwa Nimri and Fele Martínez, thereby illustrating once again that in the films written and directed by Medem it is subjectivity that provides the emotional truth. As in *Vacas*, irony undoes the myth of this happy family unit when Otto creeps into Ana's bedroom through an obstacle course made of romantic clichés, climbing out and in through windows on a stormy, moonlit night. The subjectivity signifying emotional truth combines with his emotional investment in the fantasy of his relationship with Ana and makes it real to him, but finding her asleep, however, he heads back the way he came only to find that the pragmatic Ana, who instigated the sex with her note, has bypassed romantic clichés by nipping between their rooms and into his bed before he made it back. Ana and Otto make love, but thereby become adults who take on the guilt that comes from experience, which is why, when the aforementioned family portrait reappears, it reveals their adult selves.

The guilt that Otto feels about his sexual relationship with Ana is exacerbated by the death of his mother, who once told him the love of a mother and son was forever. Her cremation prompts a romantic death wish in Otto that compels him to sled over the side of a cliff. 'Otto wanted to die and I went with him', says Ana; but the ever-pragmatic Ana jumps off in time and it is in Otto's subsequent imaginative limbo between life and death that the film reaches the transcendental state that will be revisited in the final scene of Ana's death. Between juxtapositions of life and death, memory and imagination, Otto is saved ('because I'm not dead') by his mystical encounter with a fur-clad giant called Aki who skies uphill. In this surreal limbo, Otto visits recurring moments from the past and future that include his grandfather's rescue of a German pilot called Otto found hanging from his parachute during the bombing of the Basque town of Gernika during the Spanish Civil War, and the real-life Aki's subsequent rescue of Otto hanging from his parachute in Finland. The evidence of cyclical events confounds Otto's belief that life is a single unbroken circle and allows for his revival by the love of Ana, who, running to turn back time as she did following the death of her father, finds the power to resurrect him by investing emotionally in her imagining of his resurrection. Moreover, this moment of Otto's resurrection is marked by the assonance between the name Aki and the Spanish word *aquí*, meaning 'here', which adds great portent to the coincidence of Otto later calling 'aquí' when hanging by his tangled parachute in Finland and being answered by a man called Aki. The coincidental assonance serves to link Otto's first near-death experience on the sled with his second in the Finnish trees and suggests that this transcendental 'here' is the exceptional coincidence that proves an otherwise unruly universe and is thus the point at which he and Ana must return to in order that their love may transcend death and be eternal.

Firstly, however, Otto must resolve the effect that any legacy of his Oedipal complex might have on his relationship with Ana, who wavers between maternal, sisterly and romantic designs in his imaginative limbo.

> Are you Ana?
> Yes, my child.
> Where's my mother?
> No-one knows, that depends on you.

Despite Otto's confusion, his disjunctive transcendence of his near-death experience is revealed to him as the moment when love becomes eternal, for it is in this limbic dream-space that he is nursed back to health by a woman called Cristina who is fleeing the bombing of Gernika. The character clearly recalls Suárez's character Cristina in *Vacas*, but as played by Nimri this Cristina represents Otto's subjective condensing of past and future lives and loves into one emotionally validated being. Indeed, the truth of Otto's subjectivity in this moment is emphasised by the juxtaposition of this Surreal encounter with history as presented on the television news read by Ana's mother, which recounts the official apology made by the German ambassador for the bombing of Gernika. The juxtaposition suggests that whereas objectivity about history decides that the bombing is a wrong that must be righted, a person's subjective history, which is interpreted emotionally, is always right. And as the news programme continues, Otto slips his hand up Ana's skirt, for as the Japanese title of the film has it, *Ana + Otto* and everything else is unreal. Indeed, this is also the moment when alternating chapter headings for the juxtaposed subjectivities of Ana and Otto are abandoned and the next one is titled *Ana/Otto*. The solidus can indicate separation but can also signify interchangeability, for this chapter details the estrangement of Otto and Ana while tracking their comparable efforts to be reunited in a place of transcendence beyond familial and earthly concerns. Otto steals money from his father and leaves home to live in a miserable apartment and Ana recreates his emotional imprisonment by throwing the heart he gave her into a cupboard and slamming the door, letting it bounce inside as Otto throws himself against the walls of his rented accommodation. Time passes while Ana follows every possible coincidence in the hope of finding him again. In a sequence that is rather unconvincing in its arch choreography, the juxtaposition of their positioning and subjectivities in Madrid's Plaza Mayor results in their missing each other though they both scan passers-by for each other while sitting back to back. 'There are no good coincidences left. It's my fault, I used them up too soon', says the disheartened but characteristically pragmatic Ana, who instead latches on to the coincidental appearance of Otto's schoolteacher and begins a relationship with him that will return her to her old school as a teacher. This is Ana running backwards once more to end up in the place where she first met Otto, though, ironically, it is the moment when they are furthest apart. Rather than retreat like Ana to a definite past, Otto flies into an uncertain, imaginative future because he understands that 'by leaving Ana, I'd been left without destiny' and so resolves to invent a new one.

When Otto does return to Álvaro, the father he robbed and abandoned and has since been left by Olga, there is regret and rancour until they find commonality in the notion of lost love, for Álvaro is still besotted with Olga just as Otto is with Ana. In addition, they both share an unspoken grief for Otto's mother. The film stutters to a purposeful halt in its juxtaposition of Ana sitting on a chair by an Arctic lake and Otto sitting on the sofa with his father watching old war films; yet it is from this moment of stasis rather than flux that their lives begin to re-converge around a package sent to Otto by Ana from 'Fin-landia', the land of cinematic endings. There, Ana wallows in the coincidences of not only having discovered that the German father (called Otto) of her second stepfather (called Álvaro) owns a cottage on the edge of the Arctic Circle, but that he was shot down over Spain during the bombing of Gernika. Consumed by guilt for the bombing, this Otto rescued and married a Spanish woman called Cristina, who died on the same day that their son Álvaro wrote to tell him of his meeting Ana's mother. Circles within circles is just how Ana likes it, for palindrome means 'recurring' and so many recurring names, images, incidents and circular motifs validate her theory of fate as both theoretical and tangible. Otto and Ana, whose names begin as they end, may be going around opposite edges of the self-contained world that is created by their love but they will soon meet at its top, which is within the Arctic Circle.

It is finally fitting that Otto and Ana should reunite on the night of Saint John, for the circling sun and the ceremonial erasure of the past associated with the date makes their reunion inevitable. *Los amantes del Círculo Polar* thus ends in an imaginary world that is conjured from the strength of the protagonists' imaginative desires and identified by them in the physical metaphor of the midnight sun at the arctic circle, a landscape that, like all landscapes in films written and directed by Medem, is more psychological than truly tangible. Transcendence is thus promised but withheld as Ana reacts impatiently to the news of a crashed messenger plane and breaks off her vigil, thereby missing the coincidence of her life that is Otto's parachuting into the trees on the opposite side of her lake. Always one to force coincidences by her weakness for pragmatic action rather than trusting the imagination like Otto, Ana misses the coincidence of Otto, who patiently hangs around calling '¡Aquí!' until he lucks into the coincidence of a passer-by being called Aki.

And how does Ana's story end? In the chapter called *In Ana's Eyes*, she learns that a plane has crashed and, thinking Otto dead, runs to bring him back to life but is knocked down by a bus and in her dying moments, by a massive, last emotional investment in the now unreachable fantasy of her reunion with Otto, she imagines meeting and embracing him in the apartment of his aged Finnish namesake. And how does Otto's story end? In *Otto in the Eyes of Ana*, he arrives in the village of Rovaniemi to see her hit by the bus and reaches her just in time to catch his reflection in the dilating pupils of her dying eyes. And how does *Los amantes del Círculo Polar* end? Ana dies in both stories because this is simply the way this story ends. Yet, it is at the moment of her death that she enters the limbic state that was previously visited by Otto following the crashing of his sled. When the rôles are reversed however, Otto, whose imagination lacks the pragmatism of that of Ana, is unable to bring her back to life. Thus, although in Ana's ending Otto seems to find and embrace her, he truly only embraces Ana's stiffening, staring corpse as her imagination dies with her. Here, finally, is the ironic answer to a question of love that the infant Otto wrote on his paper plane. Can love be eternal? For Otto and Ana, as for Romeo and Juliet, the answer is yes. If only, but only, in death.

Nevertheless, as the end of a circle is also its beginning, so the image of Ana's dilating pupils was a digital effect that inspired Medem to purchase his first digital camera and begin writing his next script. Although he had killed his protagonist in order to achieve it, the glimpse of transcendence offered by Otto in the eyes of Ana was also the most tangible representation of the subconscious that Medem had ever achieved onscreen. Guilt at Ana's death lingered, however, and would soon be exacerbated by the death in a car crash of her namesake, Medem's sister. The resultant grief fuelled Medem's concern at the conclusion of *Los amantes del Círculo Polar* and provoked much reflection on the responsibility of the author. But rather than shrink from the burden of authorship, he grew determined to assume and exploit the potential of auteurism for the rewards to be had by investing emotionally in fantasies that might therefore become real. Mindful of the coincidences with his own life, he sought to reverse the journey through life to death of *Los amantes del Círculo Polar* by making his next script a return journey, wherein Ana, who had died in a fade to white, was resuscitated by the fade-in from the sunlight around her reincarnated self, who Medem named Lucía. Says Medem:

> *Lucía y el sexo* is about a return to life. I wrote it in the present tense. I knew that Lucía was Ana from *Los amantes del Círculo Polar* and that's why I thought of Najwa Nimri, but I didn't include the character's past. I didn't want to know anything about Ana from before she had arrived on the island. And when she's there, she doesn't tell anyone anything. Just this one thing, that something has happened in her life and it was a tragedy. [5]

Just as Ana's name can be read both backwards and forwards, so can her life be told. Although she had just died, Ana was about to be revived by Medem, who had killed her. No cut, therefore, just dissolve and fade back in from white.

7

A ray of sun: *Lucía y el sexo* (2001)

Medem was so concerned by predictions of an adverse commercial response to the sad ending of *Los amantes del Círculo Polar* that he ran away from the pre-release anticipation of another failure like *Tierra* to the Balearic island of Formentera. He had visited the island once before, two weeks prior to heading for Finland to film *Los amantes del Círculo Polar*, when he had stayed with friends of his partner Montse Sanz named Elena and Lorenzo, but this time the ferry crossing was an escape route from what he feared was the end of his filmmaking career. He recalls that on the crossing he stood at the ship's railing and watched his shadow battling through the surf and claims this was a cleansing moment that released him from the burden of satisfying anyone but himself with the tragic end of Ana. But the image also sparked in him an idea of Ana's resurrection that he decided to recreate on film. He thus arrived on the island relatively free from the pressures connected with *Los amantes del Círculo Polar* and newly enthused by this next project. He hired a moped, toured the island and began making notes, imagining characters appearing there, having escaped from their pasts. This was where the dead Ana might end up, for example, running away from tragedy to make herself real again by dint of Medem's emotional investment in the fantasy of her reincarnation. 'I went to the island with Ana', he says [5].

Medem set himself the remit to be simple in his writing and vowed not to bother with any of his characters' pasts. His resolve echoed that of Ángel in *Tierra*, but had not the suspicion that any new lightness of being was temporary at the end of that film been borne out by the complexity and tragedy of *Los amantes del Círculo Polar*? Resolute, he stayed with Elena and Lorenzo again and began transforming his fantasy of Ana's resurrection into a story:

Ana was escaping her tragedy, the loss of her man, who I called Lorenzo. She came to this island and met three characters including Elena, who were each escaping their tragic pasts, but nobody said what had happened to them. They simply started living together like new, with the crucial element that she provided of being light. Ana wanted to live in the air, in the light, and not think of the past, neither of the future, simply live in the present without a care in the world. [5]

Medem's obsession with the light on the island of white sand beaches was intoxicating; he claims it erased responsibilities and caution. When he returned to Madrid he was gorged with ideas for a script about Ana, who he renamed Lucía, that would be called *Lucía, un rayo de sol* (Lucía, A Ray of Sun) after the song of the summer of 1970 by the Catalan group Los Diablos. As with the abandoned project of *Mari en la tierra* during the filming of *Tierra*, he had the idea of filming *Lucía, un rayo de sol* with a hand-held digital camera and just a few friends for cast and crew. The plan was to simply tell the reverse of Ana's journey from life to death in *Los amantes del Círculo Polar*. Lucía would run from death and find life. Yet the possibility of this warm and luminous ending for Lucía was so much the antithesis of what he had written for Ana that it sparked in him an awareness of his own creative potential that overwhelmed him with responsibility. Medem often speaks of how he both suffers and enjoys his prerogative as author to throw characters together, force coincidences, stretch plausibility, suggest meaning in elaborate visual conceits and manipulate narratives to the point where comprehension is determined by emotional empathy; and *Lucía, un rayo de sol* was an examination of all this. The story began in the middle because, as he states, 'I'd not wanted to know anything about the characters' [5]. It began with a paranoid woman suddenly appearing in a guest house run by Elena, who has fled to the island because she had lost her daughter, where she has gotten furtively involved with a diver with an extraordinarily large penis who swims beneath the island but with whom she never speaks. Elena is also being tracked through internet chatrooms by a psychologist who might also be the fourth character in the story, a man in a raincoat who goes everywhere by bicycle and sleepwalks during the night. Surreal, intimate and Dogme-like in its conception, the project was also intended to reunite Medem with Carmelo Gómez and Emma Suárez, both of whom were involved in its initial planning.

Looking back on a film that lacks them, however, both Suárez and Gómez are reticent to discuss what might have been. Suárez remembers the original idea was 'a little co-operative project' [14] but that Medem had trouble securing funding and its filming kept on being delayed. Gómez says he liked the original script:

> It had a lot to do with Julio, of course. Its world was essentially his, like always, but it was about four characters isolated on an island, not this baroque world he made up later with all these connections to sex, where it turns out that in order to make it work he had to show they were characters in the mind of a writer. It was amazing, you can't imagine! With just two women and two men and without saying much at all there was this incredibly powerful drama, without even leaving the house. It was so oppressive! It was magnificent! But then Julio started adding this muddle of sex and it changed the whole film. [15]

Contrary to expectations, *Los amantes del Círculo Polar* was a critical, popular and international success that positioned Medem as a commercially and critically consecrated auteur filmmaker who could suddenly attract major funding. Sogecine sought involvement in his next project and the promises of an expansive budget fuelled and distorted Medem's ambition. From this point on the tale of *Lucía y el sexo* becomes one of many project overhauls involving reworked and discarded scripts, revised and abandoned casts and innovative but over-reaching technical ambition. He promptly abandoned the aim of simplicity and wondered instead if all that he had written on the island and called *Lucía, un rayo de sol* was only half the story. Back in Madrid and buoyant with the success of *Los amantes del Círculo Polar*, he attempted the first half of *Lucía, un rayo de sol*, a backstory or prequel-of-sorts that he wrote as a novel from the perspective of a minor character called Lorenzo:

> I wrote a novel instead of a script because Lorenzo was a novelist and I wanted to feel like him and just let myself write freely. My plan was to write the past and I started to write very fast, wanting to know what it was that Lorenzo and the other characters knew about their pasts. And from that came the sex. [5]

Identifying more and more with Lorenzo, another writer, Medem positioned himself as Lorenzo, the creator of the characters on the island, which he now imagined in symbolic and psychological terms as a land mass floating freely above the past lives of characters that lay in the water beneath, a metaphor that had already informed the design of Sofía in *La ardilla roja*. The connection between this subconscious, underwater past and the conscious present above, he decided, was sex, which was also what linked the characters: sex as a source of life and joy, but also of guilt and tragedy. 'Somehow, in the fantasies that all of us have, it's sex that's the great fabulist, the great creator of situations and images, and it was with this that I wanted to play', says Medem [5].

He called Lorenzo's novel *Sexo, antes del sol* (Sex, Before The Sun). Put it together with the script for *Lucía, un rayo de sol*, remove the sub-headings, and one gets *Lucía y el sexo*. The first draft of the combined screenplay is dated 16 June 1999 (Medem 1999) and sits at the bottom of a pile of eight on a shelf in Alicia Produce, a long way down from the final shooting script, which is itself quite different from the finished film. By butting the original script and Lorenzo's novel together, the characters on the island were overwhelmed with unresolved backstories involving tragedy, guilt and provocation in a bewilderingly fragmented, deliriously spasmodic and temporally haphazard screenplay that begins with a phone call from the police asking Lucía to identify the body of someone who had died. Instead she catches a train and ferry while, in voiceover, Lorenzo the author converses with Lucía, his literary creation. Their relationship is peripheral to that of Belén, however, who suffers the attempts of her mother to liberate her sexually after she is diagnosed with autism by a psychologist called Víctor. Meanwhile, Carlos, who is also called Antonio, is seeing a psychologist called Aitana, who enjoys rough sex with Víctor. Belén and her mother, Manuela, seduce Carlos and form a perverse family unit. Belén studies psychology and babysits for Elena, who is in contact with Lucía by means of a chatroom about Mediterranean cuisine that is also visited by Lorenzo, who uses a sun '☼', not a lighthouse, as his sign. Elena flees to the island after a dog kills her daughter, meets Lucía and invites Belén to join her there, but Carlos/Antonio murders Belén and her mother and heads for the island, where he kills Víctor and has sex with Lucía. Lorenzo's running from the dog that killed Elena's daughter is juxtaposed with Lucía running from a man who might be Carlos but turns out to be just a horny Italian holidaymaker. Elena and Carlos have sex. The end. In Medem's own words this first draft was 'the most mechanical and indigestible thing I'd ever written' [5].

In the second draft he introduced the idea of Lucía's erotic encounter with the lighthouse and the hole in the ground that were put there by Lorenzo's imaginative subconscious, and crucially turned Lucía into Lorenzo's muse and reader, trapped in a cycle of both inspiring his novel and being inspired by it. Because Lorenzo was now responsible for whatever happened to Lucía, he became a buffer between Medem and her, which allowed Medem to avoid all responsibility for her fate and thereby freed him from the guilt he felt at killing Ana in *Los amantes del Círculo Polar*. Assuming the subjectivity of Lorenzo, he deleted sub-plots and minor characters that were beyond Lorenzo's subjectivity and wrote furiously, pouring out a story that validated the Surrealist technique of automatic writing by exhausting reason and drawing on the creative reserves of the subconscious:

> I drew on very dark things, things one doesn't know about oneself, but they are there, deep down. Then this fascinating relationship developed between the writer who creates the fiction and the reader who receives it. Lorenzo risks a lot because he exposes himself so much. [5]

The link between Medem's admission and his identification with Lorenzo is found in auteurist ambitions and agency as 'a mode of enunciation that describes an active and monitored engagement with its own condition' (Corrigan 1991: 104). That is to say, Medem subscribes to the cliché of authorship and auteurism that the Self must be exposed in the creation of an Other with whom the author/auteur identifies. As he states: 'I suppose there are writers who don't risk anything, who don't reveal themselves, but that's not how I do it. I wring myself dry and I guess that makes me a victim of what I write' [5]. However, for an author/auteur to position himself like this as both victim and culprit of what he creates ignores the privilege that comes from the cheat of Lorenzo/Medem pretending that the true subject of *Lucía y el sexo* could ever be Lucía, the reader. Although Medem makes a pretence of assuming the subjectivity of Lucía, he remains rootedly empathetic to that of Lorenzo, whose martyrdom for the sake of his work is treated with great indulgence.

Lucía is the reader, who Roland Barthes states should be 'the one place where multiplicity is focussed' (1982: 148), but all the strings of all the characters are tied to the fingers of Lorenzo, who is puppeteered by Medem. In response, Medem counters that the true skill of an author/auteur is empathy, 'the ability to imagine "What would I do in that situation?"' [5] and then write or film it. This, he argues, makes Lucía the true subject because it is she who puts herself in the position of others by pretending to be them. For example, she pretends to be the protagonist of Lorenzo's first novel to seduce him and is 'the girl from Malta' when she first arrives on the island. However, the question then becomes how much moral responsibility and choice does Lucía have in her actions. Is Lucía a free-thinking individual or is she just following the path that Lorenzo, a stand-in for Medem, has described for her? Medem replies:

> Lucía doesn't do anything bad. There are bad things that happen, morally bad things, but she's always able to say what she would have done in place of others, even if she would have done the same thing, which to my mind is the most interesting reaction and at heart it's what *Lucía y el sexo* is all about. It's the suggestion that by telling stories you can influence the reader and the audience. [5]

The drafts piled up until Medem ended on the eighth version of the script dated 23 May 2000 (Medem 2000). It was still a story in two halves: the first half told of a writer called Lorenzo, who transforms his experiences into stories, while the second half told of Lucía, the reader who transforms his stories into her experiences. In effect, Lorenzo writes a novel that inspires Lucía so much she imitates its protagonist in a flattering and successful attempt at seducing him. Lorenzo, who has been suffering writers block, is then inspired by Lucía to write another novel in which he, like Medem, manipulates the lives of the characters he creates, making Lucía, this lovestruck waitress from Madrid, a character in his own book and bed until their six years of romance are strangely curtailed by Lorenzo's possible death and Lucía runs away to an island. There, Lucía realises that she is Lorenzo's fictional character made flesh by the emotion he has invested in their relationship and, resolving to take control of her life story where Lorenzo left off, she goes in search of a happy ending. Consequently, when on the island, the script switches to Lucía's subjectivity as she acts upon her own imagination, thereby effecting a poignant contrast with the missing Lorenzo, an author whose imagination is only expressed in what he writes. Lorenzo aims to find her, however, by breaking out of his indulgent depression and heading to the tropical island, a much more amenable meeting-place for star-crossed lovers than the Arctic Circle, though the coincidence of their meeting is the same. Thus, Medem created another couple of separated lovers on one more of his alien landscapes, this time a floating island on which characters far from urban tensions followed their deepest instincts. Cut off from reality, they reinvent themselves, with Lucía strolling naked into adventures and relationships and Elena, the mother of Lorenzo's love-child Luna who was killed by her dog when her babysitter Belén was busy seducing Lorenzo, tentatively reacquainting herself with the outside world by using the internet as the medium of her anonymous cry for help: a plea that is answered by Lorenzo, the writer whose ability to breathe new life into characters gives her much-needed hope.

By bringing the subjectivity of Lorenzo to the fore and making what had been a minor character into the protagonist, Medem performed the paradox of assuming the responsibilities of authorship by displacing them onto his stand-in, thereby performing 'the task of inexorably blurring, by an extreme subtilization, the relation between the writer and his characters' (Barthes 1982: 144). Like the novel that Lorenzo writes, Medem's script for *Lucía y el sexo* came with two distinct advantages over *Los amantes del Círculo Polar*. 'The first advantage is that when the story gets to the end, it doesn't finish, it falls down a hole and the story resumes half-way through. The second advantage, and the greatest, is that from here one can change the course of the story. If you let me, if you give me time.' Instead of the deathly fade-out that had done for Ana, Medem/Lorenzo situated the characters and events of *Lucía y el sexo* in a constant, rewritable loop. Unlike the cyclical narrative of *Vacas*, which obliged its characters to repeat the mistakes of the past, the narrative loop of *Lucía y el sexo* allowed characters to correct them. This was a never-ending narrative that resolved the anguish of Otto in *Los amantes del Círculo Polar* because it really was an eternal love story, both structurally and thematically, that could be endlessly retold and any sad or tragic ending could be erased by starting again in the middle until the story turned out right. A film with a markedly similar narrative loop is *Lola rennt* (*Run, Lola, Run,* 1998) directed by Tom Tykwer, which allows the flame-haired Lola three attempts at saving her boyfriend from gangsters. Yet, although commonly deemed postmodernist for its fractal plot and irony, as Owen Evans argues, 'there is nothing complacent, nor cynical, nor ultimately playful about *Lola rennt* [for] Lola's running is not aimless; it has a well-defined focus. The film is about *not* passively accepting one's fate; it is all about changing it' (Evans, O., 2004: 112). As Lola lies dying at the end of the first episode, for example, she says 'That's not what I want' and Tykwer subsequently resurrects her so that she can have another go, which is essentially what Medem does with Ana, only he resurrects her as Lucía.

Enthused by the eighth draft and keen to build on the international success of *Los amantes del Círculo Polar*, Sogecine agreed a budget of four million Euros and twelve weeks of filming. The managing director of Sogecine, Fernando Bovaira, agrees that 'Spanish cinema has always

been famous for its sexual charge' [17] but insists that the erotic
potential of *Lucía y el sexo* was secondary to expectations of Medem's
profitable auteurism: 'The erotic element is there, but it's a quality film
where the emotions are more important than the sex' [17]. Nevertheless,
the scene of Lorenzo's agent Pepe (Javier Cámara) urging him to add
a lot of sex to his novel because that's what people like begs the question
of a parallel with Bovaira. 'I don't think there's any opportunistic
gambit. There could have been because I don't have any scruples about
doing so, but not Julio, because it's a film with very personal themes',
replies Bovaira [17]. In the international arthouse market, it was the
combination of auteurist credentials with explicit sexual content
that seemed to validate the investment in a production that was also
likely to clear a profit in Spain. Sex in Spanish cinema is usually either
linked with Catholic repression and male violence or frivolously
deployed as spectacle for the male gaze, but the end of the 1990s and
the new millennium had seen a surge in the youth audience that
was increasingly led by prosperous female graduates and these old
ideas of Catholic guilt and the female as object were unpopular and
threadbare. Films such as *Boca a boca* (1995), *El amor perjudica
seriamente la salud* (1997), *Cha cha chá* (1998) and *El otro lado de la
cama* (2002), which were all successful at the box office, were all
contemporary and youthful and featured strong female characters
whose attitudes to sex were mostly uninhibited and fun. At the very
least, *Lucía y el sexo* seemed likely to fit this domestic trend, while also
satisfying those critics and audiences who demanded some investment
in film as art and based their critical and commercial favours on ideas
of the director as film artist. In European cinema too, where sexual
relations between characters in self-consciously serious art films such
as Kieślowski's *Trois Couleurs*, *Irréversible* (2002), *La Pianiste* (2001),
Swimming Pool (2003), *9 Songs* (2004) and many others are
dominated by power-plays and frequently touched by madness, *Lucía
y el sexo* seemed an ideal fit.

   Unfortunately, due to the delay caused by the several drafts, Medem
had to assemble a very different cast from that which he had imagined
a year earlier. Carmelo Gómez's character Víctor had simply disap-
peared in rewrites, while Emma Suárez, who had filmed *Sobreviviré*
(1999) and *Besos para todos* (2000) while waiting for filming to begin,
found herself estranged from the project and its writer-director, with
whom her relationship temporarily soured. Instead, Najwa Nimri took
the rôle of Elena only three days before filming began and read the

script on the plane to Formentera, though upon arrival Medem ripped out all the pages in which her character did not appear and left her to tailor her performance accordingly: 'Me fui enterando de la trama sobre la marcha y, de hecho, hubo secuencias que rodé con el texto pegado a las paredes. Por eso, las sorpresas son tan reales' (Escamilla 2001: 70) (I worked out the plot as we went along and, in fact, there were scenes I filmed with my dialogue stuck to the walls. That's why the surprises are so real). The most drastic change was Medem's decision to drop Ana Risueño, the actress cast as Lucía, because he claims she did not resemble his idea of the character. In her place came Paz Vega, a Sevillian actress who was seven years younger than Risueño and had appeared in the television situation comedy *Siete vidas*. Vega performed a disastrous four-hour read-through of the entire script that only confirmed Medem's perversely stubborn belief that she was Lucía because of the appropriate way she had struggled with the character as defined by himself through Lorenzo. Lorenzo, meanwhile, was Tristán Ulloa, who Medem had kept in mind since *Mensaka* (1998) and invited to play the rôle when the actor happened to walk past a café where Medem was sitting.

Medem used his digital camera to film rehearsals, including fully-clothed sex scenes, that he concluded by assuming the rôle of psychologist and treating each of his actors in character: 'I had the feeling that the characters really had been with me. I knew that I had asked a lot of them, but I wanted to see just how far one can go as writer and as spectator' [5]. More than this, however, it was Medem's enthusiasm for filming with a hand-held digital camera that led to his decision to film *Lucía y el sexo* 'a bit like Dogme' [5] and mostly chronologically on CineAlta Hi-Definition 24P, only the third time a feature film had been shot on this format. As cinematographer Kiko de la Rica, who had made his mark with *Salto al vacío* (*Jump into the Void*, 1995), tells it, 'the idea was to follow the actors around with these little cameras' [10]. He over-exposed the image and reduced the contrast and colour saturation in order to create the bleached, heavenly look requested by Medem, who kept his actors largely separate from his crew. Says Tiko de la Rica:

> It wasn't a condition, but the work philosophy was almost 'my actors and I here, and the rest of you there'. We'd discussed everything, we knew what we had to do, and with digital cameras we could film without stopping on the sole condition that we were as discreet as possible, that

we didn't bother them, that we didn't restrict what Medem wanted them to do. [10]

Tiko de la Rica admits the influence of the Dogme 95 movement, whose manifesto advocates hand-held camerawork and claims that *Lucía y el sexo* was an experimental film for the manner in which it was shot so quickly. Reverse angle shots were immediate, for example, while the notion of a closed set became almost literal in Montse Sanz's set design of Lorenzo's apartment, which had fixed walls and ceilings instead of the usual breakaway sections and just a small hole to film through, which greatly inconvenienced the sound crew. 'We all had to be hushed and as far away as possible', remembers Tiko de la Rica [10].

Filming took thirteen weeks with a crew of fifty-nine, far removed from the tiny project that Medem had originally envisaged. The digital camera was a prototype Sony HDW-900 that proved a headache for the focus-puller, who operated the lens by remote control from behind a monitor. High-definition digital video has none of the grain associated with film, but provides a transparency to the light that Medem deemed perfect for characters who have supposedly moved to a more metaphysical plane. Another advantage of shooting digitally was the immense amount of footage that could be transferred to the hard drive of editor Iván Aledo, though the loss of clarity and the gaining of texture in the commercial cinema prints and VHS tapes would mean that, apart from the very few occasions when the film was projected digitally, it is only DVD that maintains the requisite picture quality and, therefore, the best representation of the film's mise en scène and meaning. Shooting digitally had afforded Medem all the light he wanted and the ability to shoot endlessly around his cast: 'It's very convenient, especially for filming the sex. I directed them in the shot. I wanted to see how far we could go in treating the actual filming like rehearsals' [5]. Inevitably, however, the question of seeing 'how far we could go' prompts enquiry about establishing the limits of the filmed sex scenes. Explicit sex on film is mostly a spectacle that is often categorised as pornography, while the *My Plaything* Digital Sin DVD series of interactive sex simulators even utilises the subjective camera to render the viewpoint of the male in order to increase the vicarious thrill of the spectator. The irony is that the question of how to distinguish between images that are there to excite one sexually and those that are essential to an understanding of the narrative is one that can only be answered subjectively. Or not. 'I've no idea where the limits are', says Medem [5].

The original plan was to be 'as explicit as possible' says Medem [5] but whereas he claims to have had no idea where the limits where, the cast imposed them by requesting body doubles for the scenes involving what might be termed the sexual functioning of genitalia rather than the suggestion of it. Thus the close-ups of male erections were performed by a porn actor and the penetration shots in the sex between Lorenzo and Lucía were courtesy of a Russian porn actress who plays the rôle of Belén's mother. Consequently, just as the various characters live vicariously through each other, so did Medem add body doubles to the range of alter egos and emotional substitutes that populate the film, thereby adding an ironic extra layer to its meaning that Medem claims was uniquely cinematic:

> In the editing I worked out if I could manage it or not, if the penetration could belong to someone else. And it's funny because the insinuation works the same way. You see the dick, you see her hand, and in the next shot you see her vagina, though it isn't hers, and him entering her. That mix, that's cinema! [5]

The stereotypical objectification of Lucía, which dominates the film and its marketing and which is exaggerated in her leather-and-lingerie striptease, may be understood as emanating exclusively from Lorenzo's novel *Sexo, antes del sol* and is therefore explicitly his point of view. However, the emphasis on the display of Lucía (and so Paz Vega) as erotic spectacle is such a clichéd example of 'woman as image, man as bearer of the look' (Mulvey 1992: 750) that the dominant subjectivity of Lorenzo may be mistaken for that of Medem. Indeed, although Lucía, Belén and Elena each celebrate Lorenzo's supposed sexual potency, there is no corrective female subjectivity and objectification of the male that might demonstrate this. In contrast to Lucía's full-frontal striptease for his viewing pleasure, Lorenzo offers only a parody of the female as erotic spectacle in which he pouts, tweaks his nipples and bunny-hops with his trousers around his ankles while wearing concealing black briefs and lip-synching. His spoofing of female sexuality for male viewing pleasure does not deconstruct the power-play, rather it alleviates his fear of it, while what might have constituted a critique of Lorenzo is withheld because Medem stubbornly negates any eroticism in the display of his male body. This, despite the fact that Lorenzo is supposedly seen from the subjectivity of Lucía. Indeed, reverse shots of Lucía sitting rapt and naked on the couch signify that she remains the object of desire. As in *Tierra* but unlike in *La ardilla roja* and *Los amantes del Círculo Polar*, Medem succumbs once again to the foreshortening of female subjectivity that is a recurring weakness of his films.

Lucía y el sexo may be redeemed, however, because, although Lucía proclaims undying love for Lorenzo at their first meeting, Elena has sex with him only once and describes this as 'the best fuck of my life' and Belén is up for anything that he can think of, this facile, arrogantly sexist imagining of these three females is entirely the point, because Lorenzo is the archetypal male coward in films written and directed by Medem. Like J in *La ardilla roja* he makes up for his shortcomings by indulging in the fantasy of fashioning females into gorgeous and sensual women who adore him. The problem of appreciating *Lucía y el sexo*, however, is that it is very much a self-consciously auteurist film, built on Medem's personal concerns about authorship and designed to maximise his auteurist status in an international market. It delivers a complicated muddle of subjectivities rather than the geometrical exactitude of *Los amantes del Círculo Polar* and the fact that the subjectivity of Lorenzo, the author, should ultimately prove itself dominant corroborates the trend of Medem identifying with (and being identified with) his male protagonist.

At the heart of *Lucía y el sexo* lies this complex interdependence of Medem and Lorenzo that has parallels in the relationships of the writer and the reader, the filmmaker and his audience, and the artist and the critic. In his 'Notes on the Auteur Theory in 1962' Andrew Sarris affirms that 'the way a film looks and feels should have some relationship to the way a director thinks and feels' and celebrates this interior meaning of film as 'the ultimate glory of the cinema as an art' (1992: 586–7). The film director as auteur, it would seem, is the *deus ex machina*, the god in the machine, who introduces himself into his work in order to resolve the plot. However, because those auteurs who succumb to this self-deification tend to wear themselves out on projects that become repetitively solipsistic and end up redundant, Medem certainly risked exemplifying this failing with *Lucía y el sexo*. On the other hand, the advantage of *Lucía y el sexo* was that it featured such an intimate exorcism of Medem's personal issues that he was subsequently able to move on to the political arena of *La pelota vasca* and *Aitor*.

Chief amongst these issues was the death of Medem's sister Ana in a traffic accident during production, along with his brother Álvaro's partner Olga, who was pregnant with a boy, who would have been called

Otto. This Otto, who was named after Medem's uncle, a pilot, would have been the son of Álvaro and Olga, which are the names of the parents in *Los amantes del Círculo Polar*, where Otto is played by Medem's son Peru. And, to reiterate, this was Ana, who had inspired the Ana of *Los amantes del Círculo Polar*, who had also died in a traffic accident: the Ana whose spirit Medem was busy reviving in Lucía. This was a surfeit of coincidences that brought all the fun of mixing reality and fiction to an abrupt and tragic halt. Editing of *Lucía y el sexo* was postponed until Medem felt able to return to his original task, that of resurrecting Ana in Lucía, with added urgency. This was Lucía, from the verb *lucir*, meaning to give off light. But the imperfect tense: Lucía, meaning something that used to give off light.

Born of a crisis of authorship that emerged from Medem's need to revive Ana from the tragic ending of *Los amantes del Círculo Polar*, *Lucía y el sexo* was concluded by a need to remember her inspirational namesake. In the final reunion on the island, it is clear that Lucía, Elena and Lorenzo have all learned to engage with trauma in order to reach the coincidences that might make for a happy ending, but rather than criticise their flight, if the film has a message it is the value of escaping into fantasy. Indeed, the resolution of *Lucía y el sexo* concludes a thesis on internal and external exile in the films written and directed by Medem that are all concerned with what Edward Said identified as the 'need to reassemble an identity out of the refractions and discontinuities of exile' (Said 2002: 179). Thus, in Medem's films, characters run from things not because they want to hide but because they want to be found. In *Vacas*, characters flee the Basque Country in order to live and love beyond the stricture of suffocating myth, in *La ardilla roja* they escape a traumatic past and in *Tierra* they run from the abyss of existential despair. In *Los amantes del Círculo Polar* Ana runs from life until she is found by Otto, albeit at the moment of her death, while Lucía encarnates the paradox of both desiring and fearing exile by introducing herself to the audience thus: 'My name is Lucía and I'm running away.' Running is coincidentally a natural talent for Medem, who might once have represented Spain at the Olympics, until he ran away from athletics to find himself in the study of psychiatry and a career in film. That his scripts are powered by the personal resonances that come from his identification with characters named for family members, whose subjectivity he commonly assumes in their writing, is no surprise when one considers how he also engineers coincidences by converting elements from his own life into the narrative obstacles and shortcuts that these characters encounter. As an avowed Surrealist, Medem thrives on coincidences as exceptions that confirm the rule of a truly unruly universe; as for Ana in *Los amantes del Círculo Polar*, coincidences are touchstones that link up to show him he is running in the right direction, even when they are manufactured, such as naming his second daughter Ana, who was born in 2004. But if he is going to name characters such as Peru, Sofía, Ana, Otto and Álvaro after members of his family and integrate his experiences of divorce and the death of a loved one into his solipsistic scripts, how could this not give rise to coincidences between fantasy and real life? There may be other writer-directors who do this and, for that matter, also dedicate each of their films to loved ones, but only Medem has made this integral to their understanding and essential to considerations of his auteurism.

So Medem runs, Ana runs and so do Lucía, Elena and Lorenzo. But, wanting to be found, they all end up on the island of *Lucía y el sexo*, which begins with credits being typed out on the screen: a clear statement of Medem's authorship. Behind the credits is the familiar subjectivity of an underwater camera that recalls but rejects the opening of *La ardilla roja*, for here there is a clear evolution. In *La ardilla roja* the murky water full of dead trees symbolised Sofía's troubled subconscious, but the crystal waters of this desert island are full of seaweed and glittering fish. The contrast suggests a cleansing of the psyche of the author who comes up for air on the final credit: 'Written and Directed by Julio Medem'. This deliberate surfacing from what may be interpreted as the metaphorical subconscious is then explored in the story of Lorenzo, a writer whose imaginative channelling of real events and people into his writing is upset by the real events and people that are affected by his fiction. Lorenzo is, with respect to Peter Wollen's delineation of the *homo hawksianus* (1992: 591), the *homo medemianus*, the protagonist of Medemian values in the problematic Medemian world. And if Lorenzo's story is partly a confession, then so is that of Medem, who, like Andrei Tarkovsky and John Cassavetes, insists on standing too close to the mirror. Close up, *Lucía y el sexo* is a film about solipsism and a catalogue of its writer-director's style, favourite themes and assorted auteurist paraphernalia including a plethora of personal references, structural loops and cycles, and themes of duality and chance. Visually and aurally, the film is typically neurotic and swoony, while the camera is a restless body-snatcher, appropriating the subjectivities of characters who provide variant perspectives on events. Light, symbolism and symmetries effect layered swirls of meaning. Is it any wonder that so many of Medem's characters faint?

The first cut, which the producer Fernando Bovaira rates as superior, was two hours and forty minutes with direct sound but no music. As always, however, crucial to the structuring of the final cut was the score by Alberto Iglesias, who chose the waltz, which incorporates a rigid structure and allows space for florid gestures, as an ideal accompaniment to the plot. Iglesias:

> I thought I'd relax with the waltz, but it's a paradox because a waltz, above all the Viennese waltz, has one of the most difficult rhythms there is. It's a 3 by 4 rhythm but it moves around a lot and there are times when no two beats are the same. It's as complex as Freud, which is really why Julio and I decided to adopt it as a concept. [16]

The beauty and appropriateness of the waltz also resides in its complex structuring of time. Although the music participates in the emotional narrative of the film, the changes in rhythm remind the characters, as they usually inform dancers, of how much time is left. In addition to provoking emotional responses, the waltz therefore influences the perception of an audience that is already engaged in making sense of time in its deciphering of the temporal shifts of the non-linear narrative, making it seem that time goes faster in some sequences than others. This adds immeasurably to the changing rhythms of the film by enhancing, for example, the languidness of the lovemaking when Lorenzo and Lucía first meet and think they have all the time in the world, the urgency of Lorenzo and Elena's first tryst, and the simple exhaustion in the coming to rest of the couple at the film's end. The first cut of *Lucía y el sexo* was thus re-edited to Iglesias's score until it came to rest at 123 minutes.

The film begins by breaking into the middle of a telephone conversation between Lucía, a hassled waitress, and Lorenzo, her writer boyfriend, who has lost his balance between reality and fiction and is no longer able to distinguish between them: 'I'm in a hole. I don't know how to get out', he tells her. Lorenzo's dilemma thus illustrates that which Roland Barthes explores in his essay 'The Death of the Author', which argues that 'writing is the destruction of every voice, of every point of origin. Writing is that neutral, composite, oblique space where our subject slips away, the negative where all identity is lost' (1982: 142). As Lorenzo loses his identity and slips away, *Lucía y el sexo* is revealed to be a film about the craft and imagination of writing in which the author is the victim of his trade. And, crucially, the suicide note left by Lorenzo is actually in Julio Medem's handwriting. This note clearly testifies to Medem's identification with Lorenzo as an author whose possibly manipulative mix of fantasy and reality has been the basis of his work as well as the concerns that have plagued his psyche. Furthermore, this note is also Medem's farewell to fiction prior to engaging cinematically with the politics of the Basque conflict in *La pelota vasca* and *Aitor* and his sign-off is literally on the screen. *Lucía y el sexo* is actually unique amongst the films written and directed by Medem in that it has no explicit mention of the Basque Country and, although its use of Formentera effects a representation of Otherness in relation to Spain that is similar to the metaphorical Otherness of Finland in *Los amantes del Círculo Polar*, there is no political dimension to the film besides the questing for identity that has no clear universal or political resonance. *Lucía y el sexo* thus concludes Medem's purposeful distancing from the Basque Country that he began by entering the tree hollow at the end of *Vacas*. This 'necessary strategy geared towards self-examination and self-definition [as] only through a dynamics of differentiation can an individual acquire self-knowledge' (Santaolalla 1998: 333) thus ends as Lucía travels down the hole at the end of her story that was put there advantageously by Lorenzo, 'for when [the story] reaches the end it falls down a hole and reappears in its middle' from where the plot can be changed. Hers is a return journey in every sense in which it is likely that she passes all those coming the other way from Medem's previous fictions, analysis of which therefore demands this Alice-like journey that enters the tree hollow in *Vacas* and continues on through *La ardilla roja*, *Tierra* and *Los amantes del Círculo Polar* before emerging into the sunlight through the hole that exists at the centre of *Lucía y el sexo*. In addition, this 'tunnel' through the five fictions is better described as a series of holes that represent the lack of identity of the films' protagonists, which not only relates to the emphasis on the void in Basque art and its metaphorical representation of a lack of a firm national identity, but also the personal estrangement of Medem from the Basqueness that was essential to the meaning of his work. If *Lucía y el sexo* is ultimately the least meaningful of Medem's fictions in terms of any political relevance, it nonetheless marks the point of liberty from questions of Basqueness that mark the acquiring of self-knowledge outlined in Santaolalla's incisive theory of the dynamics of differentation. That is to say, *Lucía y el sexo* delivers the paradox of being Medem's most personal film and his most objective. The critical self-analysis that undermines the self-indulgent portrait of Lorenzo illustrates a degree of detachment from the overriding concerns with Basqueness that had featured in his previous fictions, thereby allowing him to subsequently approach the question of the Basque conflict with at least a professional resemblance to neutrality.

This combination of self-analysis and self-indulgence is undermined by Barthes' insistence that 'the explanation of a work is always sought in the man or woman who produced it, as if it were always in the end, through the more or less transparent allegory of the fiction, the voice of a single person, the author "confiding" in us' (1982: 143). The clear symbiosis of Medem with Lorenzo that provides the explanation of *Lucía y el sexo* was also picked up by Tristán Ulloa, who incorporated imitations of Medem into his performance just as Nancho Novo and Carmelo Gómez had before him. Yet unlike the charismatic, romantic anti-heroes of J in *La ardilla roja* and Ángel in *Tierra*, Lorenzo is a scruffy character played subtly and cleverly by the rather ordinary-looking Tristán Ulloa, whose performance neither possesses nor expresses the animal magnetism of Carmelo Gómez, nor the wit and sensitivity of Nancho Novo. As a stand-in for Medem, Ulloa differs from Novo and Gómez by being neither tall nor dark nor particularly handsome, but like the characters they played, Lorenzo represents the darker side of imaginative creativity, becoming a cowardly fanta-sist with a martyr complex who runs away from commitment and responsibilities in order to tend his bruised creativity, who takes advantage of a mentally unstable woman and later leaves her to suffer unfounded grief. Lucía may be the catalyst for his redemption, but beyond her picturesque search for female independence it is the Freudian plight of the author that determines the direction and tone of the film, precisely because Lorenzo is also fictional, only doing what *his* author, Julio Medem, tells him to.

Lucía y el sexo is a postmodern film about authorship that recalls the works of the writer Paul Auster and the Basque author Miguel de Unamuno. In Unamuno's *Niebla* (*Mist*, 1914) the protagonist's vain search for the meaning of life leads him to confront Unamuno, who informs this character Augusto Pérez that Pérez has no control over his actions because he is fictional. Determined to prove Unamuno wrong, Pérez tries to commit suicide, but Unamuno kills him first by accidental food poisoning, only for the dead Pérez to return in

Unamuno's dream that night and taunt the author with his own presence in the novel that he is writing, thereby proving that the author is himself a work of fiction. Ultimately, as Barthes argues, the crucial subjectivity about a work such as this is that of the audience, which must disentangle meanings and decide for itself. In a similar fashion, Auster's *City of Glass* (1987) investigates the nature of authorship by interweaving stories of an author named Quinn, his pseudonymous authoring of a detective novel as Wilson, the detective in the novel named Work and, of course, Paul Auster. Like *Lucía y el sexo*, *City of Glass* begins with a phone call and a tumbling together of past and present, truth and reality; only 'much later, when [Quinn] was able to think about the things that happened to him, he would conclude that nothing was real except chance' (Auster 2004: 3). Like Unamuno's Augusto Pérez, Medem's Lorenzo and Lorenzo's Lucía, Auster's characters are engaged in a struggle between fiction and reality with their author: 'Wilson served as a kind of ventriloquist. Quinn himself was the dummy, and Work was the animated voice that gave purpose to the enterprise. [. . .] If Wilson did not exist, he nevertheless was the bridge that allowed Quinn to pass from himself into Work' (Auster 2004: 6). Yet this is all a ruse for Auster to investigate his own authorship of all three characters when Quinn takes a call from someone asking to speak to Paul Auster. 'There's no one here by that name', replies Quinn (Auster 2004: 7). Dashiel Hammett meets Kafka: Where a detective seeks the murderer, Auster seeks the nature of the character that asks the questions. This is not just a whodunnit, but a who *really* dunnit? Answer: The author.

Like Auster and Unamuno, Medem (and, by projection, Lorenzo) resembles the description offered of Proust by Barthes: 'By a radical reversal, instead of putting his life into his novel [. . .] he made of his very life a work for which his own book was the model' (1982: 144). But if Medem uses film to imagine himself as Lorenzo, it is remarkable that Lorenzo uses his novel to imagine himself as a rampant sex-god, projecting himself into Carlos 'the man with the world's biggest penis' and using a supremely phallic lighthouse '<i>' as his internet call-sign. Meanwhile, the three disciples of his godlike masculinity, Elena, Lucía and Belén, must also be considered figments of Lorenzo's fervid imagination for not only are they grateful for Lorenzo's lovemaking, they are also excellent cooks and nurturing of his creativity. Here is the chauvinist dream in triplicate: whore-cook-mother. How to redeem such an insufferable <i>? The answer lies in Lucía, like Sofía in *La ardilla roja*, being far more real than she appears and therefore resistant to the identity that Lorenzo imposes on her.

As representative of the author in the text, Lorenzo's experience of writing and madness confronts Medem with the symptoms that arise from addiction to fantasy. Lorenzo has much in common with Don Birnam (Ray Milland) in *The Lost Weekend* (1945), Jack Torrance (Jack Nicholson) in *The Shining* (1980), Sarah Morton (Charlotte Rampling) in *Swimming Pool* (2003) and Chow Mo Man (Tony Leung) in *2046* (2004). Of these Wong Kar Wai's *2046* is most comparable to *Lucía y el sexo* in that it is also a pseudo-sequel to its director's previous film about disaffected soulmates, *Fa yeung nin wa* (*In the Mood for Love*, 2001), which left him similarly frustrated at the vaccuum left by its unresolved ending. Just as Medem resurrects Ana from *Los amantes del Círculo Polar* in *Lucía y el sexo*, so Wong Kar Wai revives the protagonists of *Fa yeung nin wa* in *2046*, the parallel tale of a writer who is both masochistically unable and sadistically unwilling to return the love of a beautiful woman. Instead, Chow Mo Man displaces his real trauma onto the science-fiction tale of a time-travelling train taking people to 2046 to reclaim their memories (for 2046 is really the number of the hotel room where Chow lived and lost his one true love). The train never arrives because Chow, like Lorenzo, can never revisit the past and it is only in fiction that he can admit his life's great failing. The increasingly paranoid fiction of Lorenzo and Chow should be vicariously fulfilling, but it only frustrates the emotional isolation that leads to their emotional dependence on their imaginations. This becomes an addiction that separates them from reality and causes them to abuse the women who truly love them. In *2046* the woman is a beautiful prostitute, in *Lucía y el sexo* she is Lucía, who promises love and sex (as do prostitutes) to Lorenzo, but is also a real woman who suffers the burden of comparison with the fantasy women in his writing. Like Chow's imagining of 2046, Lorenzo's tropical island symbolises his unreachable future, for one must recall that *Lucía y el sexo* juxtaposes scenes from the future on the island that are taken from *Lucía, un rayo de sol* with the sordid backstories from the novel *Sexo, antes del sol*, wherein its author Lorenzo is inexorably trapped. In accordance with Barthes, who states 'the Author, when believed in, is always conceived of as the past of his own book: book and author stand automatically on a single line divided into a before and after' (1982: 145), Chow must abandon fiction in order to reach 2046, just as Lorenzo must do likewise if he is ever to reach the island.

Consequently, the physical terrain of Formentera is, like the memory of 2046, also a psychological landscape in which the Freudian motifs that symbolise Lorenzo's trauma are writ appropriately large in the unrequited lust between a lighthouse and a hole in the ground.

Following Barthes and as always with Medem, 'everything is to be *disentangled*, nothing *deciphered*' (Barthes 1982: 147). Medem intends that meaning is not found in the fractal narrative of *Lucía y el sexo* but in the disentangling of it by an audience that in the act of disentangling is engaged in a process of self-exploration. Lorenzo's audience/reader is, of course, Lucía, who is typically unable to distinguish between reality and fiction, and acts like a stalker of the kind that believes celebrities are their friends and even soulmates. However, the fact that Paz Vega is sexually attractive erases much of the creepiness of her first encounter with Lorenzo and suggests it is Lorenzo's fantasy that Lucía is consciously representing. It is even likely that Lucía has assumed the traits of the female protagonist of Lorenzo's first novel in order to shore up her own lack of identity and seduce him, because there is nothing more attractive to an insecure writer than flattery and imitation is its most sincere form. Lucía may seem sweet but she is deranged and so lacking in identity that she has assumed a surrogate one after reading a novel by an author to whom she subsequently declares herself romantically. Indeed, the ruse is common to stalkers, who are often the victims of emotional trauma stemming from neglect that has left them bereft of a reasonable sense of identity and, in response, commonly subsume their trauma into the fiction of their relationship with others (Flora 2004). The meeting between Lorenzo and Lucía is thus one of two voids, wherein two negatives make the plus that is their seeming escape from psychological disarray, which is also the case when the two stories that lack their other halves (*Lucía, un rayo de sol* and *Sexo, antes del sol*) meet in *Lucía y el sexo* and thereby fill the void that dominates Basque art and culture, allowing Medem to end his film at a desired distance from Basqueness and the Basque conflict.

Lucía's escape from feeling herself annulled into a relationship with a male who takes advantage of her condition to impose an identity is markedly similar to that of Sofía's relationship with J in *La ardilla roja*. Just as Lucía and Sofía search for new identities, so do the two blocked artists in need of a new muse: the writer Lorenzo and the musician J. Thus, just as J returns to writing songs after his adventure with Sofía, so Lorenzo's creative drought ends fortuitously when he buys a pack of the appropriately named Lucky Strike cigarettes and is approached by Lucía, who apparently reconnects the circuit between his sexual and his creative arousal. Indeed, the whole sequence of their meeting is overflowing with peripheral details that later resurface in Lorenzo's fiction, including the attack dog seen on the bar's television, the portentous name of Lucía's restaurant Mediterráneo across the street, and the glowing picture of the moonlit tropical island on the front of the cigarette machine that forms the backdrop to their conversation. Like J, Lorenzo is a moral rapist who latches onto Lucía as the source of his inspiration and renewed identity and thereafter their obsessive, exclusive relationship echoes both *La ardilla roja* and *Los amantes del Círculo Polar* in its observation of the manner in which a couple create and shape each other in a relationship. 'Do whatever you want to me', Lucía tells Lorenzo, who does exactly that in bursts of sexual activity. Yet Lorenzo also makes an insensitive comparison of their sexual exploits with the sex that he once enjoyed with Elena and he mixes elements of both Elena and Lucía to create the protagonist of his new novel.

This fragmentation and reconstruction of characters is emphasised in the sex scenes being based upon the aesthetics of collage and the

9 Lorenzo (Tristán Ulloa) meets Lucía (Paz Vega) in *Lucía y el sexo*

compartmentalisation of the senses that are both primary tenets of postmodernism, which holds that the individual (and the narrative) is not a unified entity but a composition of fragments. Just as *Lucía y el sexo* illustrates what Barry Jordan and Rikki Morgan-Tamosunas identify as the 'postmodern framework of the de-legitimisation of knowledges, the challenge to fixed identities' (Jordan and Morgan-Tamosunas 2000: 5), so each bout of lovemaking between Lorenzo and Lucía is composed of a montage of body parts that represents their deliriously sensual experience of blurring into each other. Lucía wakes Lorenzo by dipping her nipple to his lips and their erotic games progress into Lorenzo tasting and guessing parts of Lucía from her elbow to her anus. Lorenzo then delights in mixing these sensations by authoring the protagonist of his second novel as a hybrid collage of Lucía and Elena that combines Elena's skill with paellas, for example, with Lucía being cared for by her grandmother after the deaths of her parents and brother in a car crash: 'The restaurant became famous in Madrid thanks to the paellas of that lonely young women, who didn't speak, who still recalled her grandmother buried in the village next to her parents.' On another level, the ruse also echoes the delight expressed by Medem at seamlessly cutting between his actors and their body doubles in the editing of the same sequence and it is symptomatic of Medem's filmic rather than literary relationship with his characters that Lucía's fragmentation should be rendered on film when Lorenzo introduces a Polaroid camera into their lovemaking. Again, body parts are separated and made anonymous in the paradoxically explicit and blurry close-ups. These Polaroids correspond to the 'new beauty' that David Thomson found in the films of Jean Luc Godard and called 'the beginning of modern cinema – uncomposed, but snapped' (1998: 292). However, Lorenzo's transposition of parts of Lucía into his fiction weakens her whole identity in the real world, just as underlying this postmodernist concept of collage is the idea of an author's creation of fictional characters from details of the people in his life, which is vital to a disentangling of the films of Medem, particularly in his suspicion of fatally weakening his real-life sister's identity by transposing her into her namesake in *Los amantes del Círculo Polar*. Lorenzo's theft of Lucía's identity culminates in the shot of her naked reflection in his unplugged computer monitor suggesting she is trapped on the inside and helplessly looking out. Meanwhile, the prioritising of Lorenzo's subjectivity suggests that Elena and Belén have similarly resulted from his fearful neuroses, but his inability to engage with any of the

10 Lucía (Paz Vega) trapped in Lorenzo's novel in *Lucía y el sexo*

emotional responsibilities, psychological demands or physical consequences that arise from his relationships, which is illustrated by a cut from Lucía's blissful orgasm to Elena's painful giving birth to Luna, results in his self-absorption and destruction in morbid, masturbatory sex fantasies that prompt the knowing Lucía's estrangement from sex on the island, even to the extent of refusing to succumb to the temptation of the impressive penis that Lorenzo imagines for his alter ego Carlos.

The entangling of scenes from *Sexo, antes del sol* and *Lucía, un rayo de sol* continues with Lorenzo's memories of Elena inspiring a story about his daughter Luna, who was conceived on Lorenzo's birthday at about the same time as he was born and at the same time as he received the news of her existence at his own birthday party from Pepe, who tells him, 'If you write this well, it could be the story of your life.' Like the coincidences that Ana links up to tell the story of her life in *Los amantes del Círculo Polar*, this chain of coincidences is linked to Lorenzo's conception of his new novel and the authorial identity that prompts him to spend his afternoons with Luna and her nanny Belén (Elena Anaya). His writer's compulsion to exploit their nascent relationship for the good of his novel bests any parental responsibility he might have felt and marks Lorenzo's first appearance in his own fiction in a scene that was initially the script's first, in which he converses with Luna on the island and explores his real and fictional creation of her as well as Luna's own awareness of it:

> Would you like me to be your father?
> Can you?
> If you want me to, yes; but in secret.
> My real father!

Lorenzo urges his child in both fact and fiction to keep the secret of her biological and literary creation because, as he explains, its telling would cause the sea to drop and the mountains to be inverted, thereby revealing all the secrets that lie beneath the island. But this is exactly what happens when Lucía reads his novel surreptitiously and deduces that the fictional daughter is also real. Thinking herself the reason for Lorenzo's fresh burst of creativity, Lucía strokes his hair but Medem cuts to Lorenzo's hand stroking that of Luna, thereby indicating the author's relapse into a limbo between fiction and reality, a problem that intensifies as Lorenzo asks questions of his computer screen and Belén answers him with details of sexual fantasies that Lorenzo then provokes her into realising so that her experiences might feed his fiction. The increasingly aroused and creatively mercenary Lorenzo loses touch with reality and drifts into the fiction that he is creating as shown by his reflection emerging from the television screen to ravish Belén. His loss to his fiction is then underlined by a cut to Lucía reading the text of Lorenzo and Belén's tryst on his monitor and, in a desperate attempt at remaining his muse, stripping naked and trying to rouse Lorenzo, whose catatonic unresponsiveness with her is juxtaposed with a shot of him devouring Belén.

Most crucially, this postmodern analysis of the *deus ex machina* of the author in his fiction is revealed to be both literal and metaphorical when Belén passes Lorenzo a video of one of her mother's porn films and its back cover reveals a photograph of Julio Medem himself directing his actors. On one level, this is Medem's tongue-in-cheek, pre-emptive attack on those who might condemn *Lucía y el sexo* as pornography, but it is also Medem reminding Lorenzo exactly who controls and directs the fantasy and a clear echo of Unamuno's attempt to do the same in *Niebla*. Unamuno and Augusto Pérez, like Medem and Lorenzo, and like Paul Auster, Quinn, Wilson and Work are all collages of the author and his protagonist, just as from this point on *Lucía y el sexo* is a collage of reality and fiction in which the plight of the author who loses his identity in his writing is juxtaposed with

Lucía's isle-bound quest for hers. Lorenzo forces fate by having Belén seduce him, but his selfish, devouring nature is revealed in the symbol of the dog that kills his daughter. The link between the male ego and this dog is underlined by Elena comparing it to her boyfriend and Belén threatening it with castration, while Lorenzo gnaws greedily on a chicken bone with a bag of dog food behind him. When the dog attacks, Lorenzo panics, both as writer and as the protagonist of the novel that he is writing. Having written himself into a corner when faced with Belén's seduction of him, the dog killing Luna provides him with a perhaps appropriately clumsy plot device (cf. the machination of the crocodile attack in the Charlie Kaufman scripted *Adaptation* [2002]). He breaks a window and runs away, leaving Belén to slash her wrists with a piece of the broken pane and Lucía to try and rouse him the next morning when he can no longer distinguish between reality, dream or fiction: 'I'm not here anymore. I've gone and I can't come back.'

In a venal attempt at evading responsibility for his authorship of the tragedy, Lorenzo displaces his guilt onto Belén, her mother Manuela and Carlos by sadistically writing of them as being infected with his own perversity: 'The three of them were diseased with sex. Stinking, rotten sex.' Lorenzo writes them into a literally sickening orgy that he also joins as a victim of the compulsive and sadistic voyeurism that governs his authorship: 'That selfish, cowardly man despised himself so intensely and without mercy that he allowed himself no pardon, only death.' Lorenzo dreams of escape by killing off his characters and acts upon it by utilising the guise of Carlos in his fiction to slash the wrists of Belén and her mother. But all this degeneracy from morbid introspection is abhorred by Lucía, who berates him: 'You're sick, Lorenzo. You're sick with yourself, with your need to be a writer and nothing more.' Yet her attempt at extricating Lorenzo from his fiction by differentiating between them is ineffective partly because, as Barthes states, 'once the author is removed, the claim to decipher a text becomes quite futile' (1982: 147) and partly because Lorenzo's tapping into the creativity of the Dionysian well of his subconscious that lies beneath his frustrated Apollonian consciousness satisfies a need for meaning within the Self in his fiction that counters his loss of meaning in the real world. But Lorenzo's immersion in his own fiction leads to the madness of a nihilistic ideology, where his world, being fictional, is devoid of meaning, his physical condition is irrelevant and his location is arbitrary.

The resolution of *Lucía y el sexo* is, like all of Medem's fictions, determined by emotional investment in a fantasy making it real. Without her author Lucía has nothing to do on the island besides mope about on a moped, avoid sex as a kind of meditative abstinence and reflect upon whether the relationship she once made real with Lorenzo by the emotion she invested in it had ever inspired enough genuine love in him to cure him of his enslavement to his fiction. Heading towards the light, she inevitably ends up at the lighthouse, where she falls down the hole that seems to symbolise the first advantage of Lorenzo's story; but nothing happens. Instead of reappearing in the middle of the story, she lands bruised and sodden at the bottom of the hole. The most optimistic diagnosis is that she is real. Meanwhile, Lorenzo finds redemption by anonymously resuming his relationship with the grieving Elena via the chatroom about Mediterranean cuisine and writing a new fiction for her by e-mail, one that imaginatively bypasses grief and any obligation to take responsibility for the death of their daughter by erasing its occurrence and substituting a more satisfying ending instead. This, he tells her, is a story with advantages, for when it reaches the end it falls down a hole and reappears in its middle from where he can change the plot 'if you let me, if you give me time'. Thus the 'dead' author is revived by his reader in illustration of Barthes' dictum that 'a text's unity lies not in its origin but in its destination' (1982: 148). This collaboration between them is represented by Lorenzo's reflection in his monitor being juxtaposed with that of Elena in her computer screen while she reads as the musical motif of the waltz appears and author and reader take turns reading until their reflections are conjoined and they are both transported by the fiction towards a happy ending for Ana from *Los amantes del Círculo Polar* and all the characters of *Lucía y el sexo* that is engineered on what Lorenzo calls 'the island of dreams, where nobody dies'. Or rather, a happy middle; for just before the credits run backwards, the film ends how Lorenzo promised it would, by falling down a hole and reappearing in the chronological centre of the story, three years previously, half-way between Lorenzo's tryst with Elena and the final reunion on the island, with Elena and their resurrected infant daughter Luna strolling in the square beneath Lorenzo's apartment, while Lucía sings at his sunny window and Lorenzo writes enthusiastically beside her.

The adage that you take your problems with you wherever you go is clearly not relevant to those who escape into fiction because their fates can be transformed. This is, of course, one of the reasons why audiences watch films and, in cases such as this, the reason why filmmakers make them. *Lucía y el sexo* may finally resemble a Surrealist meditation on love, loss and longing that recalls *Un chien andalou* (1929) in its bewildering time-shifts and tangential narratives that both demand and deny rational interpretation, but it is also light, bright, flirtatious and blessed with ample nudity, which made it an excellent prospect for the international festival and arthouse circuit. It was well received in the film festivals of Toronto, London, Rotterdam, San Francisco, Karlovy, Dublin and Sundance, where its screening in the World Cinema section inspired a minor scuffle between international distribution companies. In a major investment in its potential in the American market, Palm Pictures orchestrated a gradual roll-out from New York and Los Angeles that was boosted by the scandal raised in Seattle, where, despite Medem winning the Emerging Master Award at its film festival, *The Seattle Times* and *The Seattle Post-Intelligencer* refused to carry advertising for the unrated film. A cut and rated version was also prepared and released to cinemas and on DVD alongside the unrated version that Fernando Bovaira claims was made with Medem's full agreement: 'If Julio had told us he didn't want to cut the film, we wouldn't have cut it. We had his complete authorization' [17]. This excision of the most explicit scenes of sexual arousal and activity suggested that Medem was eager to tailor his work to the market, even to its detriment, for the censored and rated version is severely weakened by the absence of realism in the sex scenes and the lessened emphasis on sex means that the film's title indicates a tease rather than a treatise. The cut version was more successful, however, as only 1% of the 35,000 screens in North America play subtitled fare and very few of these accept unrated films. The official box office for the USA and Canada combined totalled € 1,646,614 (almost a third of the € 5,255,843 total take to date) (Sogecine 2004). *Lucía y el sexo* was also profitable for Metro-Tartan in the UK (€ 588,000), where a teaser campaign saw a series of ads appear in the lonely hearts column of *The Guardian* newspaper beginning 'Lucia seeking sex . . . ' (Anon 2002: 43), which totally misrepresented the character. *Lucía y el sexo* was distributed throughout Europe and the new markets of Croatia, Turkey and Israel. Its marketing was based upon a summery and sexually bedraggled portrait of Paz Vega perched on her moped with the blurred lighthouse behind her, though the tease of an uncovered nipple that was thought charmingly sexy in most of Europe was nervously airbrushed out in the UK, North America and elsewhere.

Reviewers were either besotted or bemused, though Medem remains adamantly proud: 'I love Lucía very much. She's the character of mine I love the most' [5]. At this journey's end of exile from the Basque Country and its labyrinthine conflict, Lorenzo accepts the joy as well as the burden of authorship on behalf of his creator, and fabricates an optimistic new beginning for Lucía, Elena and Luna, one that was commercially very successful. Redemption, resurrection and profit were therefore combined in Medem's engineering of a second chance for Lorenzo and, of course, Ana. The coincidence of Elena passing beneath Lorenzo's window provided a new link in the chain that Ana once claimed could be used to tell the story of her life. Like Lola in *Lola rennt*, Lorenzo, it is hoped, has learned enough from the mistakes in one life to not commit them in another. This was a metaphysical hope made tangible in a final fade to white that now inspired Medem to return from this peaceful distance from the Basque Country to deal with the subject of the Basque conflict head on with what he believed was objectivity and self-knowledge. From a perspective that seemed far enough away to enable both 'the exile's detachment' that is diagnosed by Edward Said (2002: 185) and the 'dynamics of differentiation' that are described by Isabel Santaolalla (1998: 333), Medem now proposed symmetry as a solution to the conflict of the Basque Country that he now returned to with *La pelota vasca*. Having completed his journey into exile, he was returning to his roots.

8

Framing fearful symmetry: *La pelota vasca: la piel contra la piedra* (2003)

The crack of a hard rubber ball against a concrete wall is the opening shot of Medem's documentary *La pelota vasca: la piel contra la piedra*. The sound is an aural symbol, an onomatopoeic metaphor for a notion of the suffering 'skin' of the Basque people and the intransigent 'stone' of the Basque conflict. *La pelota vasca* is a polyphonic patchwork of speakers on this subject, whose range of perspectives and depth of feeling are interwoven in an inclusive montage that, in terms of finding a solution, is both open-minded and, inevitably, open-ended. It is also a stylish transposition of the structure and themes of the fictional films that Medem had written and directed into the documentary genre for the purpose of elaborating some symmetrical order out of the crushing complexity of its subject. Conceived of as merely a preparatory personal project for *Aitor: la piel contra la piedra*, Medem's long-cherished 'opera of the Basque conflict' [1], *La pelota vasca* came about because of the Basque elections of May 2001, when Spanish national television's reporting had seemed to Medem to carry 'an unacceptable bias' [2] that allowed Spanish nationalism to criminalise Basque nationalism. In beginning *La pelota vasca*, Medem claimed he had no greater ambition than to prepare himself for *Aitor* by interviewing those with memories and opinions to spare about the history, cultural identity and politics of the Basque Country, but it became a project that would provoke and inspire months of argument in the Spanish media, turning Medem into a rallying point for those who believed that freedom of expression and dialogue about political affairs was being stifled by a singular and censorious policy of containment and dogmatism, while, for others, he became the perpetrator of an apology for terrorism that demanded censure.

The origins of *La pelota vasca* lie in 1996, when Medem had left the Basque Country to live in Madrid after separating from his wife during the filming of *Tierra* and suffering the death of his father as well as the commercial and critical disappointment of *Tierra*. 1996 was also the year that Felipe González's PSOE government was voted out of office and the centre-right Partido Popular came to power under the presidency of José María Aznar. Medem spent several weeks in his brother's apartment in Paris and wrote two scripts, one about hate and one about love. The first was *Aitz: viaje al fondo del mar* (*Aitz: Journey to the Bottom of the Sea*) and the second was *Los amantes del Círculo Polar*. In writing *Aitz*, Medem had aimed to examine his confused ideas about the Basque Country he had just abandoned, but he was disturbed by an ability to hate that dominated the characters whose subjectivities he characteristically assumed in their writing. With *Los amantes del círculo polar* he focussed on his own experience of lost love, both conjugal and paternal, and proposed instead the idealisation of an eternal love in writing a mature and melancholic film whose commercial and critical success would establish his international status. *Aitz* remained in limbo while Medem made *Lucía y el sexo*, another commercial triumph that effected a poignant contrast with Medem's distress at the death of his sister during its making. The light and space of the natural setting of Formentera in *Lucía y el sexo* also jarred with the claustrophobia that Medem observed in, 'el auge del nacionalismo ultraespañol de Aznar, que se ha ido haciendo insoportable en su confrontación totalitaria contra el nacionalismo vasco'(Medem 2003a: 35) (the rise in the ultra-Spanish nationalism of Aznar, who has become unbearable in his totalitarian confrontation with Basque nationalism). Nevertheless, although the intense solipsism of *Lucía y el sexo* seemed to many to underline Medem's wilful indulgence in panacean fantasy, the physical and thematic distancing from the Basque Country had allowed him to develop what he claimed was the objectivity necessary for a reworking of the script of *Aitz* around ideas about the contemporary Basque Country.

Urging himself not to hate in the process of assuming once more the subjectivity of his characters, Medem worked on a rewrite of *Aitz* that he titled *Aitor: la piel contra la piedra* (*Aitor: The Skin against the Stone*). *Aitor* is a Basque word that stems from *aitz* (stone) and speaks of a mythic sense of masculinity. *Aitor* can also mean father and, in assuming the rôle of Aitor in his writing, Medem was perhaps facing up to middle age and the mantle of responsible fatherhood that had been left vacant by the death of his own. In creating the character of Aitor, Medem was also haunted by the figure of the grandfather Manuel Irigibel in *Vacas*, whose children and grandchildren had been torn between two rival families. Like Manuel, Aitor was a character who thrashed against the suffocating traditions of Basque masculinity that are integral to notions of Basque identity and nationhood, but whereas the effort turned Manuel insane, Aitor's superior strength, impartiality and symbolic crusade created a magical realist uprising that caused an army of the dead that lives inside the Basque forests to sing to him in a chorus of reconciliation and forgiveness as they fell from the trees. The script became an opera, the complexity and scale of which meant that Medem decided upon a preparatory documentary approach to the subject to be called *La pelota vasca: la piel contra la piedra*. The documentary and the fiction were to function as siblings, brother fact and sister fiction, for they shared the same surname (*la piel contra la piedra*) as well as a concern for rendering the Basque conflict through different subjectivities. *La pelota vasca* would be in honour of the mythic Aitor, who, due to Medem's efforts at equanimity during the writing of the script, had become a character unable to hate and therefore at an equal distance from all sides in the Basque conflict. The documentary would even be shot and edited from the point of view of Aitor, this character incapable of hate and devoid of bias, prejudice and suspicion, allowing Medem to reconcile his creative energy with the subject of hate. It would also require his complete immersion in the conflict that still tied him to his birthplace and the Basque side of his family that he describes as being 'very united around the idea of Basqueness. They treat it with great pride, which seems to me a noble and interesting sentiment' [4].

Born in San Sebastian, Medem carries a mix of German and Valencian blood from his father, and Basque and French blood from his mother. The family moved to Madrid in time for Medem to begin his secondary school education and for Medem, as for many Basque artists and filmmakers who moved to Madrid, Basqueness became a thing of curiosity and longing accompanied by a sentimental but superficial affiliation to Basque nationalist beliefs. After leaving school, he studied at the University of the Basque Country and graduated in 1985, but a decade later he returned to Madrid, where he still resides. *La pelota vasca* was not just a way to confront aspects of the Basque Country that he believed were blocking political negotiations but had also been a long time clogging his own creativity. Within the Basque conflict he identified the 'devastador problema moral de la violencia [y] un grave y crónico trastorno de origen político que en los últimos años ha desembocado en la actual guerra (política) entre los Gobiernos español y vasco' (2003a: 35) (the devastating moral problem of violence [and] a grave and chronic disorder of political origin that in recent years has resulted in the actual (political) war between the Spanish and Basque governments). At the start of filming for *La pelota vasca* he admitted that his personal search for hatelessness seemed frivolous when compared to the situation of 'todas aquellas personas que tienen motivos profundos para odiar; me refiero a los que sufren en propia carne y alma la violencia relacionada con el conflicto vasco' (2003a: 35) (all those people with deep reasons to hate, those who suffered in their body and soul the violence related to the Basque conflict), but he started filming anyway, using the privilege and status of his auteurism to secure access to many interviewees.

Without knowing if the material could ever be compiled into a commercially viable documentary, Medem shot *La pelota vasca* between May and July 2002 with two small digital cameras and a team of ten including executive producer Koldo Zuazua, production assistant Silvia Gómez, assistant director (and Medem's partner) Montse Sanz and co-interviewer Ione Hernández. Zuazua, like Medem, was born in San Sebastian, though he first met the director in Madrid in December 2001 while working alongside Montse Sanz on *Piedras* (2001). Zuazua recalls that Medem described *La pelota vasca* as 'an enriching project that would help him to contemplate reality in a more objective manner' [13]. Medem financed the project with his profits from *Lucía y el sexo* after applications for funding were rejected by ICCA (Institut Catalá del Crèdit Agrari) and FORTA (Federación de Organismos de Radio y Televisión Autonómicas). To his own money was added a bank loan based on the pre-sale of transmission rights to Basque television that was later joined by investment from Canal Plus, which agreed a three-episode documentary series, and three private donations from Medem's brother Álvaro, the independent producer Pedro Zaratiegi and Mireia Lluch, daughter of the socialist Catalan politician Ernest Lluch killed by ETA, who offered Medem her inheritance so that he might finish what she considered to be a worthy and important film.

The project was based in San Sebastian and the team was strengthened by the addition of researcher and interviewer in Euskera Maider Oleaga, who compiled a dossier of suitable interviewees based on a list of a hundred profiles drawn up by Medem. Medem wrote an

11 Julio Medem during the filming of *La pelota vasca: la piel contra la piedra*

open letter describing his intentions to these potential interviewees and with Zuazua and Oleaga began contacting these people by telephone and e-mail as well as in person because, as Zuazua states, 'there was a lot of distrust, fear and rejection, and there were profiles that we never got to fill' [13]. Medem wanted to film in wide open natural landscapes to achieve a sense of space and depth that was redolent of the primary motif and theme in Basque art and scultpure and also suggestive of the complementary aesthetic of juxtaposition by being quite opposite from the usual documentary convention of interviewing politicians and academics against dark, claustrophobic backgrounds such as bookshelf-filled offices. Medem hoped that the natural, supposedly neutral locations would prevent any subliminal visual bias to their testimonies and believed that his isolation of each individual erased the tensions that might have arisen from a background containing anything that could be identified as a symbol of oppression or authority. It was also important that the Basque landscape have this protagonism because of its defining rôle in accounts of its history, conflicts and individuals; thus Zuazua spent a great deal of time scouting locations and matching interviewees to spaces that often had to be examined and approved by their bodyguards. The interviews lasted an average of forty minutes but some took five hours. Medem's intention was always to interview as many people as possible from all sides of the Basque conflict and then edit them together to create a dialogue where previously none had been possible: 'I wanted a polyphony. I wanted the maximum possible diversity' [4]. Thus he travelled Spain with a camera and a CD of music by the Basque composer and singer Mikel Laboa playing on such a constant loop that it imposed itself on his mental editing of the film and became the natural soundtrack to the documentary. He learned the skill of interviewing as he went along, but there were complications with those who agreed to be interviewed but then refused to be included in the edit. Medem attempted to maintain his objectivity in the venture by staying at what he described as 'a fearful distance' [4] while his commitment to the project fed off awareness that it was allowing him the rare privilege of interviewing these people. Silvia Gómez asserts that 'Julio was personally committed to being objective. He had his ideas, but there were never any political discussions about the purpose of the project, quite the contrary' [7].

Crucial support for the project came from the Basque author Bernardo Atxaga, who expressed full and clear empathy with Medem's undertaking, having himself been at the forefront of the cultural analysis of the modern Basque Country with debate over his novels *Obabakoak* (a major influence on *Vacas*), *El hombre solo*, *Esos cielos* and *El hijo del acordionista* (see Jones 2006). Medem asserts that the positioning of Atxaga as preface and postscript of *La pelota vasca* was deliberate and symbolic:

> Atxaga can comment on the Basque Country because he holds this position of objectivity. He can describe all sides of the Basque conflict through the subjectivity of the characters he creates. In that sense, Atxaga represents me. He's the person with whom I identify. [4]

Again, therefore, as in his fictions, Medem identified himself in his text by an act of empathy with Atxaga that also elevated his own status as filmmaker to that of the author credited with revitalising the modern Basque language in his literature. Medem's identification with Atxaga clearly reflected his own ambitions to revitalise Basque cinema that he had championed as a film critic on the newspaper *La voz de Euskadi* and it helped turn *La pelota vasca* into a project with far greater ambitions than he had originally imagined. Thereafter he aimed to complete two or three interviews a day, his intention being 'ver el odio sin odiarlo' (2003a: 35) (to see hate without hating it). He conducted two thirds of the interviews himself with Oleaga doing those in Euskera and Ione Hernández interviewing the families of convicted members of ETA on the coach trip to their prison in Huelva, southern Spain. Hernández, who is also from San Sebastian, had known Medem since appearing as an extra in a film that he had edited in 1988 called *La espalda del cielo*. She claims she was hired because 'Julio realised very early on that the documentary was excessively political and was missing the real pain of the victims but, because of the recent death of his sister, it was too difficult for him to face the victims so he asked me to go on the coach' [11]. She spent three days on the coach there and back with the families but waited outside the prison while they spent half an hour inside and ended up with seven hours of footage. She describes the coach as 'a very enclosed environment that makes one feel like an intruder' [11] but sympathises very strongly with her interviewees: 'I wanted to capture the human side and the tragedy of these people whose pain is beyond any political conflict' [11].

Medem set about structuring the footage from a total of 103 interviews in the editing, for which he deliberately assumed full responsibility, while Zuazua got on with securing the rights for newsreel, film clips and photographic images. Missing and missed, as the film's preface would make clear, were members of the ruling Partido Popular with whom Medem had been negotiating since the second week of filming, Fernando Savater of the *Basta Ya!* anti-terrorist social movement, and current members of ETA as well of the Association of Victims of Terrorism, a group which would later be vociferous in their condemnation of the documentary when picketing the Spanish Film Academy Awards ceremony in January 2004. Medem assembled a marathon rough cut on his home computer in the editing studio adjacent to what was his apartment building near Madrid's Plaza Mayor. In the midst of editing, the taskbar of his computer screen held numerous trial edits, some of which would become whole scenes in *La pelota vasca*, while others were exercises in rhythm, effect and juxtaposition. He also considered an unedited clip of the testimony of ex-terrorist Anika Gil in which she spoke disgustedly of being tortured by Spanish security forces. Come the September 2003 release of *La pelota vasca*, the inclusion of this speaker would provoke many critics into questioning the validity of her declaration and its inclusion in the documentary. For an opposite view, Ione Hernández argues that Gil's testimony was truthful because she spoke in Euskera but quoted her torturers in Spanish: 'That's where you realise she hasn't invented anything' [11].

However, the testimony spoke of a different problem for Medem, who feared undermining the authenticity of the speaker by editing. This quandary, which has long plagued documentary filmmakers, was especially problematic for Medem because of its relation to his emphasis on competing subjectivities in his fictions:

The premise of the documentary is pure objectivity. The aim is not to manipulate anything, to just show the faces and hear the testimonies. But what happens is, while you're editing, your point of view emerges. Even though you don't want it to, it does. [4]

Gradually, he felt the speakers in *La pelota vasca* taking sides with their testimonies being increasingly polarised around what he described as 'Basque nationalism and the anti-Basque nationalism of the Spanish government' [3] while he struggled to remain resolutely impartial at its centre. As these sides drew further apart, the innate controversy of the visual and aural debate opened up a void at the centre of the documentary that was exacerbated by the absence of key spokespersons from ETA and the Partido Popular. Instead of being invalidated by this lack, however, *La pelota vasca* exalted this void as evidence of its relation to the tradition of its represention in Basque art. Ultimately, Medem's isolation in the editing process, both physically at his computer and psychologically in his determined equidistance from both sides, saw him latch onto the metaphor of a bird that flies in a straight line through the void at the centre of the conflict and use the animal catalyst as a symbol of his own subjectivity:

I looked for the film's dignity and tried to maintain the necessary distance and out of that came this idea of the bird flying through this gorge. Well, that's me. Here I am. And around me are all the sides of the Basque conflict. [4]

The metaphor also inspired Medem's somewhat obtuse essay on the production of *La pelota vasca* that he called *Un pájaro vuela dentro de una garganta* (2003a: 35) (A bird is flying through a gorge).

Medem assembled *La pelota vasca* as if it were a jigsaw by dividing out the pieces in sections. First, he placed the testimony of the multi-faceted Bernardo Atxaga at the corners; but between Atxaga's opening description of the Basque Country as an isolated archipelago and his closing hopes for it to become a multicultural city there remained cacophony rather than polyphony. Sorting through the mass of opinions, experiences and reflections was a complex and gargantuan task. Says Medem:

The first time I looked through it all I felt very humble. I had no idea how to make a film from it all until I started editing. Then I just felt lost, overwhelmed and suffocated by the project, by the responsibility of dealing with all these marvellous and necessary voices. I couldn't see the film in my head. I could only see a million ways of putting it together. [3]

Undeterred, he employed an assistant and began piecing together the edges of this jigsaw with geographical, linguistic, racial and cultural arguments invoked for and against the cause of Basque nationalism, separatism and independence. He grouped declarations that corresponded to specific chapters in Basque history, matching and juxtaposing testimonies that explained and argued how the Basques reside in seven provinces with three on the French side of the Pyrenees and four on the Spanish side that bear the collective name Euskadi, a term invented in 1896 by the father of modern Basque nationalism Sabino Arana to identify a utopian, autonomous Basque nation that remains both a nationalist dream and a political aim. In addition, many Basques invoke the term Euskal Herria, meaning 'the land of the Basque speakers' (which features in *La ardilla roja* when J pointedly gives a false address), to describe their linguistically-determined territory and cause because, as politicians frequently protest and academics constantly puzzle, the Basque language of Euskera (and therefore, perhaps, those who speak it) cannot be linked to any other. The question of the language and the inclusion of Euskera-speaking interviewees immediately added colour and shape to Medem's picture, for the language was sharp and angular in sound, staccato in its rhythms and echoed in the soundtrack by the voice of Mikel Laboa.

The accumulation of history gave an irrefutable solidity to the documentary with speakers explaining to offscreen interviewers (for Medem, Hernández and Oleaga are never seen and their voices are never heard) that the Basques had lived according to ancient laws and privileges called *Fueros* that they defended and lost in the Carlist Wars of the nineteenth century. Consequently, the 1890s saw the establishment of the Basque Nationalist Party (PNV), which responded to Carlist defeat and the immigration of non-Basques to the Vizcaya province with a nationalism that advocated the reinstatement of the *Fueros* and the dominion of Euskera. Then, in a poignant and pointed montage, Medem demonstrated that the fledgling Basque film industry had supported this aim with propagandist travelogues and rural melodramas that celebrated a romantic notion of a unique landscape and nationhood that was threatened by industrialisation and immigration. The origins of the present conflict emerged as speakers argued the history of the Spanish Civil War (1936–39) and the dictatorship (1939–75). Newsreel from the Basque-language television channel ETB1 and film archives began to intercede: Gernika is bombed and people flee through smoke, protestors are beaten back by police, smoking metal knots of cars are doused with hoses and coffins draped in flags are passed over crowds. And then, believing he had the edges to the puzzle firmly interlocked, Medem proceeded to sort the colours of myriad political differences. Contrary to the authorial control of characters in his fictions, he now faced the unwieldy consequences of having promised freedom of expression to his interviewees. In addition, if his care with chronology had provided a relatively impartial context for their declarations, his response to the subject now under debate was inevitably coloured by his own memories of the Basque Country. By 1958, the year of his birth, some Basques had committed themselves to the realisation of an independent Basque state based on an interpretation of Marxism and militancy for the sake of cultural and linguistic emancipation. The group they formed was EKIN, which begat ETA, which became violent in its campaign in 1968, the same year that Néstor Basterretxea and Fernando Larruquert released the epic Basque documentary *Ama lur* (*Tierra madre/Motherland*) (Stone 2006). *Ama lur* recorded and celebrated the cultural identity of the Basque Country in a 103 minute montage of musical and rural customs and traditions that was a crucial reference point for Medem, whose inclusion of several excerpts from *Ama lur* testifies to his ambitious positioning of *La pelota vasca* within the contentious but illustrious tradition of documentary filmmaking in the Basque Country.

Following Franco's death in 1975, Spain's transition to democracy and the 1978 Constitution that allowed for the declaration of a Statute of Autonomy for the Basque Country in 1979, the first autonomous PNV Basque government had taken up the challenge set by *Ama Lur* and dedicated itself to the task of preserving, re-building and promoting Basqueness by revitalising the indigenous film industry by investment in documentaries and features that had provided funding and apprenticeships for many, including Medem. That the history of Basque cinema is integral to *La pelota vasca* and its creator is complicated, however, because conflicting definitions of the Basque Country have been the subject of Basque cinema since its inception. Film reached the Basque Country at the end of the nineteenth century at the same time as nascent nationalism met socialism, when the growing urban population was becoming separated from its rural customs. Cinema was thus a kind of lifeline because the mythic Basque utopia was still visible on film. Short, silent travelogues and films about folklore promoted a unique cultural heritage and became a weapon in the cause of Basque nationalism, because the more authentic was the illusion of nationhood in the cinema, the more deeply felt was the lack of *real* nationhood by the audience when the lights came up (Stone 2001: 133–8). Franco's victory in the Civil War had brought fierce oppression to bear, however, including strict censorship and the outlawing of Euskera. In response, Basque filmmakers sought to create an equivalent visual language by applying the theories of Soviet cinema to the documentary medium in which they replicated the sharp angles and aggressive, intellectual montage of films such as Eisenstein's *Strike* (1924) and *Battleship Potemkin* (1925). Basque documentaries such as *Pelotari* (1964) were visual metaphors for the otherwise forbidden, sharp, staccato language of Euskera. Though rarely seen except in private film clubs that were a cover for political debate, these documentaries maintained the clandestine cultural legitimacy of Basque identity at a time when political expression was impossible. Nevertheless, many Basque activists in the early 1970s made a pragmatic decision to define Basqueness in terms of sensibility rather than language and so supported Euskera as an ideal but not a vital characteristic of Basqueness. The generous funding of an indigenous Basque film industry allowed filmmakers with no knowledge of the language such as Imanol Uribe and Medem to begin making films on Basque themes, as well as prompting production of the kind of period epics and rural dramas that Medem would deconstruct in *Vacas*. The move also imposed a definition of Basque cinema as one that was eligible for funding but was also maintained by a powerful documentary tradition in films such as Uribe's *El proceso de Burgos* (*The Burgos Trial*, 1979) (Stone 2001: 138–40) that would inform and influence *La pelota vasca*, which ironically was not funded by the Basque Ministry for Culture.

The 1980s and 1990s saw the Basque Nationalist Party (PNV), which had governed in coalition with the Socialists since 1985, gradually settle for autonomy rather than independence while the 1988 Ajurea Enea Pact, which was signed by all political parties except Herri Batasuna, proposed a commitment to non-violence and the reintegration of like-minded members of ETA. The Civil Guard were replaced by an autonomous police force but the GAL (Anti-Terrorist Liberation Groups with suspected backing from the Spanish government) were responsible for the deaths of at least twenty-seven alleged members of ETA. ETA was said to be losing faith, cause and members; but by the late 1990s there were signs of its re-organisation. During the two years in the making of *La pelota vasca*, ETA continued its violent activities while separatist political parties won up to 16% of the vote in regional Basque elections. The Basque-language newspaper *Egunkaria* was closed in February 2003 after state evidence suggested it was linked to the financing of terrorism and the Batasuna party was banned for similar reasons. While Medem edited, numerous key members of ETA were arrested in France, Aznar joined the 'crusade against terrorism' alongside George Bush and Tony Blair, and public demonstrations demanded peace in the Basque Country and Iraq. Until the 11 March 2004 bombing of commuter trains in Madrid by Islamic fundamentalists, however, Aznar had assured the voters that Spain was going well, and with 2004 the year of a royal wedding and, supposedly, the re-election of the Partido Popular, dissenting voices were at best spoilsports and at worst traitors. Thus, it was not so much the identification of Medem's single point of view in *La pelota vasca* that would eventually rankle but his inclusion of so many, for Medem's target polyphony was always bound to prove unacceptable to those who took dialogue to signify disunity.

Throughout 2003 there was also great debate over the Ibarretxe Plan and its call for the transfer of the Basque Country to a state of 'free association' with Spain. This plan was deemed unconstitutional by the Spanish government but its supporters still campaigned for its implementation and Medem chose to insert a description of this plan close to the conclusion of *La pelota vasca*. The jigsaw remained incomplete, however, as the two large pieces of ETA and the Partido Popular were missing. Many other ommissions, such as the anti-ETA demonstrations that followed the killing of the civil servant Miguel Ángel Blanco, would be corrected in the seven-hour Spanish DVD version of the documentary that may prove to be the most abiding legacy of the entire project, but the commercial release was inevitably identified as lacking. Nevertheless, Medem claimed:

> There's a sense to how the film is edited with the people who are included and even those who aren't. To remove something doesn't always mean to erase it. Sometimes silence is more visible, more audible. [4]

Indeed, the centrality of this lack was yet another indication that the documentary could be meaningfully contextualised within tradtitions of Basque art, sculpture and film. Although *La pelota vasca* includes discussion of the purpose of terrorism during democracy that is inevitably devalued by the absence of ETA and the Partido Popular, the absence of both does maintain the illusion of symmetry. If both had appeared the documentary would have been complete, but if either had appeared the documentary would have been imbalanced: as neither of them appear, the documentary is paradoxically incomplete but balanced. However, it also is precisely this dual absence that makes it seem as if the PP and ETA are equidistant reflections of each other, when one is a radical terrorist group and the other is a democratically elected government.

All these problems and consequences attest to the inevitable fact that the structuring of any 'raw' footage is arguably the necessary evil of any documentary, because raw material cannot articulate without structure and a filmmaker cannot structure without adding a point of view. Thus Medem ran the risk of expressing a perspective that would invalidate the authenticity of the footage. On the other hand, films commonly impose a framework on history and the more linear the narrative, the more comprehensible becomes that history, no matter how chaotic that period or event really was. While propagandists strive to maximise the linearity of the political discourse of their films, less partisan filmmakers must negotiate between real events and their representation, which gives rise to a critical and theoretical debate that would duly flare around Medem's 'intrusion' into politics. Shooting on digital video had simplified the editing process because the material could be re-edited indefinitely without expense or damage, but this also complicated matters by providing an infinite number of combinations that could be speedily constructed, saved and compared with others, thereby drawing out the aesthetic considerations that Medem initially attempted to suppress. In his defence, Medem argued that he had assumed the consequences of his authorship in the editing:

> There comes a time, in the most visual moments perhaps, that you have to assume subjectivity. I don't add my own voice, but I do create these montages. Maybe it's paradoxical, but if I accept the responsibility and don't try to disguise it, that's different, that's acceptable. [4]

The most controversial aspect of the documentary was not these montages, however, whose political meaning was thus severely underestimated, but the cutting into the declarations of his speakers. By choosing to edit out all the excess within a single take of an interviewee, their pauses, repetitions and variety of common and involuntary vowel noises associated with careful thought processes were all excised, resulting in tiny jumpcuts. Medem called these ellipses 'cortes visibles' (visible cuts) [3] and argued that they were to save time and increase the rhythmic intensity: out went spaces between words and phrases to allow for the clearing of a murky memory or the redirection of a sentence. The resultant elliptical passages offered jolted heads and hands that aroused suspicion of manipulation, but Medem argued he was purposefully springing the trap of such criticism:

> I don't hide the cut. I prefer it to be seen. These are instances of trust that I permit myself with the audience. I'm like a journalist who records the whole interview and then edits out the pauses. You'd never read the little noises and coughs made by interviewees, would you? You'd never write all the 'umms', right? [4]

On the one hand, such declarations of puposeful and privileged authorship demand that *La pelota vasca* be located within the auteurist trajectory and framework of Medem's fictions, especially because *La pelota vasca* combines Medem's typical thematic obsessions with Self and Otherness, conflicting subjectivities, duality, myth and the imagining of nationhood within a structure based upon symmetry and juxtaposition that relates to traditions in Basque cinema. On the other hand, just as John Grierson, the controversial father of the documentary form, claimed of his own somewhat less than truthful documentaries, 'here we move from the plain descriptions of natural material to arrangements, rearrangements and creative shapings of it' (Hardy 1979: 20), so Medem's arrangements and creative shapings of his footage were a declaration of personal involvement that allowed for bias and even an overt political point of view. More objectively, however, it is understandable and ironic that *La pelota vasca* should be accused of bias, because subjectivity is one of the primary elements of Medem's films. During the editing of *La pelota vasca*, it seemed that the documentary would either express a point of view, which was bound to enrage observers on one side or another, or it would not, which would disappoint and confuse those taken with Medem's auteurism. Shooting on digital video and editing on his home computer may have reduced costs and so exalted his independence and auteurism, but the point of view and creative shapings associated with such authorship constituted a set of auteurist conventions that any ambitions to dealing neutrally with the subject matter of the Basque conflict ironically required him to reject. Medem's gambit, so it seemed, would be inevitably scuppered by the paradoxes, even oxymorons, of authorial impartiality and auteurist anonymity.

Nevertheless, by a process of juxtaposing his interviewees, Medem whittled the 103 speakers down to the sixty-nine that suited a commercial running time of 115 minutes. A chronological if at times conflictive account of the Basque conflict was employed to educate audiences and so prepare them for the debate. Medem then divided the documentary into sections that corresponded to different styles of *pelota*, changing the rhythms as the speakers appear like *pelotaris*, hitting the film forward, letting the ball be struck by the next speaker. The interviewees were initially to be linked by the hand-held digital camera swooping up past their heads into the sky, a cut, and a downward glide onto the next speaker, but this proved unworkable in the editing process and would instead be collated for the final sequence in which the camera soars up and past all the speakers in a montage that precedes a majestic glide above the rural and urban landscape of the contemporary Basque Country. This bird-like protagonism of the camera tallied with Medem's thematic and visual conception of the film because its perspective represented his own ambition, but it also underlined the paradox of subjective objectivity that would prove so controversial on its release, when the video cut was transferred to 35mm film in time for the special screening within the Zabaltegi section of the 2003 San Sebastian Film Festival.

Between locking the final cut and the premiere, Medem expanded the documentary into three 55-minute episodes for pay-TV channel Canal Plus and a seven-hour DVD. In addition, there was the 968-page book of the film that Medem dedicated, as he does the documentary, 'to the Basques, to each and every one of the Basques' (Medem 2003b: 7). These synergetic products were all based on the same material but were radically different in their use of it. In sum, this multimedia project was a priceless archive of voices that revealed a glut of independent narrative structures and a surfeit of resource material for further debate about the Basque conflict. In retrospect, they also constituted a celebration of auteurist endeavour. 'And I've paid for it all. The book, the documentary, the DVD. It's the most personal and most independent project I've ever done', said Medem [4]. But even before its screening, *La pelota vasca* was rebounding on its maker with the first critical questions aired in the Spanish media by distrustful interviewees and suspicious politicians indulging in suppositions about its content. Perfectionism, dismay at the missing interviewees, frustration at the limited running time and uncertainty about the response were certainly all factors that contributed to Medem's nervousness prior to the San Sebastian Film Festival. To pre-empt some criticism and prepare the interviewees, Medem organised screenings for many of the participants beforehand. Amongst the audiences for these previews were the journalist Iñaki Ezquerra and Gotzone Mora, spokesperson for *Profesores para la Libertad* (Teachers for Freedom), who both demanded their interviews be removed because they considered the documentary presented a biased view of the victims of terrorist threats. Their bitter and vociferous rejection of the documentary ignited a controversy that was fanned by reactions from politicians and media commentators. Medem refused to cut Ezquerra and Mora from the film but did remove their testimonies from the accompanying book. Mora began legal action (Anon 2003) and, in an attempt to postpone debate until after the premiere, Medem issued his own press release on 17 September 2003 in which he urged the press and public to wait to see a documentary that he assured them was committed to ending violence and inspiring political debate. This missive drew immediate criticism, however, and also disappointed those who were expecting Medem to step into the public arena instead of allowing his documentary to speak for itself. Medem referred the wary, disappointed and angry back to *Un pájaro vuela dentro de una garganta* (Medem 2003a), but in the context of the burgeoning debate and sharpening focus on Medem's intentions this did little to assuage fears and quieten criticism that *La pelota vasca* might be a solipsistic dabble in potent political issues by a filmmaker who, it was argued, had no personal, academic or professional credentials to justify his intrusion in the debate. Neither did it help matters when Medem made statements to the press that edged him close to martyrdom: 'He ido con las manos y los ojos limpios a dar voz a todos' (Aldarondo 2003) (I've gone with my eyes and hands clean to give a voice to everyone). Meanwhile, members of the Partido Popular and the San Sebastian Town Council asked Odón Elorza (Chairman of the Council and the San Sebastian Film Festival, who himself provides testimony in *La pelota vasca*) to reconsider the screening of the documentary at the Festival. Elorza replied that *La pelota vasca* was 'a valuable cinematographic project' and the screening was maintained (Gibbons 2004).

Although the premiere in San Sebastian seemed logical and to many provocative, Medem had been aiming for Cannes and, when editing dragged on, had worked towards Berlin instead. The Venice Film Festival also came and went until the aptness of its premiere in his birthplace became obvious. Then, without having seen it, Pilar del Castillo, Spain's Minister for Culture, described *La pelota vasca* as suspicious. Medem responded by describing her to the Spanish press as 'una majadera y una irresponsable que me llama terrorista' (Fiestras 2004) (an irresponsible idiot who is calling me a terrorist). Indeed, Medem was becoming increasingly outspoken about the subject of his documentary and such politicians:

> They define a single line of thought. It's very clear in the case of the Basque Country. If you don't see the Basque Country as they tell you, if you differ in any way, that makes you their enemy. But right now I'll say what I feel. The attitude of the Spanish government towards the subject of the Basque Country is very dangerous. [4]

Koldo Zuazua claims that in the week before the Festival the phone lines at Alicia Produce were blocked and members of staff received personal threats. Legal actions to paralyse the premiere were also initiated, which made the media presence at the event predictably overwhelming. The screening took place in a cinema packed with interviewees, politicians, critics and journalists that Zuazua ruefully recalls as 'a social happening that would never have been possible before *La pelota vasca* because the political situation was such that these people couldn't sit around a table together, couldn't even be in the same room' [13]. Medem arrived with his partner Montse Sanz in what were the ultimate hours of her pregnancy and took to the stage with the characteristic gesture of folding his arms tightly to form a comforting embrace of his own torso. He attempted a nervous smile and surrendered to a ransom of flashes that demanded he accept authorship of the documentary about to be shown.

The *pelota* match that begins *La pelota vasca* is viciously fast. The white *pelotaris* career against green walls and as each echo of their strikes subsides a line-by-line preface appears onscreen:

> This film is intended to be an invitation to dialogue. This film is based on respect for all opinions. This film is independent, entirely the result of personal initiative. This film supports the victims of violence connected with the Basque conflict. This film will always regret the absence of those who did not want to participate.

The declaration is then replaced by a cut to a panorama of the lustrous but overcast Basque landscape, while the balance between landscape and voices is symbolised by the camera hovering in slow-motion shots of the writers, politicians and musicians that make up the first group of speakers. Unfortunately, as the preface makes clear, a few key speakers are missing and this polyphony of Basqueness is already doomed to incompletion. An inevitable failure in terms of its own ambition, *La pelota vasca* is nevertheless a triumph of cinematic brokerage over naive endeavour in which sixty-nine interviewees are sixty-nine square pegs in the single round hole of a film by Julio Medem.

As the first to speak, the Basque author Bernardo Atxaga's initial description of the Basque Country as a place of many islands instead of a single nation is like a deep breath before the argument starts. Atxaga speaks with wit and wisdom, perhaps consciously giving Medem what he wants: an imaginative visual metaphor. Indeed, as

12 Bernardo Atxaga opens the discourse of *La pelota vasca: la piel contra la piedra*

successive speakers appear it becomes evident that Atxaga's metaphorical archipelago is an inspiring framework for Medem, whose island-hopping between speakers has probably already happened too quickly and left part of his audience behind. This is a dizzying journey for an audience expecting the familiar polarisation that comes with discussion of Basque themes, though the journey does become a steady glide through the centre of a gorge that symbolises the void, in which the camera's flight between the walls of ancient rock symbolises the bird, which is itself the visual metaphor for neutrality and objectivity that illustrates equidistance and suggests that Medem's documentary will aim to maintain the middle path between successive interviewees grouped around political, historical, social and moral themes. None of the speakers knew while being filmed who would precede or follow them in the final cut, but their trust is what Medem also counts on from his audience when the logic of the sequencing is clearly the product of sleight of hand in the editing. For example, Javier Elzo (Professor of Sociology in the University of Deusto) sits beside his bodyguard, whose back is to the camera, and provides his opinion of the Basques before José Ignacio Ruiz de Olabuenaga (Professor of Sociology and Political Science) cuts in with 'es decir . . . ' (that's to say . . .) despite the fact that his explanation is not entirely complementary to that of Elzo. The notion of dialogue is therefore artificial and the lack of context for this structural experimentation is disorienting. In addition, although speakers are uniformly eloquent in their intellectual and emotional responses, they respond to questions that are never heard and there is no clear indication that interlinked comments are in response to the same question. Furthermore, these aforementioned tiny jumpcuts in the middle of testimonies are both an admission of inevitably manipulative authorship and a pre-emptive strike at reactionary critics that testifies to Medem's auteurist endeavour: his *pelota*, his rules. Although Medem has argued that this is merely journalistic convention, the ellipses do create a disconcerting fragmentation of the speaker, whose declaration inevitably appears to have been simplified, or worse, censored. Despite the fact that the jumpcut is a key element of the aesthetic experimentation in Basque documentaries such as Néstor Basterretxea and Fernando Larruquert's *Pelotari* (*Pelota Player*, 1964), the effect saps the potential for gaining the trust of sceptical spectators. Medem cuts out pauses in order to hurry to his destination, but runs the risk of moving too fast and separating himself from those who are unsure whether to follow.

Soon, however, a tranquilising corrective is offered by a montage of slow-motion *pelotaris* and a respite from the piecemeal lecture in the company of an urbane Orson Welles, whose 1955 documentary series for the BBC *Around the World with Orson Welles* has long been championed (by French critics at least) as some kind of missing link in his travels between American and European cinema. In the Iberian episode, the wry, self-indulgent and inimitably convivial Welles observes a bullfight with a bohemian inflection to his envy, before, as he describes it, placing his camera on the frontier between France and Spain to provide a Basque panorama like that which begins *La pelota vasca*. It is a second start to Medem's documentary, which dispenses with politics for a moment (as does an ingenuous Welles) and picks up stragglers with the humour and warmth of Welles wandering into a town square, where his meditations on Basqueness suggest that 'all we know for sure is what a Basque is not' before he cluelessly concludes that Basques are like Native Americans. Medem then cuts to a painting by the artist Vicente Ameztoy, whose work was a major inspiration on *Vacas*, and follows it with a verse from the *bertsolari* Xabier Euzkitze, a traditional, improvising Basque poet. Subsequent images of the work of the Basque sculptors Jorge Orteiza and Eduardo Chillida, whose work more abstractly expresses Basqueness in relation to space, the elements and the landscape, together with clips from the aforementioned documentary *Ama Lur*, suggest a deliberate recourse to song, art and film, for their juxtaposition with the academic and political account of history adds a human scale to the age-old debate that, albeit somewhat ironically, removes abstraction. This is the point at which the chronological to-ing and fro-ing of *La pelota vasca* is superseded by intra-history, history at first hand.

Subsequently, Eduardo Madina's strangely resigned description of being blown up by ETA introduces tangible human suffering to the documentary. His recollection of losing his leg in the terrorist attack also signals a shift in the focus of *La pelota vasca* from the collective to the individual that is accompanied by a correlative change from the recital of dogma to a more conversational dialectic. This move away from party lines towards the interlinking testimonies of individuals united by fate, chance and circumstance allows for the elements most associated with Medem's fictions to come to the fore. The declarations become a fateful labyrinth in which various characters are bound to each other by the duality of the Basque conflict that is evidenced by the Basques on both sides of the debate. Here too is the body and soul divide with speakers able to separate physical actions from their emotions in dispassionate descriptions of violence or conscience-less accounts of performing atrocities. As Harry Barnes (ex-director of the Carter Centre for Conflict Resolution) explains, it is necessary to find the grains of truth on both sides of the conflict for discussion to begin: so here is Medem's attempt at finding symmetry in the dialogue, argument and conflict that binds the speakers together more than it separates them.

However, perhaps the most problematic element of the documentary is the interpolation of caption-less clips from fictional films. Authentic newsreel of the bombing of the Basque town of Gernika by the Condor Legion on the 26 April 1937 is accompanied by the tensed vocal chords of Mikel Laboa, whose voice descends like a bomb from a howl to a growl. Next, a *pelota* match is played by amputees. But then a clip from the film *Ogro* (1980) that recreates the 1973 assassination of dictator-in-waiting Admiral Carrero Blanco is included as well as an excerpt from *Yoyes* (2000), a biography of the eponymous female ETA activist, that depicts a re-enactment of the celebrations for the bombing of ETA activists by actors, whose singing is taken up by real-life revellers on the returning newsreel. The later intercession of clips from films such as *Ama Lur*, *El mayorazgo de Basterretxe* (1929) and *Vacas* suggests that Medem is foregrounding the rôle of film in the myth and history of the Basque Country, but his use of fiction that is not identified as such creates a tension that the use of captions could have pre-empted. Most disturbingly, the inclusion in a newsreel montage of two scenes from *Días contados* (1995), the first featuring Carmelo Gómez as a rogue ETA terrorist shooting a policeman in the back of the head and the second of a car-bomb that obliterates a vagrant, are injurious to the trust of any spectators who are unaware of the deployed fiction and may therefore be manipulated into an emotional response to these fictional killings that will affect their response to the real ones and the documentary as a whole. Indeed, writing in *El País*, José Luis Barbería observed that Medem 'renuncia a mostrar las diferencias entre las víctimas reales de carne y hueso y las víctimas imaginarias' (2004: 36) (renounces the differences between real flesh and blood victims and imaginary victims).

On the other hand, any analysis of *La pelota vasca* must also take into account the history of filmmaking in the Basque Country, wherein the union of political thought and action with film theory and practice propagated a forceful faith in documentary as an instrument of record and propaganda that contributed to a cultural offensive against the conventions of the centralised film industry during and after the dictatorship. Besides strikingly-angled shots and jumpcuts, this counterplot aesthetic also deliberately included the blurring of fact and fiction in such films as *La fuga de Segovia* (*The Segovia Breakout*, 1981) (Stone 2001: 140–1) as a response to what was perceived as the same mix in the Francoist NO-DO newsreel. The more experimental characteristics of *La pelota vasca* may therefore be seen to maintain several traditionally oppositional techniques associated with Basque cinema at the same time as the elaborate structural conceit of the symmetrical positioning of protagonists is a characteristic of films written and directed by Medem. Just as the content, style and aesthetic of *La pelota vasca* resonates with references to a clandestine and pugnacious tradition of Basque documentary filmmaking, so Medem's most emphatic montage is a collage of tug-of-war teams and oarsmen, excerpts of head-butting rams and men from Asier Altuna's metaphorical short film *Topeka* (2003). The montage also includes grainy black and white documentary shots of cows being killed by sledgehammer that are taken from Antton Merikaetxebarria's documentary *Oldarren zurrumurruak* (*Rumores de furia*/*Rumours of Fury*, 1973) and accentuate the power of the montage because they recall those in Sergei Eisenstein's *Strike* (1925), in which the killing of bulls is juxtaposed with shots of strikers being butchered. Indeed, Medem's use of the images in no way dilutes Merikaetxebarria's intention that his film symbolise his view that 'en el pueblo vasco nos matan como a bestias' (Roldán Larreta 1999: 178) (in the Basque Country they kill us as if we were beasts); on the contrary, Medem's montage serves to enforce it. The history and techniques of political cinema, beginning with Eisenstein's theories of intellectual montage and including Basque documentary and fiction are therefore all referenced by Medem, who identifies the cinematic representation of the Basque conflict as an integral part of that same conflict.

Where the mix of fact and fiction is perhaps most obvious to an audience is with the inclusion of clips from Medem's own *Vacas*. For example, a montage of newsreel that features a victim of a bomb blast who has lost a leg beneath the knee is followed by the axe hitting the log beneath the bare feet of Carmelo Gómez in *Vacas*. Although the connection appears opportunistic and crass, it does make sense when the montage concludes with Kandido Uranga playing Gómez's rival in *Vacas* and hurling his axe into the forest, because the axe (with a snake coiled around it) symbolises ETA and therefore, to Medem, signifies hate: the same hate that he claims to be determined to expunge from the dialogue. The political argument of *Vacas* was underappreciated in its day but its cycles of desire, fear and violence are the same motors of the Basque conflict as are debated in *La pelota vasca*. References to *Vacas* thus attest to the long-standing commitment of Medem to the subject of the Basque conflict and the obsessive reworking of such themes that makes *La pelota vasca* so decisive in any analysis of his auteurism. Cycles, symmetries, dualities, juxtaposed points of view, competing subjectivities, fate, chance and a unifying context of natural symbolism are all present in the visual and aural thesis of *La pelota vasca*, as is the cyclical link to *Vacas*, which in turn demands a retrospective analysis of Basqueness in all his films.

Music is another vital element in the thesis of *La pelota vasca*. The challenge to Medem of working without long-time composer-collaborator Alberto Iglesias was alleviated by the gift of the CD *Gernika zuzenean 2* from Mikel Laboa, an old friend of his mother's family. This often ethereal and sometimes shrill compilation CD features Laboa accompanied by the Youth Orchestra of Euskadi and the San Sebastian Choral Society. Laboa in performance is even featured in a montage in *La pelota vasca* that uses his gutteral cries to symbolise the fraught progression of the Basque Country through the political transition in Spain from dictatorship to democracy. Like Atxaga, Laboa is another representative of the point of view of Medem and his wordless singing returns us to the ancient voice of mankind as an expression of emotion that anthropologists believe began in imitation of birdsong. The bird's-eye view of the Basque conflict is thus combined with this avian imitation on the soundtrack, while the bird that Medem says flies through the gorge is not just a symbol of equidistance but also a link with the catalogue of symbolic animals from his previous films (respectively, cows, squirrels, beetles, reindeer and dogs).

Medem continues his grouping of speakers as if making poker hands of picture cards, ploughing on through the post-dictatorship transition to democracy and the rise of the PSOE, the 1996 election victory of the Partido Popular and the renewed radicalisation of Basque activists. However, it is at this point that the dialogue is stalled by allegations of torture and the problematic testimony of the aforementioned Anika Gil, whose disgust at what she describes causes violin shrieks on the soundtrack to represent her plight. Medem's concentration on female suffering, which is a constant element in his fictions, then extends to his juxtapositioning of the testimonies of Cristina Sagarzazu (widow of the Basque policeman Ramón Doral who was killed by ETA in 1996) and Jasone Manterola (wife of a convicted and imprisoned ETA terrorist). The comparison evoked by the juxtapositon of these two women is a challenging view of victimhood in which the balance of suffering is predicated upon equating one woman's widowhood from a terrorist killing to the distress of the wife of a jailed terrorist. As Paddy Woodworth has pointed out, the moral debate is clearly won by Sagarzazu, who claims the worst she can conceive is of her son taking up arms in revenge (Woodworth 2004). Female suffering may feature prominently in Medem's films as it does in much of Spanish and Basque cinema, for centuries of staunch Catholicism and ingrained machismo have rendered the mother a figure of sacrifice and endurance, but the equidistance that Medem aspires to here faces its most difficult challenge and its most vociferous critics.

On the whole, however, Medem's political stance is indistinct throughout, though some inclination to the left is detectable in the prominence awarded the Ibarretxe Plan and the presentation of certain historical events is generous to one perspective and frugal with another. A discussion of the GAL, for example, culminates in a rhetorical question about the mastermind behind it all that is answered by a cut to Felipe González, who was President of Spain and leader of the PSOE at the time of the GAL. An audience in Spain howls with knowing laughter at this punchline that Medem probably should have resisted. Even so, expecting Medem to be wholly impartial is perhaps unfeasible when several of the academics who speak are clearly estranged from objectivity by a subjectivity that comes from their physical presence and spoken declarations and, in the case of Elzo, is underlined by the presence of his bodyguard. Where subjectivity is arguably beyond criticism is in the simple and thoughtful declaration of Eduardo Madina, the General Secretary of the Young Socialists of Euskadi and a victim of an ETA attack in which he lost a leg. Madina expresses incomprehension at the Basque conflict and surprise that the person who blew up his car does not share that confusion: 'He should ask himself what is Euskadi. [. . .] He should look at it from other perspectives and ask himself if what he's doing resolves anything or is it preventing a resolution'. Madina appears in the middle of the debate about definitions of the contemporary Basque Country as a symbol of those who live with the consequences of violence and his suffering makes him an irrefutable spokesperson for human rights. In addition, his example eradicates the doubts and criticisms about the practicalities of equidistance that were raised when critics argued equidistance is not a viable response when hate sanctions the killing of children and civilians because the movement required to maintain equidistance between an extremist terrorist organisation and a right-of-centre democratically elected political party obliges the director to err too much to one side. That is to say, in finding the equidistance between ETA and the Partido Popular, Medem may be obliged to move to a point on the left that imbalances his objectivity. But this criticism is only valid if it is limited to the blinkered range of political bickering. The simpler questions posed by Madina's testimony suggest the greater humanist context in which Medem's attempt at equidistance struggles to function.

Frequent aerial shots of the Basque Country remind audiences to reflect on the scale of the conflict as well as it context; but just as several of the testimonies are stale rhetoric, so shots of luminous green and snowy landscapes suggest over-determined reflections of the nationalist celebration of rural Basqueness. In contrast, montages of riots, bombs and brutality provide repetitive illustrations of urban upheaval until a series of dissolves between declarations of the word 'frustration' suggests that Medem is approaching a dead-end, for even at close to two hours *La pelota vasca* still feels like a trailer for the extended DVD, which at seven hours is still no more than a warm-up to the continually postponed debate. Ultimately, what impresses most about *La pelota vasca* is its seemingly infinite variety of faces, voices and points of view. Atxaga's final, hopeful play on words that Euskal Herria (the land of the Basque speakers) will become Euskal Hiria (the city of the Basques) is indicative of a place that he says 'does not belong to anyone, but belongs to everyone', Territories and the violence that defines them thus dissolve in the final montage of cameras taking flight from their subjects that Medem edits to the powerfully surging score, with his camera swooping up past the heads of terrorists, politicians, historians, journalists, musicians, authors, wives, fathers, daughters and sons: victims all. The montage conveys an emotional, melancholic charge, for the film declares it is ending when its work has just begun, though many spectators will take from *La pelota vasca* exactly what they bring to it. On the other hand, *La pelota vasca* may not provide answers but it does suggest a way to attain them. It is not, as many have supposed (Medem included), an all-inclusive dialogue about the

Basque conflict, but it is an impassioned call for the one that might follow. Initially what followed the festival screening was a five-minute standing ovation during which a visibly overcome Medem was embraced by Daniel Múgica, whose recollection of his father's killing by ETA features in the documentary. Medem claimed the project had been vindicated: 'In the Festival I managed something that I hope will be useful to unblock the debate, which is much greater than the film' [4]. Many agreed that the documentary seemed like an honest attempt at presenting the complexity of the issue, but the division of opinions that were mostly regardless of the aesthetic qualities of the documentary took root in the Basque and Spanish press and media. Many criticised, even ridiculed Medem's ambition, never mind that an attempt at conflict resolution by the recognition and demonstration of symmetry was nothing new to this writer-director who had juxtaposed three generations of two rival families in *Vacas* and explored opportunist schizophrenia in *La ardilla roja*, the Apollonian-Dionysian divide of a man in *Tierra*, the severing of soulmates in *Los amantes del Círculo Polar* and the firework fragmentation of an author into his own characters in *Lucía y el sexo* in order to examine the conflict within a divided Self that is his most enduring theme. On 23 September 2003, *La razón digital* featured an article by Fernando Savater comparing Medem to Leni Riefenstahl, the director of Nazi propaganda films (Navarro 2003: 13), while Gustavo Rivas in *La voz de Galicia* offered a particularly contentious analogy: 'Es como si la hace sobre los campos de concentración nazis y habla el gauleiter que dirige el campo y también el judío y luego dicen que no toman partido' (Franco 2003) (It's as if the film were about the Nazi concentration camps and the gauleiter who controls the camp speaks as well as a Jew and then the makers say they don't take sides). 'Everything that's happening around *La pelota vasca* is dealt with within' [4] surmised Medem, but the fact that he did not conduct all the interviews himself provided many critics with a stick to beat him for daring to tackle such a complex theme while remaining ignorant of the Basque language. For many critics, Medem's Basqueness seemed a pose and a linguistically ignorant one at that. They demanded to know how someone who had left the Basque Country when just a child could dare comment on a place from which he was distanced. They claimed his lack of Euskera was not just a symptom of having grown up in Madrid but an impediment to his understanding that effectively invalidated the entire venture: this monolingual, quarter-Basque simply had no right to comment on Basque issues and should stick to fiction.

In truth, the charge made by linguistic dogmatists is difficult to dodge, for Basque claims to nationhood and a separate identity are inextricably linked to the status of the Basque language. By now, almost half the population of the southern Basque Country has at least moderate knowledge of the once-forbidden Euskera and there are Basque-language radio and TV stations. Medem admitted he had begun studying the language twice but had been unable to stay with it: 'You start out thinking it's not too bad, but it soon gets very complicated. I was busy with other things and couldn't give it the dedication it needed, but I'll go back to it' [2]. Whether the language barrier should have prevented the film from being made was also debated in the Spanish press and was one of the few areas in which Medem's response was less than solid, as if he were not quite convinced of his credentials either. The argument loses force, however, when one remembers that the documentary includes interviews conducted in English, a language that Medem had, at the time, also failed to learn without accusations of being unqualified to conduct those interviews through an interpreter. Moreover, the international trajectory of the documentary meant that such linguistic considerations were irrelevant for audiences who depended on subtitles for the entire film.

On 26 October 2003 the controversy overboiled Spanish borders when the first screening outside Spain took place during the London Film Festival. Medem appeared at the National Film Theatre trailing Spanish television news teams and journalists who had sniffed out the rumour that the Spanish Embassy in London had described him as *persona non grata* and rescinded the subsidy it annually offered to the Festival for the hospitality of its Spanish guests (Marín 2003). Medem expressed bewilderment: 'And now, who am I? I bring a film that's classified as Spanish by the Ministry for Culture and come here as if I've been disinherited, like an exile. Have they kicked me out of Spanish cinema?' [4]. Nevertheless, in the following week's *Time Out* magazine, the ovation awarded Medem by his audience was described as 'the most moving moment' of the Festival (Andrew 2003: 21). Medem's supporters advocated freedom of artistic expression and the rights of an auteur to opine, but in its well-intentioned way this skewed the defence towards a counter-claim of explicit personal bias. Most Spanish reviews focussed on the furore; a few foreign critics looked at the film more closely. Paul Julian Smith voiced his concern in *Sight and Sound* that Medem had fallen into the category of 'those who offer apologies for [. . .] violence' (2004: 45), but *The Guardian* stated that 'far from taking a pro-nationalist line, the film makes extremely uncomfortable viewing for the Basque Country's nationalist government, never mind ETA' (Gibbons 2004) and *Time Out* described *La pelota vasca* as 'a film of enormous courage, conviction and intelligence' (Andrew 2004: 19).

The polemic made *La pelota vasca* the most commercially successful documentary in the history of Spanish cinema with an opening weekend of € 216,661 on 32 screens and a quadrupling of the original number of commercial prints that resulted in a gross of € 1,599,881 in 2003. (Abad 2004: 104). Nevertheless, Alejandro Ballestero of the Partido Popular and spokesperson for the controlling body of Spanish national television called for Medem to return the € 510,000 that he had received for a recent broadcast of *Lucía y el sexo* (R.G.G. 2003) and the nomination of *La pelota vasca* for the Goya for best documentary in the Spanish Film Academy Awards was like petrol on a fire. On the front page of the national Spanish newspaper *ABC* of 1 February 2004, the morning after the ceremony at which *La pelota vasca* had not won the award for best documentary but Medem had been alluded to by several of the prize-winners, there is a photograph of Medem struggling towards the venue with cameras blocking his way and a wreath of microphones around his neck. On the lapel of his leather jacket he wears a sticker matching 'No to terrorism' with 'Yes to freedom of expression' that features a Greek mask silenced with a cross across its mouth. The Association of Victims of Terrorism (AVT) had waged a press campaign against the nomination for *La pelota vasca* and two hundred of its members had lined up behind banners and candles (Bravo 2004: 54), while, in response, Medem had referred to the ceremony as 'la pesadilla que me espera' (EFE 2004) (the nightmare that awaits me) and issued two takes of a press release in which he expressed his rejection of terrorism and his solidarity with the victims 'sin esperar nada a cambio' (EFE 2004) (without expecting anything in return). The Goya for best documentary went to José Luis López Linares's *Un instante en la vida ajena* (2003) and Medem thereafter assumed a distance from the hysteria that was taken as dignified by some and arrogant by others but which was, in truth, exhaustion exacerbated by the chores of baby-care, for a girl had been born to Montse Sanz following the premiere of *La pelota vasca* at the San Sebastian Film Festival. Medem had named her Ana, for his deceased sister and the infant heroine of *El espíritu de la colmena* (1973), which had been fêted for its thirtieth birthday during the Festival. Born like her father in San Sebastian, Ana was Basque, instead of the Madrid-born *madrileña* that Medem had expected and he characteristically took her birth for a coincidence that symbolised the renewal of his links with the Basque Country. Ana, like *La pelota vasca*, was as a tangible vindication of the revitalisation of his Basqueness and his commitment to its culture and progress. As he concluded: 'For whatever reason, I now feel like I belong to the Basque Country' [5].

9

Work in progress

By April 2004, *La pelota vasca* was still causing aftershocks and reflection in all who had participated in its production. Koldo Zuazua was 'content, but not proud; actually rather disturbed' [13] while Medem declared 'it's very ironic, but thanks to the Partido Popular I can now pay all my debts' [5]. Moreover, the debate about the Basque conflict had extended beyond Spain as the film played in international festivals. Meanwhile, a somewhat reclusive Medem saw out his prior commitments by filming television advertisements for an electric goods company that offered meaningful looks between a couple on an island that resembled the one from *Lucía y el sexo* and ended with washing machines perched on rocks like the skeletal bishops in Buñuel's *L'Âge d'or* (*The Golden Age*, 1930). He added a three-minute postscript to *La pelota vasca* as part of the *Hay Motivos* project, in which thirty Spanish filmmakers offered brief visual essays on the social problems that they considered most pressing in the weeks running up to the national elections of March 2004 (Piña 2004: 34) and he bowed out of directing a five-minute love story set in the 13th *arrondissement* that was to have been one of twenty in the compilation film *Paris, je t'aime* (2006). He also took part in the project *50 Minutes* sponsored by Nescafé in which five Spanish directors partnered new filmmakers in making short films based on incidents in the lives of the veterans. Medem's protégé was Daniel Sánchez-Arévalo, who based *La culpa del alpinista* on a story by Alicia, Medem's daughter, who also played a central rôle. Medem still spoke of someday making *Aitor*, for anything less would have suggested defeat, but production assistant Silvia Gómez, for one, was convinced that his next project would be 'a comedy called *Caótica Ana* , although he doesn't know it yet' [7].

Later, Medem explained that *Caótica Ana* was a film about reincarnation in which the eponymous Ana was based on his real-life sister, who had also been the inspiration for Ana in *Los amantes del Círculo Polar* and, following her death, for Lucía in *Lucía y el sexo* too:

> Wherever she goes, Ana disorganises what's organised. She disorders order but is completely unaware. She's the type of person who leaves a wake, but she's spellbound. It has a lot to do with reincarnation. She discovers under hypnosis that she's been reincarnated eighty times. These are the things that the film is about. [5]

The repetition of themes, characters and obsessions typical of Medem in *Caótica Ana* includes his characteristic reworking of personal experiences and family histories, but with at least five years between its release and that of *Lucía y el sexo* it may be that audiences, critics and academics will demand something more original of his fiction and, following *La pelota vasca*, a great deal more awareness and commitment to social and political concerns. There was also the risk that *Caótica Ana* would seem evasive and ultimately so familiar that it would line Medem up to be knocked down by the argument that European writer-directors with aspirations to auteurism tend to wear themselves out on projects that become repetitive and end up redundant. On the other hand, the journeying away from the Basque Country that was constituted by Medem's progressive exile in his first five fictions did allow for the dynamics of differentiation that powered his return with *La pelota vasca*, and it may therefore be that *Caótica Ana* was the mini-exile that would enable Medem to refresh his objectivity about the Basque conflict before heading back into the fray with *Aitor*. Moreover, the juxtaposition of subjectivities that symbolises balance, symmetry and duality and is the most enduring characteristic of his films, might also explain his decision to make the counterweight of a seemingly light and frivolous film before attempting the serious, complex and undoubtedly controversial *Aitor*.

Meanwhile, in lieu of both *Aitor* and *Caótica Ana*, what only remains to be performed in this retrospective of his work to date is a comparison of the films he has written, directed and even edited with his own, early declaration in his critical writing for *La voz de Euskadi* that a unique Basque cinema should be distinguished by 'un cierto espíritu del País Vasco, una estética genuina y distinta [y] un peculiar sentido narrativo' (1983a: 25) (a particular spirit of the Basque Country, an authentic and distinct aesthetic [and] a particular understanding of narrative). Clearly the emphasis on subjectivity as the basis of an emotional truth that is distinct from the bias of historical accounts, together with structural ploys that illustrate themes of symmetry and duality, is representative of a Basque sense of Otherness that incorporates the divisions between the Basques themselves. Also Basque is his frequent focus on the void that is emphasised by circular motifs and holes, which, with Freudian symbolism intact, frequently feature in films whose protagonists are concerned with closing cyclical narratives and countering their own lack by fabricating soulmates that become real by the infusion of emotion. This is also the naive but laudable endeavour of *La pelota vasca*, in which Medem attempted to fill the void created by the Basque conflict by inserting a constructive dialogue. In addition, the situating of human characters in relation to the natural landscape, often under the watchful eyes of animals, effects a mostly ironic reflection on its relevance to nationalism when the landscape is Basque, as in *Vacas* and *La pelota vasca*, and a consideration of objectivity through exile when the landscapes are alien, as on the journey away from the Basque Country that passes through the campsite of *La ardilla roja*, the vineyards of *Tierra*, Finland in *Los amantes del Círculo Polar* and the floating island of *Lucía y el sexo*, only to end up back where he started, in the Basque Country with *La pelota vasca*.

Whether Medem's Basqueness and, by extension, the Basqueness of his films, is inevitable and natural or deliberate and posed is illustrative of an auteurist trajectory founded upon the mix of truth, lies, history and myth in both the plots and themes of his fictions and his creation of their scripts. Where the characters he creates commonly mythologise their identities and make them real by the investment of emotion, thereby illustrating the radical Basque nationalist campaign for an independent homeland, so Medem has aspired to a concept of auteurism that is based upon the highly personal connections to his films, devotion to themes that draw on Nietzsche, Freud, Surrealism and magical realism, the development of a style that relates to aesthetic traditions in Basque cinema and narrative experimentation in contemporary arthouse cinema, and the benefits of independence gained through the use of new technologies, self-financing and co-production deals. And now, finding after five fictions and one documentary that he resembles the mythological auteur, Medem faces the task of maintaining what is a deeply felt condition that can only be safeguarded by his imagination.

Options for Medem include the seemingly 'all or nothing' gambit of
Aitor, from whose inevitable controversy he may never recover, but
which, if successful in artistic and commercial terms (that seem
doubtful given its hermetic complexity, especially in terms of potential
sales to international markets), would take him beyond the political
expropriation of the film and any bad feeling in the Spanish media.
Success for *Aitor* on any level, whether international, critical or cult,
might even revitalise the argument that Basque cinema is not Spanish
cinema, whose industry, audience and critical and academic followers
have already co-opted many Basque films and filmmakers prior to
Medem. Another possibility is that his auteurist trajectory will flourish
at a different level, with his enthusiasm for new technologies and the
synergetic distribution of its products being extended to innovative
distribution strategies incorporating new media that will require and
hopefully repay him to assume greater responsibility in the production
and financing of his features. Then again, there is a middle ground in
which the films he writes and directs will remain stylish and affecting
illustrations of universal themes, produced and marketed in collusion
with companies that can both foster and channel his creativity. The
worst would be if he repeats himself by making films about the kind
of personal concerns that he has already exhausted, until the films he
writes and/or directs keep their style but lose their meaning,
occasionally satisfying an international and/or domestic audience with
a taste for erotically-charged navel-gazing.

The story of Medem is not one of a filmmaker enclosed by a
particular period of European, Spanish or Basque history, nor one
defined by a movement or genre. Rather, Medem is a work in progress,
busy constructing himself as auteur in the likeness of his own
ambition. This has been the story of Medem learning the responsibilities of authorship while enjoying the privileges of auteurism. It is
a tale of maturing themes and technique told in colour, light and sound,
of cows and squirrels and beetles, of cowardly *aizkolari* and arrogant
angels, of a circular motif caught in eyes that entangle and reflected in
pupils that dilate, of floating islands and a hollow Earth, of Arctic
Circles and Basque balls, of coincidences, destinies, dreams and, above
all else, of the filmmaker who does the telling. Finally, therefore, this
book must end where it began, with Medem's admission that he
imagines 'my best work is still to come' [5], for his promise breaks and
widens the circular narrative made from his first few films, making
room for whatever he does next:

I'm in a period of expansion right now, feeling very explosive and decisive. I don't want to limit myself at all. I don't hold back, or at least I don't hold much back. Restraint is not one of my virtues. I see people much younger than me who have this degree of self-control, with everything in its place. Fine, you can be young and have self-control, but that's not how I see myself. I believe in perfection. You have to reach for perfection. But right now I can't make a perfect work. I'm still searching, exploring. [5]

Filmography

Audience and box-office figures courtesy of Sogecine.

El ciego
(Spain) 1974, 8mm short [*The Blind Man*]

Los jueves pasados
(Spain) 1977, 8mm short [*Thursdays Past*]

Fideos
(Spain) 1979, 8mm short [*Noodles*]

Si yo fuera un poeta (Antonio Machado)
(Spain) 1981, 8mm short [*If I Were a Poet (Antonio Machado)*]

Teatro en Soria
(Spain) 1982, 8mm short [*Theatre in Soria*]

Patas en la cabeza
(Spain) 1986, 13 min.
Production company: Grupo Delfilm
Director: Julio Medem
Screenplay: Julio Medem
Producers: Julio Medem and Luis Campoy
Cinematography: Gonzalo F. Berridi
Editing: Julio Medem
Music: Iñaki Arkarazo
Costume design: Álvaro Machimbarrena
Art direction: Álvaro Machimbarrena
Filming location: San Sebastian
Leading players: Joaquín Navascués (aka.Will More), Carmen Barrera, María
    del Mar Pérez de Olarra

San Sebastián: dentro del mar
(Basque Country) 1986, documentary short

Las seis en punta
(Spain) 1987, 16 min. [*Six O'Clock Sharp*]
Director: Julio Medem
Screenplay: Julio Medem
Producer: Julio Medem
Cinematography: Gonzalo F. Berridi
Editing: Julio Medem
Sound: Iñaki López Salanova
Music: Alberto Iglesias
Make-up and hair: Karmele Soler
Filming location: Tolosa, Guipúzcoa
Leading players: Eneko Irízar, Nicola Beller, Montxu Odriozola

Martín
(Spain) 1988, 30 min. [*Martin*]
Production company: Elías Querejeta for TVE.
Director: Julio Medem
Screenplay: Julio Medem and Juan Manuel Chumilla
Cinematography: Gonzalo F. Berridi
Editing: Raúl Casado
Music: Alberto Iglesias
Make-up: María Luisa Cabrera
Costume design: Maiki Marín
Set design: María José Martínez
Filming location: Madrid
Leading players: Miguel Ángel García Fuentes (Martín), Laura Bayonas (Julia
    Lemos), Paloma Cela (mother), José Segura (father), Raúl Freire (old hunter),
    Juan Manuel Chumilla (young hunter)

El diario vasco
(Basque Country) 1989, Documentary short

Vacas
(Spain) 1992, 96 min. [*Cows*]
Production company: Bailando con la luna for Sociedad General de Televisión
    S.A. (Sogetel)
Producers: Fernando de Garcillán and José Luis Olaizola
Budget: 165,000,000 ptas.
Director: Julio Medem
Screenplay: Michel Gaztambide and Julio Medem
Story: Julio Medem

Cinematography: Carles Gusi
Editing: María Elena Sáinz de Rozas
Special Effects: Reyes Abades
Art Direction: Rafael Palmero
Make-up: Gregorio Mendiri
Costume Design: María José Iglesias
Music: Alberto Iglesias
Leading players: Emma Suárez (Cristina), Carmelo Gómez (Manuel, Ignacio
and Peru Irigibel), Ana Torrent (Catalina), Txema Blasco (Manuel), Karra
Elejalde (Ilegorri and Lucas), Klara Badiola (Madalen), Kandido Uranga
(Carmelo and Juan Mendiluze), Pilar Bardem (Paulina), Ane Sánchez
(Cristina as a child), Miguel Ángel García (Peru as a child)
Filming Locations: Valle del Baztán (Navarre), Elizondo (Navarre)
Premiere: 26 February 1992
Audience: 152,031
Box-office: 370,703 €
Main Festivals and Awards:
Tokyo 1992 (*Golden Grand Prix*),
Turin 1992 (*Best Film*), London (BFI) 1993 (*Sutherland Trophy for the most
original and imaginative first film shown in Great Britain*), Alexandria 1993
(*Best Film and Best Photography*), Beauvais 1994 (*Jury Award*), European
Film Awards 1992 (*Nominated for Best Debut Film*), Spanish Film
Academy Awards 1992 (*Best Debut Film*), Sant Jordi Awards (*Best Debut*),
Spanish Film Writers' Circle (*Best Script*)

La ardilla roja
(Spain) 1993, 114 min. [*Red Squirrel*]
Production company: Bailando con la luna for Sociedad General de Televisión
S.A. (Sogetel)
Executive Producer: Fernando de Garcillán
Production Manager: Ricardo García Arrojo
Budget: 200,000,000 ptas.
Director: Julio Medem
Screenplay: Julio Medem
Cinematography: Gonzalo F. Berridi
Sound: Julio Recuero
Editing: María Elena Sáinz de Rozas
Special effects: Reyes Abades
Make-up: Gregorio Mendiri
Music: Alberto Iglesias and Txetxo Bengoetxea
Original Songs: *Elisa* and *La ardilla roja*, lyrics by Julio Medem, sung by Txetxo
Bengoetxea
Choreographer: Ana Medem

Set Design: Satur Idarreta
Leading players: Emma Suárez (Sofía/Elisa), Nancho Novo (J), María Barranco
(Carmen), Karra Elejalde (Antón), Carmelo Gómez (Félix), Cristina Marcos
(Girl with blue hair), Mónica Molina (Girl with red hair), Ana Gracia
(psychiatrist), Elena Irueta (Begoña), Susana García Díez (Elisa), Ane
Sánchez (Cristina), Txema Blasco (neurologist), Chete Lera (Salvador),
Gustavo Salmerón (Luis Alfonso)
Filming Locations: San Sebastian, San Martín de Valdeiglesias (Madrid),
Pelayos de La Presa (Madrid), Usanos (Guadalajara), Valsaín (Segovia), El
Pardo (Madrid), Madrid.
Premiere: 21 April 1993
Audience: 178,228
Box-office: 478,223 €
Main Festivals and Awards:
Cannes 1993 (*Youth Audience Award and Audience Award for Best Foreign
Film*), Gerander 1994 (*Special Jury Award and Critics Award*), Denver 1993
(*Special Award*), Fort Lauderdale (*Golden Palm Award*), Santa Fe de Bogota
(*Premio de Oro*), Bucharest (*Best Film and Best Script*), Luis Buñuel Awards
1994 (*Cinematographic Creation of the Year*), Premios Ondas (*Best Spanish
Film*), Spanish Film Academy Awards 1994 (*Best Original Score*), Sant Jordi
Awards (*Best Spanish Film and Best Actress* [Emma Suárez])

Océano de sol
(Spain) 1994, Music video for Antonio Vega

Hola, ¿estás sola?
(Spain) 1995, 92 min. [Hello, Are You Alone?]
Director: Iciar Bollaín
Story: Julio Medem

Tierra
(Spain) 1996, 125 min. [*Earth*]
Production company: Lolafilms S.A. and Sociedad General de Televisión S.A.
(Sogetel)
Producer: Fernando de Garcillán
Associate Producer: Manuel Lombardero
Budget: 380,000,000 ptas.
Director: Julio Medem
Screenplay: Julio Medem
Cinematography: Javier Aguirresarobe
Camera Operator: Carles Gusi
Stills Photographer: Teresa Asisi
Assistant Director: Txarli Llorente

Editing: Iván Aledo
Direct Sound: Gilles Ortion
Sound Editor: Polo Aledo
Special Effects: Reyes Abades
Costume Design: Estíbaliz Markiegi
Art Direction: Satur Idarreta
Make-up: Karmele Soler
Music: Alberto Iglesias
Music Producer: Lucio Godoy
Original Song: *Sólo para locos* by Marc Parrot
Non-original Songs: *Terra* sung by Caetano Veloso, *Túmbala si puedes* by
    Barbería del sur, *Izar Ederra* by Ruper Ordorika
Leading players: Carmelo Gómez (Ángel Bengoetxea), Emma Suárez (Ángela),
    Karra Elejalde (Patricio), Silke (Mari), Nancho Novo (Alberto), Txema Blasco
    (Tomás), Ane Sánchez (Ángela's daughter), Juan José Suárez (Manuel),
    Ricardo Amador (Charly), Pepe Viyuela (Ulloa)
Filming Locations: Cariñena, Cosuenda, Paniza, Tobed and Calatayud (all
    Zaragoza), Funes (Navarre), Peñíscola (Castellón)
Premiere: 14 May 1996
Audience: 226,174
Box-office: 717,729 €
Main Festivals and Awards:
Cannes 1996 (*Official Selection*), Sao Paulo 1997 (*Special Prize*), Uruguay
    1998 (*Best Film*), Spanish Film Academy Awards 1997 (*Best Original Score*,
    Best Special Effects), Fotogramas de plata (*Best Actress* [Emma Suárez] *and
    Best Actor* [Carmelo Gómez]), *El país de las tentaciones* (*Best Film, Best
    Director, Best Actress* [Emma Suárez])

Making of 'Airbag'

(Spain) 1997, documentary short on making of Juanma Bajo Ulloa's *Airbag*
    (1997)

Los amantes del Círculo Polar

(Spain-France) 1998, 112 min. [*Lovers of the Arctic Circle*]
Production company: Le studio Canal +, Alicia Produce, Bailando con la Luna,
    and Sociedad General de Cine S.A. (Sogecine)
Producer: Fernando Bovaira
Executive Producers: Fernando de Garcillán, Enrique López Lavigne and Txarli
    Llorente
Budget: 400,000,000 ptas.
Director: Julio Medem
Screenplay: Julio Medem
Cinematography: Gonzalo F. Berridi

Camera Operator: Mario Montero
Editing: Iván Aledo
Production Design: Itziar Arrieta, Satur Idarreta, Estíbaliz Markiegi and
    Karmele Soler
Art Direction: Satur Idarreta and Montse Sanz
Direct Sound: Sergio Corral
Sound Editor: Polo Aledo
Music: Alberto Iglesias
Non-original Song: *Sinitaivas* by J. Rixner, L. Jauhiainen, G. de Godzinsky,
    sung by Olavi Virta Ja Harmony Sisters
Costume Design: Estíbaliz Markiegi
Make-up: Karmele Soler
Special Effects: Molina FX
Casting: Sara Bilbatúa
Leading players: Najwa Nimri (adult Ana), Fele Martínez (adult Otto), Nancho
    Novo (Álvaro), Maru Valdivielso (Olga), Peru Medem (child Otto), Sara
    Valiente (child Ana), Victor Hugo Oliveira (adolescent Otto), Kristel Díaz
    (adolescent Ana), Pep Munné (Javier), Jaroslaw Bielski (Álvaro Midelman),
    Rosa Morales (Sofía), Joost Siedhoff (Otto Midelman), Petri Heino (Aki)
Filming Locations: Helsinki, Lohja and Rovaniemi (all Finland), Madrid
    (Spain)
Premiere: 28 August 1998
Audience: 752,396
Box-office: 2,827,371 €
Main Festivals and Awards:
Venice, Toronto, Bastia (France), Toulouse (*Young Audience Award*),
    Goteburg, Brussels, Sundance, Manchester, Dublin, Cartagena (Colombia),
    San Diego, San Francisco, Dallas, Washington DC, Philadelphia, Moscow,
    Hong Kong, Havana, Singapore, Jerusalem, Karlovy Vary, Napoli, Noosa
    (Australia), Tokyo, Sao Paulo, Valladolid, Gramado (*Kikitos Awards for Best
    Director, Best Screenplay, Best Music, Critic's Prize and Public Prize*),
    Ondas Awards (*Best Film and Best Actress* [Najwa Nimri]), Spanish Film
    Academy Awards 1999 (*Best Editing and Best Original Score*)

Lucía y el sexo
(Spain-France) 2001, 123 min. [*Sex and Lucía*]
Production company: Alicia Produce, Canal + España, Sociedad General de
    Cine (Sogecine), Sogepaq, Studio Canal, Televisión Española (TVE)
Producers: Fernando Bovaira and Enrique López Lavigne
Executive Producers: Anna Cassina and Luis María Reyes
Budget: 4,000,000 €
Director: Julio Medem
Screenplay: Julio Medem

Cinematography: Kiko de la Rica
Sound: Agustín Peinado
Sound Editor: Polo Aledo
Make-up: Gregorio Ros
Music: Alberto Iglesias
Original Songs: Nacho Canut and Olvido Gara (*Mr Hyde visita el túnel del amor*), Carlos Jean (*Give Me The Seventies*) and Mala Rodríguez (*Yo marco el minuto*)
Non-original Song: Joan Manuel Serrat (*Romance del Curro 'El Palmo'*)
Editing: Iván Aledo
Casting: Sara Bilbatúa
Art Direction: Montse Sanz
Costume Design: Estíbaliz Markiegi
Assistant Costume Design: Sofía Medem
Body Doubles: David Bulnes (Lorenzo), Diana Suárez (Lucía)
Leading players: Paz Vega (Lucía), Tristán Ulloa (Lorenzo), Najwa Nimri (Elena), Daniel Freire (Carlos/Antonio), Elena Anaya (Belén), Silvia Llanos (Luna), Diana Suárez (Madre de Belén), Javier Cámara (Pepe), Juan Fernández (Jefe), María Álvarez (Nurse), Alesandra Álvarez (Luna age 1), David Bulnes (porn actor)
Filming Locations: Formentera and Madrid
Premiere: 22 August 2001
Audience: 1,216,162
Box-office: 5,255,843 €
Main Festivals and Awards:
Toronto, Río de Janeiro, Sundance, Rotterdam, Seattle (*Emerging Master Award and Space Needle Award for Best Director*), San Francisco, Jerusalem, Karlovy Vary, Seul, Toulouse, Paris, Dublin, Manchester, Ondas Awards (*Best Actress* [Paz Vega]), Spanish Film Academy Awards 2002 (*Best New Actress* [Paz Vega], *Best Original Score*), Sant Jordi Awards (*Best Actress* [Paz Vega]), Spanish Actors Union (*Best Supporting Actress* [Elena Anaya])

Clecla
(Spain) 2001, 3 min.
Short film for Internet notodofilmfest.com
Leading player: Alicia Medem

La pelota vasca: la piel contra la piedra
(Spain-Basque Country) 2003, 117 min. [*Euskal pilota: larrua harriaren kontra/ Basque Ball: The Skin against the Stone*]
Production company: Alicia Produce with the participation of EITB (Basque Television) and Canal +

Executive Producers: Julio Medem and Koldo Zuazua
Production Manager: Koldo Zuazua
Production Assistants: Mikel Huércanos, Maite Alberdi and Silvia Gómez
Director: Julio Medem
Assistant Director: Montse Sanz
Screenplay: Julio Medem
Interviewers: Julio Medem, Maider Oleaga and Ione Hernández
Camera Operators: Javier Aguirre, Daniel Sosa Segura and Ricardo de
     Gracia
Original and Non-original Music: Mikel Laboa and Pascal Gaigne
Editing: Julio Medem
Editing Assistants: Carlos Rodríguez, Yago Muñiz, Enara Goikoetxea
Direct Sound: Pablo Bueno
Sound Editing: Sounders Creación Sonora
Visual Effects: Iván Mena
Researcher: Maider Oleaga
Featured speakers: Bernardo Atxaga, Xabier Arzalluz, Txiki Benegas, Txetxo
     Bengoetxea, Julen de Madariaga, Odón Elorza, Iñaki Gabilondo, Carlos
     Garaikoetxea, Anika Gil, Felipe González, Juan José Ibarretxe. Fermín
     Muguruza, Arnaldo Otegi, Gregorio Peces Barba, Alec Reid, Eduardo
     Madina, Daniel Múgica
Premiere: 20 September 2003
Audience: 377,235
Box-office: 1,794,793
Main Festivals and Awards:
San Sebastian, Guadalajara (Mexico) (*Best Documentary*), XII Basque Cinema
     Awards (*Best Documentary*), London, Sundance, Hong Kong, Bogotá,
     Buenos Aires, Cuba

¡Hay motivo!
(Spain) 2004
Segment *La pelota vasca*.
Download: http://www.clubcultura.com/haymotivo/video18.htm
Main festivals and Awards:
San Sebastián 2004, Toulouse Cinespaña Festival 2004, Turia (Special Award)

La culpa del alpinista
(Spain) 2004, 14 min. (*The Mountaineer's Fault*)
Director: Daniel Sánchez Arévalo
Original idea and screenplay: Julio Medem
Short film part of project *50 Minutes* sponsored by Nescafé

Caótica Ana

(Spain) 2007 [*Chaotic Ana*]
Production company: Alicia Produce, Sociedad General de Cine (Sogecine)
Production management: Koldo Zuazua
Budget: 9,000,000 €
Director: Julio Medem
Screenplay: Julio Medem
Cinematography: Mario Montero
Editing: Julio Medem
Music: Alberto Iglesias
Casting: Sara Bilbatúa
Art Direction: Montse Sanz
Costume Design: Estíbaliz Markiegi
Leading players: Manuela Vellés (Ana), Charlotte Rampling (Justine), Bebe
    (Linda), Ash Newman (Anglo), Nicolas Cazalé (Said), Matthias Habich
    (Klaus), Leslie Charles (Jovoskaya), Gerrit Graham (Mr. H), Lluís Homar
    (Ismael), Raúl Pena (Lucas).
Filming Locations: Arizona, New York, Madrid, Fuerteventura

Also advertising spots for Heineken, Balay and Audi

Bibliography

Where no date of publication is available for websites, the date given in parentheses corresponds to the date of access.

Abad, Ignasi (2004), Baja el público, el cine español sube, *Fotogramas*, Febrero 2004, p. 104.

AHDEL (2000), The American Heritage Dictionary of the English Language, 4th edn. Houghton Mifflin Company. Online: http://www.bartleby.com/61/14/A0531400.html. Accessed 22.12.05.

Aldarondo, Ricardo (2003), He ido con las manos y los ojos limpios para dar voz a todos, *Diario Vasco*, 13.09.03, reprinted online, www.terra.es/cine/actualidad/articulo.cfm?ID=5088. Accessed 12.09.04.

Allinson, Mark and Jordan, Barry (2005), *Spaniah Cinema: A Student's Guide*, Hodder Arnold.

Althusser, Louis (1984), *Essays in Ideology*, London, Verso.

Andrew, Geoff (2003), LFF, *Time Out*, October 29–November 5, p. 21.

—— (2004), Basque Ball: The Skin Against The Stone extended run, *NFT programme* (May), BFI, p. 19.

Anon. (1997), Tierra, *Revista Canal Plus*, http://socios.las.es/~ibravo/articulos/articulo_c+.htm. Accessed 01.08.04.

Anon. (2002) *The Guide* (*The Guardian*), May 4–10, p. 43. Scans generously provided by Victoria Pastor.

Anon. (2003), Gotzone Mora emprenderá acciones legales esta semana contra Julio Medem, *El semanal digital*, www.rebelion.org/spain/030922medem.htm. Accessed 08.12.03.

Anon. (2004), Alejo Carpentier cumple cien años, *BBC Mundo*, http://news8.thdo.bbc.co.uk/hi/spanish/misc/newsid_4126000/4126885.stm. Accessed 26.12.04.

Arana, Sabino (1965), ¿Qué somos?, *Obras completas*, Buenos Aires, Editorial Sabindiar-Batza, pp. 627–8.

Atxaga, Bernardo (1998), *Obabakoak*, Barcelona, Ediciones B.

Auster, Paul (2004), *City of Glass*, Great Britain, Faber & Faber.

Auty, Chris (2004), Days of Heaven, *Time Out Film Guide*, 12th edn., Penguin, p. 276.

Barbería, José Luis (2004), La mirada virgen de Medem, *El País*, 22.09.04, p. 36.

Barthes, Roland (1982), The Death of the Author, in *Image, Music, Text*, London, Flamingo, pp. 142–8.

Bravo, Julio (2004), Pegatinas, premios y traca final, *ABC*, 02.02.04, p. 54.

Breton, André (1962), *Manifestes du Surréalisme*, Paris, Jean-Jacques Pauvert.

—— (2000), As in a Wood, in Hammond, P. (ed.), *The Shadow and its Shadow: Surrealist Writings on the Cinema*, San Francisco, City Lights Books.

Carpentier, Alejo (1995a), On the Marvellous Real in America, in Zamora, Lois Parkinson and Faris, Wendy B. (eds), *Magical Realism: Theory, History, Community*, Durham, Duke University Press, pp. 75–88.

—— (1995b), The Baroque and the Marvellous Real, in Zamora, Lois Parkinson and Faris, Wendy B. (eds), *Magical Realism: Theory, History, Community*, Durham, Duke University Press, pp. 89–108.

Corrigan, Timothy (1991), *A Cinema Without Walls: Movies and Culture After Vietnam*, New Brunswick, New Jersey, Rutgers University Press.

Dickie, John (2004), *Cosa Nostra: A History of the Sicilian Mafia*, London, Hodder.

Doane, Mary Ann (1992), Film and the Masquerade: Theorising the Female Spectator, in Mast, G., Cohen, M. and Braudy, L. (eds), *Film Theory and Criticism*, 4th edn., New York, Oxford University Press, pp. 758–72.

EFE (2004), Julio Medem escribe una carta abierta 'ante la pesadilla' que le espera en la gala de los Goya', www.elmundo.es/elmundo/2004/01/30/cultura/1075462696.html. Accessed 30.1.04.

Escamilla, Bárbara (2001), Lucía y el sexo: Fantasía y libre instinto, *Cinemanía*, 71, pp. 68–74.

Evans, Owen (2004), Tom Tykwer's 'Run Lola Run'; Postmodern, Posthuman or Post-theory?, *Studies in European Cinema*, 1(2), pp. 105–15.

Evans, Peter William (1999), 'Furtivos' (Borau, 1975): My Mother, My Lover, in Evans, P. W. (ed.), *Spanish Cinema: The Auteurist Tradition*, New York, Oxford University Press, pp. 115–27.

—— (2004), Contemporary Spanish Cinema, in Ezra, E. (ed.), *European Cinema*, New York, Oxford University Press, pp. 250–64.

Ezra, Elizabeth (2004), A Brief History of Cinema in Europe, in Ezra, E. (ed.) *European Cinema*, New York: Oxford University Press, pp. 1–17.

Figueiredo, Fidelino de (1932), *As dues Espanhas*, Lisbon, Editora Europa.

Fiestras, Joseba (2004), Soy vasco y español, y ser vasco en España es muy
    difícil, http://cine.elcorreodigital.com/datos/festivales/sso3/noticias/27.
    html. Accessed 11.11.04.
Fink, Bruce (1999), *A Clinical Introduction to Lacanian Psychoanalysis*, USA:
    Harvard University Press.
Flora, Carlin (2004), The Stalker in All of Us, in *Psychology Today*, http://
    cms.psychologytoday.com/articles/pto-20041013-000003.html. Accessed
    16.12.04.
Flores, Ángel (1995), Magical Realism in Spanish American Fiction, in
    Zamora, Lois Parkinson and Faris, Wendy B. (eds), *Magical Realism: Theory,
    History, Community*, Durham, Duke University Press, pp. 113–16.
Fonseca, Isabel (1996), *Bury Me Standing: The Gypsies and Their Journey*,
    London, Vintage.
Foreman, Gabrielle P. (1995), Past-On Stories: History and the Magically Real,
    Morrison and Allende on Call, in Zamora, Lois Parkinson and Faris, Wendy
    B. (eds), *Magical Realism: Theory, History, Community*, Durham, Duke
    University Press, pp. 285–303.
Franco, Camilo (2003), Medem hizo con el nacionalismo vasco lo que
    Riefenstahl con Hitler, www.lavozdegalicia.es/hemeroteca/noticia.jsp?
    CAT=126&TEXTO=2014324&txtDia=24&txtMes=9&txtAnho=2003.
    Accessed 05.12.03.
Gabilondo, Joseba (2002), Uncanny Identity: Violence, Gaze, and Desire in
    Contemporary Basque Cinema, in Labanyi, J. (ed.), *Constructing Identity in
    Contemporary Spain: Theoretical Debates and Cultural Practice*, New York,
    Oxford University Press, pp. 262–79.
Gacto, Enrique (1988), Entre la debilidad y la simpleza: la mujer ante la ley,
    Historia 16, 145, pp. 24–32.
Gibbons, Fiachra (2004), Medem's Basque Documentary Sparks Bitter
    Controversy, http://film.guardian.co.uk/festivals/news/0,11667,1047302,
    00.html. Accessed 21.01.04.
Gray, John (2002), *Men are from Mars, Women are from Venus*, Great Britain,
    Harper Collins.
Haltof, Marek (2004), *The Cinema of Krzysztof Kieślowski: Variations on
    Destiny and Chance*, Great Britain, Wallflower.
Hardy, Forsyth (1979), *John Grierson: A Documentary Biography*, London,
    Faber & Faber.
Heredero, Carlos F. (1997), *Espejo de miradas: entrevistas con nuevos
    directores del cine español de los años noventa*, 27 Festival de Cine de Alcalá
    de Henares.
Hooper, John (1995), *The New Spaniards*, England, Penguin.
ICAA (2003), Report on the Spanish Film Industry from Instituto de la
    Cinematografía y de las Artes Audiovisuales. Online: http://www.mcu.es/
    jsp/plantilla_wai.jsp?id=1&area=cine. Accessed 11.12.04.

Intxausti, Aurora (2004), Mercedes Sampietro advierte del peligro de la militarización del pensamiento, *El País*, 04.02.04, p. 37.

IUDLP (2004a), Indiana University Digital Library Program, www.dlib. indiana.edu/variations/scores/abf1877/txt0005.html. Accessed 12.10.04.

—— (2004b), Indiana University Digital Library Program, www.dlib. indiana.edu/variations/scores/abf1877/sc020066.html. Accessed 12.10.04.

James, Nick (2005), Being Boring, *Sight and Sound*, Vol.15:11, p. 3.

Jones, Helen (2006), *To be known it has to be told: The Literary Fiction of Bernardo Atxaga*, PhD dissertation, University of Wales, Aberystwyth, 2005.

Jordan, Barry and Rikki Morgan-Tamosunas (1998), *Contemporary Spanish Cinema*, Great Britain, Manchester University Press.

—— (2000), *Contemporary Spanish Cultural Studies*, Great Britain, London.

Juliá, Santos (2004), *Historias de las dos Españas*, Spain, Taurus.

Kael, Pauline (1985), Circles and Squares, in Mast, G. and Cohen, M. (eds), *Film Theory and Criticism*, 3rd edn. New York, Oxford University Press, pp. 541–52.

Labanyi, Jo (1995), Modernity and Cultural Pluralism: Postmodernism and the Problem of Cultural Identity, in Graham, H. and Labanyi, J. (eds.) *Spanish Cultural Studies: An Introduction*, New York, Oxford University Press, pp. 396–406.

Lacan, Jacques (1991), *The Four Fundamental Concepts of Psychoanalysis*, Great Britain, Penguin Books.

Lázaro Reboll, Antonio and Willis, Andrew (eds) (2004), *Spanish Popular Cinema*, New York, Manchester University Press.

Marín, M. (2003), Artistas vascos ponen el dinero retirado al Festival de Londres, *El país*, 25.10.03.

Marroquín Ruiz, Alberto, Julio y el cine: sitio web no oficial de Julio Medem, www.juliomedem.org. Accessed 2003–6.

Martínez Expósito, Alfredo (2004), Julio Medem y la poética del compromiso, *Alpha*, 20, 121–34. Online: http://www.scielo.cl/scielo.php?script=sci_arttext&pid=S0718-22012004000200008&lng=es&nrm=iso&tlng=es

Matthews, J.H. (1976), *Towards the Poetics of Surrealism*, New York, Syracuse University Press.

Medem, Julio (1983a), Cine Vasco: Una historia interrumpida, *Cinema 2001*, 3, XII, pp. 21–9.

—— (1983b), La puesta en escena: fundido en negro, *La Voz de Euskadi*, 16.07.83, p. 35.

—— (1983c), El último dinosaurio, *La Voz de Euskadi*, 19.06.83, p. 26.

—— (1984a), *La Voz de Euskadi*, 16.09.84, p. 21.

—— (1984b), *La Voz de Euskadi*, 22.09.84. p. 35.

—— (1984c), La creatividad en desuso, *La Voz de Euskadi*, 14.03.84, p. 44.

—— and Michel Gaztambide (1991), *Vacas*, script on file in offices of Alicia Produce, Madrid.

—— (1992), *La ardilla roja*, script on file in offices of Alicia Produce, Madrid.

—— (1995), *Tierra*, script on file in offices of Alicia Produce, Madrid.

—— (1997), *Mari en la tierra: diario de un personaje*, Barcelona, Planeta.

—— (1998), *Los amantes del Círculo Polar*, script on file in offices of Alicia Produce, Madrid.

—— (1999), *Lucía y el sexo*, first draft of script on file in offices of Alicia Produce, Madrid.

—— (2000), *Lucía y el sexo*, eighth draft of script on file in offices of Alicia Produce, Madrid.

—— (2001), *Lucía y el sexo: guión cinematográfico*, Madrid, Ocho y Medio.

—— (2003a), La memoria (Un pájaro vuela dentro de una garganta. Trayecto), *El País*, 18.09.03. p. 35. Reprinted online, www.canarias-alternativa.org/lector.asp?doc=pelotavasca.txt.

—— (2003b), *La pelota vasca: la piel contra la piedra*, Madrid, Aguilar.

—— (2003c), Tras las acusaciones contra su documental: comunicado íntegro de Julio Medem, www.elmundo.es/elmundo/2003/09/17/cultura/1063809825.html. Accessed 17.09.03.

—— (2004) Aitor, guión cinematográfico en dos partes, 2nd version, Madrid.

Mulvey, Laura (1992) Visual Pleasure and Narrative Cinema, in Mast, G., Cohen, M. and Braudy, L. (eds), *Film Theory and Criticism*, 4th edn., New York, Oxford University Press, pp. 746–57.

Navarro, Nuria (2003), Entrevista con Julio Medem, director de cine: la democracia se está precipitando al abismo, *El periódico*, 11.12.03, p. 13.

Nichols, Bill (2000), Film Theory and The Revolt Against Master Narratives, in Gledhill, C. and Williams, L. (eds), *Reinventing Film Studies*, London, Arnold, pp. 34–52.

Nietzsche, Friedrich (1873), On Truth and Lies in a Nonmoral Sense (*Über Wahrheit und Lüge im außermoralischen Sinn*), http://www.publicappeal.org/library/nietzsche/Nietzsche_various/on_truth_and_lies.htm. Accessed 20.05.04.

—— (1993) *The Birth of Tragedy Out of the Spirit of Music*, trans. Shaun Whiteside, London, Penguin Books.

—— (1999), The Birth of Tragedy, *The Birth of Tragedy and Other Writings*, Geuss, R. and Speirs, R. (eds), New York, Cambridge University Press, pp. 1–116.

Nowell-Smith, Geoffrey (1968), *Visconti*, New York, Doubleday and Company.

Orr, John (1998), *Contemporary Cinema*, Great Britain, Edinburgh University Press.

—— (2004), New Directions in European Cinema, in Ezra, E. (ed.), *European Cinema*, New York, Oxford University Press, pp. 299–317.

Pascal, Blaise (2004), *Pensées*, http://housatonic.net/Documents/309.htm. Accessed 12.04.05.

Pearson, Keith Ansell (2005), *How to Read Nietzsche*, London, Granta.

Perriam, Chris (2003), *Stars and Masculinites in Spanish Cinema: From Banderas to Bardem*, New York, Oxford University Press.

Piña, Begoña (2004), La élite del cine replica al gobierno con un filme sobre la España de hoy, *La Vanguardia*, 05.02.04, p. 34.

R.G.G., El PP pide a Medem que se disculpe o devuelva el dinero cobrado por emitir 'Lucía y el sexo' en TVE, *El país*, 25.09.03, reprinted online, www.aideka.tv/Serviciosinformativos/prensasentencia/25-09-03/4Comis Control-240903.jpg. Accessed 30.09.03.

Rodríguez, María Pilar (2002), *Mundos en conflicto: aproximaciones al cine vasco de los noventa*, San Sebastián, Universidad de Deusto.

Roh, Franz (1995), Magic Realism: Post Expressionism, in Zamora, Lois Parkinson and Faris, Wendy B. (eds), *Magical Realism: Theory, History, Community*, Durham, Duke University Press, pp. 75–88.

Roldán Larreta, Carlos (1999), *El cine del País Vasco: de Ama Lur (1968) a Airbag (1997)*, San Sebastián, Ikusgaiak 3, 1–407.

—— (2003), *Los vascos y el séptimo arte: diccionario enciclopédico de cineastas vascos*, San Sebastián, Filmoteca Vasca.

Said, Edward (1994), The Mind of Winter: Reflections on Life in Exile, in Robinson, M. (ed.), *Altogether Elsewhere: Writers in Exile*, Boston, Faber & Faber, pp. 137–49.

—— (2002), Reflections on Exile, in *Reflections on Exile and Other Essays*, Cambridge, Mass., Harvard University Press, pp. 173–86.

Sala, Teresa (2001), Vicente Ameztoy 'Cada cuadro que pinto es un nuevo intento de sorprenderme a mí mismo', *Euskonews & Media*. http://www.euskonews.com/0129zbk/elkar1290ies.html. Accessed 20.11.05.

Sánchez, A. (1997), Women Immune to a Nervous Breakdown: The Representation of Women in Julio Medem's Films, *Tesserae: Journal of Iberian and Latin American Studies*, 3(2), pp. 147–61.

Santaolalla, Isabel (1998), Far From Home, Close To Desire: Julio Medem's Landscapes, *Bulletin of Hispanic Studies*, LXXV, pp. 331–7.

—— (1999), Julio Medem's '"Vacas": Historicizing The Forest', in Evans, P. W. (ed.), *Spanish Cinema: The Auteurist Tradition*, New York, Oxford University Press, pp. 310–24.

Sarris, Andrew (1985) Notes on the Auteur Theory in 1962, in Mast, G. and Cohen, M, (eds) *Film Theory and Criticism*, 3rd edn. New York: Oxford University Press, pp. 527–40.

—— (1992), Notes on the Auteur Theory in 1962, in Mast, G., Cohen, M. and Braudy, L. (eds), *Film Theory and Criticism*, 4th edn., New York, Oxford University Press, pp. 585–8.

Schatz, Thomas (1992), 'The Whole Equation of Pictures' from The Genius of the System, in Mast, G., Cohen, M. and Braudy, L. (eds), *Film Theory and Criticism*, 4th edn., New York, Oxford University Press, pp. 654–8.

Smith, Paul Julian (1996), Julio Medem's 'La ardilla roja' (The Red Squirrel): A Transparent Society?, *Vision Machines: Cinema, Literature and Sexuality in Spain and Cuba, 1983–1993*, London and New York, Verso, pp. 128–45.

—— (2000) Between Heaven and Earth: Grounding Julio Medem, *The Moderns: Time, Space and Subjectivity in Contemporary Spanish Culture*, New York, Oxford University Press, pp. 146–61.

—— (2004), The Basque Ball: Skin Against The Stone, *Sight and Sound*, Vol.14.5, p. 45.

Sogecine (2004), Budget and box-office statistics relating to films of Julio Medem, received by e-mail, 10.6.04.

Stone, Rob (1998), Designing Women: 'Vertigo', 'Carmen' and 'La ardilla roja', *Tesserae*, IV, pp. 173–82.

—— (2001), *Spanish Cinema*, Harlow, Longman.

—— (2004a), Julio Medem's Basque Balls: 'Pelota Vasca', *Vertigo*, Vol. 2.6, pp. 46–8.

—— (2004b), *Flamenco in the Works of Federico García Lorca and Carlos Saura: The Wounded Throat*, New York and Lampeter, Edwin Mellen Press.

—— (2006), Mother Lands, Sister Nations: The Epic, Poetic Propaganda Films of Cuba and the Basque Country, in Dennison, S. and Song Hwee Lim (eds), *Remapping World Cinema: Identity, Culture and Politics in Film*, Wallflower, pp. 65–72.

Thompson, David (2004), Stop Making Sense, *Sight and Sound*, Vol.14.5, pp. 28–31.

Thomson, David (1998), *A Biographical Dictionary of Film*, Finland, André Deutsch.

Tremlett, Giles (2003), Anyone for Pelota?, *The Guardian*, 23.10.03, pp. 16–17.

Triana Toribio, Núria (2003) *Spanish National Cinema*, London, Routledge.

—— (2004) 'Santiago Segura: Just When You Thought That Spanish Masculinities Were Getting Better . . . ', in *Hispanic Research Journal*, Vol.5:2, pp. 147–56.

Unamuno, Miguel De (1999), *Niebla*, Spain, Espasa Calpe Colección Austral.

Vallejo Ugarte, Asier (2002), Francisco Escudero, una muerte prematura, in *Filomúsica*, 30, July 2002. Online: http://www.filomusica.com/filo30/escudero.html. Accessed 28.10.05.

Vincendeau, Ginette (1998), Issues in European Cinema, in Hill, J. and Church Gibson, P. (eds), *Oxford Guide to Film Studies*, New York, Oxford University Press, pp. 444–5.

White, Anne M. (1999), Manchas negras, manchas blancas: Looking again at Julio Medem's 'Vacas', in Rix, R. and Rodríguez Saona, R. (eds), *Spanish Cinema: Calling the Shots*, (Leeds Iberian Papers), Leeds, Trinity and All Saints, pp. 1–14.

Williamson, Dugald (1999), Language and Sexual Difference, in *The Sexual Subject: A Screen Reader in Sexuality*, London, Routledge, pp. 107–25.

Wollen, Peter (1992), The Auteur Theory, in Mast, G., Cohen, M. and Braudy, L. (eds), *Film Theory and Criticism*, 4th edn., New York, Oxford University Press, pp. 589–605.

Woodworth, Paddy (2001), *Dirty War, Clean Hands: ETA, the GAL and Spanish Democracy*, Yale University Press, New Haven and London.

—— (2004), commentary with Rob Stone, *Basque Ball*, Region 2 DVD, Metro-Tartan.

Zulaika, Joseba (1988), *Basque Violence: Metaphor and Sacrament*, Nevada, University of Reno Nevada Press.

—— (2004), In Love with Puppy: Flowers, Architecture, Art, and the Art of Irony, *International Journal of Iberian Studies*, 16.3, pp. 145–58.

Index